INDIA AND THE WORLD IN THE FIRST HALF OF THE TWENTIETH CENTURY

This book examines how India was placed and placed itself in the world during the first half of the twentieth century in a period of global turmoil and set against the subcontinental contest for independence. In situating India in the world, it looks not just at current foreign policy studies, but also at geopolitics, World War experiences, theoretical and strategic approaches, early foreign policy institutional transitions and the role of Indian civil and foreign diplomatic services. The work explores history and theory with a focus on cosmopolitanism beyond nationalism.

The use of extensive sources from archives in UK and Russia – especially in different languages, mainly German and Russian – lends this volume an edge over most other works. The book will be useful to professional academics, historians including military historians, security specialists, literary specialists, foreign policy experts, journalists and the general reader interested in international issues.

Madhavan K. Palat has been Editor, *Selected Works of Jawaharlal Nehru*, New Delhi, since 2011. He was earlier National Fellow at the Indian Institute of Advanced Study, Shimla, Visiting Professor of Imperial Russian History at the University of Chicago, and taught Russian and European History from 1974 to 2004 at the Jawaharlal Nehru University, New Delhi. He has published on Russian social, literary and political history of the nineteenth and twentieth centuries. He has edited *Social Identities in Revolutionary Russia* (2001) and co-edited the *History of Civilizations of Central Asia*, vol. 6 (2005). His recent articles include, 'The Grand Inquisitor and the Holy Fool,' Foundation Day Lecture, ICHR, 2014, and 'The Interesting Ideas of Eric Hobsbawm,' NMML Occasional Paper, 2013.

INDIA AND THE WORLD IN THE FIRST HALF OF THE TWENTIETH CENTURY

Edited by
Madhavan K. Palat

Routledge
Taylor & Francis Group
LONDON AND NEW YORK

First published 2018 by Routledge

2 Park Square, Milton Park, Abingdon, Oxfordshire OX14 4RN

52 Vanderbilt Avenue, New York, NY 10017

Routledge is an imprint of the Taylor & Francis Group,
an informa business

First issued in paperback 2019

British Library Cataloguing-in-Publication Data
A catalogue record for this book is available from the British Library

Library of Congress Cataloging-in-Publication Data
A catalog record has been requested for this book

ISBN: 978-1-138-28256-8 (hbk)
ISBN: 978-0-367-88658-5 (pbk)

Typeset in Sabon
by Apex CoVantage, LLC

FOR MAHESH RANGARAJAN

CONTENTS

CONTRIBUTORS

Rakesh Ankit teaches History at the Law School in OP Jindal Global University, Haryana, India. He did his undergraduate and postgraduate studies at Delhi and Oxford and his doctorate at Southampton. His doctoral thesis titled *The Kashmir Conflict: From Empire to the Cold War, 1945–66* was published by Routledge in 2016. His current research focuses on aspects of 'India in the interim, 1946–49.'

Amit Das Gupta is Senior Researcher at the Universität der Bundeswehr, München, Germany. Earlier he was affiliated with the Germany Institute of the University of Amsterdam, the Institute for Contemporary History, Department Berlin, Foreign Office, and Jacobs University Bremen. After a first book about West Germany's South Asia policy between 1949 and 1966, he has authored a political biography of Foreign Secretary Subimal Dutt and co-edited a volume on the Sino-Indian War 1962. Currently, he is working on a monograph on the impact of officers of the Indian Civil Service on Indian foreign policy after independence.

Pradip Kumar Datta is Professor at the Centre for Comparative Politics and Political Theory, School of International Studies, Jawaharlal Nehru University, New Delhi, India. Earlier he taught English Literature and History and was Professor at the Faculty of Political Science at University of Delhi, India. His work has concentrated on identity formations, Hindu–Muslim antagonisms in Bengal, and literary and political cultures to see what produces the modern duality of both violent and co-existing identities. He is currently studying Tagore's Viswabharati as an early experiment in an alternate global habitation. He has written, co-authored, and edited several books including *Indian Political Thought* (co-edited, 2013); *Heterogeneities:*

Identity Formations in Modern India (2010); and *Carving Blocs: Communal Ideology in Twentieth Century Bengal* (1999).

Madhavan K. Palat has been Editor, *Selected Works of Jawaharlal Nehru*, New Delhi, since 2011. He was earlier National Fellow at the Indian Institute of Advanced Study, Shimla, Visiting Professor of Imperial Russian History at the University of Chicago, and taught Russian and European History from 1974 to 2004 at the Jawaharlal Nehru University, New Delhi. He has published on Russian social, literary and political history of the nineteenth and twentieth centuries. He has edited *Social Identities in Revolutionary Russia* (2001) and co-edited the *History of Civilizations of Central Asia* (2005). His recent articles include 'The Grand Inquisitor and the Holy Fool,' Foundation Day Lecture, ICHR, 2014, and 'The Interesting Ideas of Eric Hobsbawm,' NMML Occasional Paper, 2013.

Srinath Raghavan is Senior Fellow at the Centre for Policy Research, New Delhi, India, and Visiting Professor at Ashoka University, Haryana, India. He is the author of *India's War: The Making of Modern South Asia, 1939–1945* (2016); *1971: A Global History of the Creation of Bangladesh* (2013); and *War and Peace in Modern India: A Strategic History of the Nehru Years* (2010). He has edited and co-authored three further volumes on India foreign and security policies. He is a recipient of the Infosys Prize in Social Sciences (2015).

A. R. Venkatachalapathy is Professor at the Madras Institute of Development Studies, Chennai, India and has taught at the universities of Tirunelveli, Madras, and Chicago, and held research assignments in Paris, Cambridge, London, and Harvard. He was the ICCR Chair Professor in Indian Studies at the National University of Singapore (2011–12). He was awarded the V.K.R.V. Rao Prize (History, 2007). He has published on the social, cultural, and intellectual history of colonial Tamil Nadu in both English and Tamil. His publications include *The Province of the Book: Scholars, Scribes, and Scriblers in Colonial Tamilnadu* (2012) and *In Those Days There Was No Coffee: Writings in Cultural History* (2006); he has also edited books on Madras, anthologies of Tamil poetry, and translations of Tamil literary works.

PREFACE

This volume is presented to Mahesh Rangarajan by a group of his colleagues in appreciation of his tenure as Director of the Nehru Memorial Museum and Library between 2010 and 2014. It was all too brief, but memorable withal. He further enlivened an institution that had once been one of the liveliest of academic centres in Delhi. He almost compulsively collected private archives to enrich the by-far most valuable repository of private archives in the country. Suddenly it seemed as if every book that scholars of the twentieth century in India might look for could once again be found in this library. Seminars, lectures, and conferences of outstanding quality followed each other in such quick succession that organisers were sometimes sent scurrying in search of an appropriate hall; and these lectures were sent out on the internet and published as Occasional Papers. He welcomed scholars of all ages, from the doctoral student who had just completed a thesis to the advanced scholar, to speak at these events. He persuaded those who may not be considered social scientists by strict definition to address audiences of chiefly social scientists. Although the library fostered mainly the study of Indian history of the twentieth century, non-historians and historians in every field of specialisation both spoke and attended. The pleasure of recall is tinged with regret; and perhaps we shall remember it all the more vividly for its exemplifying Nietzsche's dictum: 'only that which does not cease to hurt remains in memory.'

Most of the chapters are revised versions of lectures delivered at the library. Many of those who would have contributed could not do so because notice was too short and they were otherwise committed, but they were enthusiastic in support. I am most grateful to them for such encouragement. Many others could not be invited in spite of their readiness to contribute, I am sure, had they been asked. The reason is that this volume was to be a surprise present to Mahesh; and it would have been illogical to broadcast a secret. I trust that those friends and colleagues would forgive me for engaging in such conspiracy while advocating and pursuing the openness of academic exchanges.

PROLOGUE

The theme of this volume is India and the world, and the world and India, how India placed herself in the world as she mobilised herself for the new role and made the transition as an independent nation and state, and also how and where the global struggles placed India, and in one important sense, did they place India? The chapters are grouped into three pairs: (1) the global context; (2) looking out from India; and (3) the making of foreign policy, especially of the diplomats, in those heady years of transition.

The global context is dealt with in two contributions, by Palat on geopolitics and Raghavan on India's place in American strategy during the Second World War. The geopolitical theorisation, which stretched from the late nineteenth century to the middle of the twentieth, was preoccupied with planetary power, how an integrating world would be run and from which centre or centres of power. It was an epoch of both superlative creativity and barbarism, as perhaps befits a global power struggle of such dimensions. It is customary to cast it as a three-cornered contest between liberalism, communism, and fascism; but geopolitical theory effectively reduced it to a bipolar competition between the Western world with its diverse alliances and the Axis powers. Strangely, the Soviet power bloc did not quite make the grade as making a realistic bid for global dominion, neither during the inter-war years and the Second World War nor after it. It is revealing how, when that process was underway, India was utterly marginal to global strategists. But then so were Latin America, most of Africa, China, and Southeast Asia. Empires were collapsing, but the developing world was still remote from the global power play, a collection of objects in the game. But, in each specific context, they were significant for the resources that they could deploy. Raghavan's chapter shows well how the USA had a clear role for India in the war effort, and it was so different from the British anxiety merely to hold on to empire. American planners saw all too well that a nationalist mobilisation would further, not hinder, their cause. They also understood that nationalism could be of use as much after the war, and that colonial rule had had its day.

The next pair of chapters consists of perspectives on the world from two immensely influential and representative Indians from the world of literature, journalism, and politics, Tagore and Periyar. They are as unlike each other as may be imagined, yet they converged in expressing the aporias of nationalism and the imperatives of global citizenship; they were arrestingly avant-gardist, albeit in entirely different ways; and, as it to be expected, they attracted controversy and fruitful comment. It is of some interest that there were no geopolitical theorists in India, indeed there could not be, but one like Tagore could experience the agony of humanity, both before and during the First World War. His imagination was global and it was more than merely cosmopolitan, as Datta's chapter explicates; and his foreboding of impending catastrophe was unusual, more akin to the apocalyptic visions of so many European thinkers of the time. Tagore's anxiety over the narrowness and limitations of a particular type of nationalism is well known; but Datta has shown well how Tagore explored being both rooted, as in Santiniketan, and global. He chose to be embedded in the world, not just the nation, and he assumed for himself a performative rather than passive role with that conviction.

While Tagore sensed the apocalypse, Periyar belonged to that form of the global that was iconoclastic, experimental, and utopian, so much of which was spawned by the Russian Revolution, but which belonged in a wider sense to the European avant-garde. Venkatachalapathy has offered us an account of his voyage of discovery and of experimentation as he travelled to the Soviet Union and Europe in the disturbed conditions of the early thirties. He has left us a diary; unfortunately only parts of it have been found; but we are fortunate to have an exegesis of it here. His visit to the Soviet Union was beset with so many uncertainties, and, like so many others, he was a bemused and sometimes naïve observer of its innovations. His further travels in Germany took him to such unlikely spaces as nudist colonies, in which he participated without inhibition as befitted a person of such utopian passions. It is singularly interesting that one who is associated always with a Dravidian nationalism should have been quite as globally oriented as Tagore, but with a wholly different trajectory. Equally significantly, their global commitments were not derived from international socialism or communism, the usual route in that epoch to a global consciousness, although Periyar had a most unusual engagement with communism.

The final pair of chapters have been chosen for illuminating that most important aspect of the transition to independence, the institutional structures and its personnel for pursuing a foreign policy. As a colony, India did not have a foreign policy, and still less did it engage in strategic planning. Indian nationalism was limited to itself; and virtually only Nehru, Subhas Bose, and Krishna Menon may have reflected on the world beyond in terms of strategy for an independent state. But once the task was set out, an independent foreign policy establishment and strategic thinking had to be instituted. The personnel came from the Indian Civil Service, necessarily, but the global vision was provided by Nehru. We are fortunate to have two chapters, with considerable archival research in multiple languages, on the framing of foreign policy as seen through the eyes of Subimal Dutt, sometime foreign secretary, and on the experience of establishing diplomatic relations with the Soviet Union. Amit Das Gupta has already given us a vast tome, a biography, of Subimal Dutt, and this chapter reveals not only visions but as much the institutions and the persons that were to play their roles. Rakesh Ankit has focused on the opening of the embassy in the Soviet Union and Vijaya Lakshmi Pandit's experience as the first ambassador there. Indo-Soviet relations have been studied or commented on so extensively for their later bonhomie; but this first phase of it was very special. It was at a time when there was no bonhomie, when Stalin looked on Indian nationalists with suspicion, not the least because Nehru had taken India into the Commonwealth, the Indian armed forces were still headed by British officers, and Indian communist insurgencies were being suppressed. Like all founding moments, it was a difficult time, and fraught with enormous uncertainties. For that reason, these two chapters are so illuminating, for they focus specifically on the diplomats, not just Nehru.

1

GEOPOLITICS AS THE THEORY OF WORLD DOMINION

Madhavan K. Palat[*]

The word *geopolitics* used to refer to the discourse on the competition for the dominion of the world from a single centre of power. As such it was elaborated in Germany, Great Britain, and the United States from the 1870s to the 1940s although the word itself was coined only in 1899 by Rudolf Kjellén in Sweden. It has ceased thereafter to be a coherent doctrine of world politics and now denotes little more than regional rivalry and global power in general, largely because the competition for global dominion has been moving relentlessly in favour of power centred in the United States, substantially so from 1945 and especially so from the 1980s. The doctrine has been understood or presented in many different ways, but its core perhaps consisted in: (1) the unity of world politics leading to the competition for domination, and (2) the principal agent of the competition being the global power bloc, perhaps better known by its German equivalent, the *Grossraum*.

However, theorists have stressed varying aspects of the concept or concepts according to their peculiar national experience or ambition. Thus, the German Friedrich Ratzel[1] and the American Nicholas Spykman[2] have focused on the state as a living organism that must grow lest it die; Karl Haushofer in Germany acquired a dubious reputation as a champion of *Lebensraum*, or living space for growth and expansion;[3] the British geographer Halford Mackinder dwelt at length on the history of the rise of Britain to emphasise the relation between sea and land power;[4] and all of them spoke of the boundaries of the state as permanently fluid and unstable. As a science geopolitics has been seen as a branch of political geography; but it has been deplored as a pseudo-science for providing sundry seemingly geographical arguments for Nazi territorial expansion and conquest and for even bringing political

4

geography into disrepute.[5] The Grossraum, or the power bloc, is not considered central to geopolitical theory in most accounts.

But it is worth doing so, and Mackinder is of enduring interest for having identified just such power blocs that would compete globally; in the course of that exercise he detailed the manner in which they would cohere and the resources that they would be able to deploy for the contest. His global power blocs of the future were composed of Eurasia and Africa on the one hand and the Americas on the other. These large landmasses were separated by oceans, deep and wide, which entailed relating sea and land power. He was little concerned with the other issues, not at all with Lebensraum, and even sea power was of secondary significance in his projections for the future. He had accorded sea power such overweening importance as part of his historical explanation of British supremacy: but it has been misread as the primary focus of his theory of the global future. More than Haushofer or even Spykman, Carl Schmitt followed Mackinder in his account of the power blocs that would compete for dominion.[6] In spite of being a Nazi apologist, Schmitt disavowed Lebensraum[7] and paid little attention to the organic theory of the state; and he examined the nature of sea and land power only to record the fading of the decisive role of sea power.[8] James Burnham in 1941 examined the three blocs or superstates locked in combat: the Allied, the Axis, and the Soviet,[9] which recalled Rudolf Kjellén's classification of the 1890s.[10] With the Axis being extinguished and the British Empire subsiding, America and the Soviet Union were left in the field and the clarity of Cold War bipolarity emerged, again in the work of James Burnham who analysed Soviet post-war strategy in such terms in early 1944,[11] and generally of American strategic planners from 1943 to 1944.[12] As geopolitical theory morphed into Cold War theorisation through a series of papers by Burnham, George Kennan, and others, the core remained the rivalry between power blocs, variously known as Grossraums, super-states, or superpowers; but just as sea power and Lebensraum seemed essential to geopolitics, so also ideology distinguished Cold War theory.

The unity of the world

Geopolitics is premised on a conceptualised unity of the world; and geopolitical strategy had to be global strategy, the counterpart to the global geography advocated by celebrated geographers like Paul Vidal de la Blache,[13] Elisée Reclus, Friedrich Ratzel, and above all Halford

Mackinder, all in the quarter century before the First World War. A geo-politics of specific regions of the world would do violence to the concept, be it a geopolitics of East Asia, of Central Asia, or of the Middle East or of Europe, although it is employed in that fashion to denote the power struggles of the post–Cold War world. A single world and its human population has been imagined in so many different ways since the sixteenth century, and the chronology of the development of such a consciousness has been laid out in so many scholarly inquiries that it would be futile to catalogue them. But the claim specific to geopolitical theory was that both the process of 'discovery' and of colonial conquest had drawn to a close by the last third of the nineteenth century; henceforth all strategies of power, whether political and military, or economic and cultural, or even the purely creative in the arts and letters,[14] had to be global in their awareness and competitive ambition. It was no longer given to anyone to remain purely European, to carve out separate empires, to retreat into 'tradition,' and still less to ascend into the mists of Shangri-La. A unified world that could not expand outward except into space must reorder itself toward internal cohesion through intensified competition between power blocs. The multiple centres of global power must inexorably amalgamate into smaller numbers but larger units; the final contest must be in some sense bipolar or between two centres; and ultimately a hegemon must emerge. The much-cherished sovereignty of states, especially of national states, must submit to this relentless logic and subordinate itself to power blocs that would compete for mastery. Geopolitical theory sought to explicate this process and identify the players.

The portents of global unity were sensed in many different ways. Friedrich Ratzel, who died in 1904, formulated something akin to a law of amalgamation of small states into bigger and bigger ones[15] until he arrived at the conclusion that 'There is on this small planet sufficient space for only one great state.'[16] His admirer, Rudolf Kjellén, chose to quote the British prime minister, Salisbury, on the law of large states becoming larger and small states smaller, coupled with Marx's dictum that the factory grew at the expense of handicraft.[17] With exceptional clarity he saw a single global politics, its hierarchy of states, the distinction between great powers and world powers, and the world powers as an 'aristocracy' that ruled the world. Like true aristocracies, they were not subject to law which they framed as they chose.[18] George Curzon, fresh from his Indian mint, assured his audience in 1907 that 'As the vacant spaces of the earth are filled up, the competition for the residue is temporarily more keen. Fortunately, the process is drawing towards a natural termination.' By 'fortunately' he meant that the anarchy of international rivalries was about to be replaced by the international law of a few world powers,[19] which he assumed was less anarchic. In 1910 Frederick Jackson Turner noted that the forces that had shaped America were disappearing, that colonisation and the advance of the frontier were coming to an end, and that a new 'imperial republic' had emerged.[20]

More than anybody else, Halford Mackinder saw the world now as a 'closed system' when the decisive advantage of sea power and global explorations, which he called the Columbian epoch, had come to end, and he foresaw a world of intensified and destructive competition:

> From the present time forth, in the post-Columbian age, we shall again have to deal with a closed political system, and none the less that it will be one of world-wide scope. Every explosion of social forces, instead of being dissipated in a surrounding circuit of unknown space and barbaric chaos, will be sharply re-echoed from the far side of the globe, and weak elements in the political and economic organism of the world will be shattered in consequence. There is a vast difference of effect in the fall of a shell into an earthwork and its fall amid the closed spaces and rigid structures of a great building or ship.[21]

In 1911 he advocated an 'imperial' vision to the teaching of geography, which may be misunderstood as yet another contribution to strategies of empire. But it was significantly more, in spite of its opaque manner of presentation. He imagined a unified perspective of the world for an effective imperial strategy and demanded a scientific geography that would permit the strategist to view the world as one, to see the relation of the various parts to the whole.[22] He derided the earlier mode of descriptive geography that collated information about locations into gazetteers; he called for a new, unified, and causally explanatory one.[23] He distinguished the literary creation, which was for hearing, from geography, which was for seeing, for 'the mapping of the "scheme of things entire" on the surface of the globe.'[24] He waxed eloquent on the power of vision in the manner of Wordsworth recounting his enslavement to the 'bodily eye,' 'the most despotic of our senses';[25] and Marxists may be disconcerted that even an imperialist like him could pronounce: 'The special virtue of thought by visualisation is that it prompts doing rather than merely knowing.'[26] It was an arrestingly panoptical vision of the globe, one that would have delighted Bentham and should have tempted Foucault, although, to the discomfiture of some of his admirers, spatial configurations of power seemed secondary to temporal or historical structures in his work.[27]

With the approach of global dominion, geopolitical theory was popularised in America in the 1940s down to *Life, Time, Reader's Digest, Harper's Magazine*, and Warner Brothers;[28] and the new-found unity of the world was repeatedly emphasised. Robert Strausz-Hupé noted that 'Global war has shown the continents and oceans to be parts of one closely meshed world political design.'[29] Andreas Dorpalen paraphrased it to mean 'the doctrine of power on earth,'[30] while Andrew Gyorgy stressed the emergence of a few gigantic states over the surface of the globe.[31] Nicholas Spykman reminded his compatriots that 'the total earth's surface has, today, become a single field for the play of political forces,' and that it had in effect become so since the late nineteenth century.[32]

Post–Cold War scholarship has reverted to that theme. John Agnew sets the tone well with his Mackinderian emphasis on seeing: 'The use of visual language is deliberate. World politics was invented only when it became possible to see the world (in the imagination) as a whole and pursue goals in relation to that geographical scale.'[33] His sometime student, Gearóid Ó Tuathail, has described it as 'ocularcentrism,' the Foucauldian 'governmentalisation of geography' made possible by the world becoming a 'closed space' and a single system which must or may be viewed with 'Cartesian perspectivalism' from the outside and as a totality.[34] Edward Soja noted that history constructed sequences while geography saw simultaneities, and appropriately enough he has cited Jorge Luis Borges: 'What my eyes beheld was simultaneous, but what I shall now write down will be successive, because language is successive.'[35]

The definition of the centres of power in geographical terms accounts for the prefix to the word. The alternative theories of contestation throughout the twentieth century and beyond have employed varying concepts for identification: in Cold War theory it was the ideological, as democracy versus totalitarianism or the historically evolved global structures of capitalism versus socialism; in race theory it posited the purity of the race against miscegenation and pollution, or the Aryan against lesser races; and in civilisation theory it set power blocs defined by cultural attributes against each other, but primarily the Western against a major challenger, the Orthodox or the Slavic, or latterly, the Islamic. Geopolitical theory valorised the territorial over the ideological, racial, or cultural; and it flourished in those centres that could nurse a realistic ambition of world dominion, Imperial Germany, and the Third Reich on the one hand, and the British Empire and the United States jointly on the other. But at different moments and in variable hierarchies of significance, geopolitical theories were supplemented and fortified by these ideological, civilisational, and racial doctrines.

Significantly, the Soviet Union did not compete for world dominion and challenge the United States: until 1945 it confined itself to carving out a space for survival as a socialism in one country; thereafter it was limited to ensuring a protective glacis in East Europe, sustaining a few impoverished client states around the globe, nurturing an unexpectedly lasting friendship with India, and both befriending and neutralising China as best it could. After 1945, its proudest boast was not that it was the centre of World Revolution, but that it had survived the terrifying Nazi onslaught as a state, probably as a nation, and as a socialism of its unique brand. In its self-understanding, its achievement lay in its virtually miraculous survival, not in its shaping of the world. As such, it was more nearly a partner to the US structuring of the world after 1945, prickly and truculent during the Cold War, dismembered, sullen, and submissive after 1991 as just Russia.

Grossraum

This has been translated more often than not as large space, which is literal and mocks the concept itself. It would be more satisfactory to understand it as power bloc, of the kind that the Allies, the Axis, and the Japanese Greater East Asia Co-Prosperity Sphere constituted during the Second World War, or of the Western and Eastern blocs, NATO and Warsaw Pact, during the Cold War. It denoted an unequal alliance or union of sovereign states under the military, political, and ideological leadership of a single state and in opposition to one or more such blocs. Colonial conquest could be considered in this category for its global reach, and John Agnew's important work has described it as 'civilisational geopolitics';[36] but it has been excluded here with good reason. The Grossraum sought to structure all of world politics by reducing the number of players ideally to two, at worst one or two more, and it subordinated developed sovereign states to the ultimate sovereign, the leader in the manner of America or the Third Reich. Colonial empires, in spite of their global spread, were driven by piecemeal expansion on the ground, ever so often by 'men-on-the-spot,' with the limited objective of securing a colony rather than reordering the world. By the end of the eighteenth century they had already structured a global politics of competition with each other for acquiring territory, zones of influence, trade concessions, and investment opportunities. But no single empire or even an alliance between them thought in terms of restructuring global politics for domination from a single centre or even from two of them. They were bereft of the global vision that distinguished geopolitics.[37] But by the late nineteenth century the world had been carved up between these empires, it had become a 'closed system,' as Mackinder noted, and these imperial centres would now turn on each other. As these elimination rounds, or world wars, loomed, geopolitical visions superseded imperial ones, and strategies for domination from a single centre of power emerged.

As may be expected, the transition from the imperial to the geopolitical vision occurred imperceptibly, yet it is clearly visible. The most obvious may be found in the British Empire owing to its immense reach, with planners like Curzon shifting from imperial strategy as governor-general in Calcutta to the global as foreign secretary in London. As governor-general he was full of mobile frontiers and plans to extend influence in Tibet, Central Asia, Iran, and the Indian Ocean, besides upholding paramountcy over the princely states in India. But from London he was busy drawing boundaries to make and unmake states in East Europe and demoting them to the status of protectorates.[38] Mackinder preceded him, without having to make the transition from imperial to geopolitical strategist. He never did apply the term geopolitics to his own views; but he rejected the term 'imperialist' as limiting, and he preferred 'imperial' in the sense of geopolitics and even today's 'global.'[39]

Mackinder propagated the idea of the Grossraum, *avant la lettre*. He did so by positing the final opposition of the Atlantic to the Eurasian power blocs and of the necessity of the one overwhelming the other. It was a bipolarity that was to lead to unipolarity. But he blurred his remarkably clear vision by presenting it in terms of sea power versus land power, of British imperial strategy, and of the need to study geography as a new discipline. In fact, none of these elements was central to the notion of two power blocs approaching their final moment of reckoning. He was followed by Karl Haushofer in Germany during most of the first half of the century, and by Nicholas Spykman in America in the thirties and forties. They discussed the possible composition of the two power blocs; with variations these overlapped at the most significant points; but the decisive claim in each case was that the global power struggle would be conducted by two power blocs, the Atlantic and the Eurasian, and that one of them would prevail.

Mackinder's lecture of 1904 to the Royal Geographical Society is usually identified as the source of this central geopolitical argument. He began by defining the two power structures in terms of sea power and land power; by ascribing British supremacy to her mastery of the seas; and by warning that this era was coming to a close with modern technology, especially of railways. Sea power had been superior to land power for allowing easy access to and power projection at all corners of the globe. Land communication was cumbersome and immensely expensive by comparison. But it had not always been like that. In Mackinder's analysis, until the fifteenth century when the seas were mastered, the greatest empires on earth were based on land power; and he illustrated his argument with the terrifying images of Chinggis Khan and of Timur rather than of Alexander, the usual European favourite for visions of world conquest. His preferred exempla could be relied upon to send a shiver down every civilised spine. Associating land empires with barbarity induced the appropriate mood to peer at Germany and Russia looming as the new land empires. From the fifteenth century, sea power had enabled European expansion; but that 'Columbian' epoch, as he called it, was now coming to a close. Railways would make communication on land as effortless and efficient as on the waterways; land power would equalise with sea power; and the British Empire would lose its advantage. Leo Amery from the audience then added perhaps the most important insight of all: air power erased geographical advantage altogether; for 'It will not matter whether they are in the centre of a continent or on an island; those people who have the industrial power and the power of invention and of science will be able to defeat all others.' This was as early as 1904, when air power still seemed to belong in science fiction.[40] Indeed, in 1907, H. G. Wells rose to the occasion with a novel on a world war decided by air power.[41] In the Armageddon that ensues, China is plunged into civil war, India rises in insurrection, Japan goes through a social revolution, and jihad seizes the world from the Gobi to Morocco. As the sole survivor of this holocaust, Japan conducts repeated raids on various parts of the world; and the technology of air power is so simplified that it enables and engenders guerilla warfare everywhere.

For long this was the core of the geopolitical argument. Sea power was necessary but no longer sufficient. It must combine with all other technologies and resources, on land and in the air, natural resources and economic enterprise, but most of all human skills, to achieve an optimum for dominion on the planet. British supremacy was coming to a close; it was about to be challenged by American, German, and Japanese power; to these would be added nationalism in India and China and elsewhere,[42] and even the jihad as H. G. Wells had suggested or foreseen. The British Empire had enjoyed no more than primacy: it was due to be replaced by the worldwide dominion of the one that could optimally assemble resources.

From this followed any number of combinations for the future. Sea power was represented by the United States and the British Empire and its dependencies, and their alliance was taken for granted. Japan was the third sea power, and its orientation could not be predicted. Mackinder suggested both possibilities, that it could be aligned with America and the British Empire against Russia, or that it could dominate both China and Russia and become that fearsome monster, a combined land and sea power.[43] But the immediate question was the manner in which land powers would move. The most significant ones were Russia and Germany, and both were rivals to British and American power globally. If either of them acquired sea power in addition to the upgraded technologies of land power, not to mention air power, each of them would become a potent threat. Before 1914, Germany aspired to just such a fusion of continental and sea power; she hoped to connect all the land routes up to the British Indian Empire through the Balkans and Turkey, at least up to Iraq through the Berlin-Bagdad Railway; and she simultaneously constructed a navy to compete with the Royal Navy. If Germany were to dominate Europe from the North Sea to the Adriatic, as so many plans proposed, this would be a continental and naval bloc of formidable power. If Germany could also link her African empire to Iraq and the Ottoman Empire, as yet other plans proposed, she would be overwhelming. If, to top it all, Germany were to ally with the vast Russian land empire, Anglo-American strategists faced the nightmare of a single Eurasian heartland from the Atlantic to the Pacific and extending along Africa down to the Indian Ocean, all of it complemented by sea power and bearing down on the rest of the world. In this manner the bipolar contest between the Eurasian and Atlantic powers was identified. To Anglo-American strategists, it was obvious that any coalescence between Germany and Russia must be disrupted; to German strategists it was equally clear that such a fusion was imperative. The rest of the world was to be arranged around either of these poles.

All subsequent geopolitical theorisation on the structure of world power was built on this central axis, the opposition between two centres of power, the Eurasian and the Atlantic and their forthcoming elimination round. Mackinder focused his attention on the Eurasian

Heartland with Russia as the 'pivot area' and suggested that those beyond it could move either way. The states on the Eurasian continent but outside the 'pivot' of Russia were termed the 'inner marginal crescent.' These were the great European states, including Germany, and beyond Europe it took in Turkey, the Middle East, India, China, and Korea, and other states on the continent. All of them faced both inward to the Continent and outward to the seas, and as such were both land and sea powers, albeit of secondary or tertiary rank with the exception of Germany. Beyond these were the scattered lands of the oceans, which he called the 'outer insular crescent.' The outer crescent consisted of Britain, the United States, and Japan principally, but it included Australasia, Indonesia, Africa, and the rest of the Americas. The Atlantic would form a bloc of the outer and inner crescents against the pivot area of Russia. But the uncertainty lay with Germany in the inner crescent and Japan in the outer crescent. They could move both ways: in different combinations they could unite with Russia, either by alliance or by conquest. Germany and Russia could unite, or Japan could independently dominate both China and Russia. The neat bipolar opposition did not quite hold, especially with Japan being a possible third pole.

In 1919, with the experience of the War behind him, Mackinder's attention was fixed almost wholly on the danger of the unification of the Eurasian Heartland.[44] As he saw it, it was only by a whisker that such a fate had been avoided; but in another war that may no longer have been possible. This time, the danger would come from Germany, less from Russia; but as always in the form of Germany uniting the Heartland. British sea power had finally defeated Germany, but he saw its limits all too clearly, not only with railway construction but now with air power also.[45] His solution was to separate Germany and Russia, especially by a string of states wedged between the two,[46] which was in fact Allied, especially French, policy in the inter-war years.

It is one of the strengths of Mackinder's analyses that he fused geopolitical argument with moral legitimation as he shifted focus from the British Empire to a Grossraum of a 'league of democracies.' His lecture of 1904 pointed to the loss of British naval supremacy and with it of British supremacy in general, and he foresaw new technologies of rail and air power (Amery on air power in 1904) in which Britain would not enjoy an automatic advantage. British power would rest on something more than Empire; and for the rest of his life Mackinder stressed the need to invest in human resources, working-class improvement, and pedagogy in general.[47] As early as 1911 he identified the forthcoming self-rule in India through British education, justice, and peace, which would add India as a willing partner to the 'league of democracies' composed of Britain and the Dominions. This was something more than the usual civilising mission of colonial dogma. It did not suffice to point out that India was safely under the heel of the British. A Grossraum of his making must be coherent in ideology to be effective in strategy, and a free and democratic India as a willing member of the Grossraum would be a strategic asset of incalculable value.[48] He did not elaborate: it was too radical a thought for a convinced imperialist, eugenicist, and racist as early as 1911;[49] but it portended imperial mortality. He disparaged the narrowness of both nationalism and even of mere Empire.

After the War, the tasks seemed more obvious. His democratic Grossraum must become a power that maintained the law among nations exactly as a state must preserve order among its citizens; and he predicted a 'world empire' that would be democratic also.[50] In principle, he was proposing the need for the sovereign of the kind that is associated with the name of Carl Schmitt.[51] Predictably, this world empire or democratic Grossraum would be led by the United States and the British Empire in tandem; the British Empire would consist of the Dominions and the United Kingdom in democratic association followed by the rest of the Empire in a theoretically undefined status but nonetheless in a worldwide democratic league. It was now 1919, and he was not so sanguine about India as an individual and perhaps independent member of a 'league of democracies' as he had been in 1911. He preferred to see India as the Raj, *tout court*. He adhered to the principle of a democratic Grossraum but compromised on India.

He drew on democratic ideals within British conservatism and European Christian Democracy to frame the ideological contrast between his democratic Grossraum and its tyrannical opponent in the Heartland. These democracies would be structured as local communities; they would be united through the equally democratic principle of federalisation; and the pyramid would rise from the city and the province through the nation to the League of Nations. It is not surprising that in the late nineteenth century this convinced conservative could work apparently harmoniously with the equally committed anarchist, Peter Kropotkin, in the Royal Geographical Society, which also welcomed another celebrated anarchist, Elisée Reclus. One end of the argument favoured global unity; but the other end saw it as an aggregation of local communities.[52] He imparted passion to cold strategy by supplying the familiar ideological, cultural, and psychological stereotypes that have become familiar throughout the century. As a professional British imperialist, Mackinder both flaunted British democracy and roundly denounced German imperialism and German tyranny without a trace of anxiety over inconsistency. He contrasted a homely British individualism to a robotic German 'Organised Man-Power.'[53] The British and Germans engaged in capitalist competition as decreed by Adam Smith, but the Germans were predatory and he likened them to 'cannibals.'[54] Bolshevik socialism and its threatened class war combined with German militarism. The Heartland could be united, not only as a monstrous land power but also through a witches' brew of militarist and socialist ideologies stirred in Prussian and Russian cauldrons. To round it off, he declaimed: 'German Kultur and all that it means in the way of organisation, would have made that German domination a chastisement of scorpions as compared with the whips of Russia.'[55] With that anti-Teutonic anti-Slavic diatribe he outlined something akin to the 'Free World' as he took leave in effect of British imperialism while complacently extolling the virtues of the British Empire.

Kjellén, in Sweden, speculated along almost identical lines during these early years until the twenties. But he stood closer to the ground and saw three rather than two power blocs unlike Mackinder, who, as a British imperial strategist, stood on a higher peak as it were and saw farther into the distance. Kjellén classified the leading powers in terms of world powers and great powers. As early as 1897 he suggested that the world would be divided into three autarkic regions, united by railways and led by America, Germany, and Japan. He also classified them, like Mackinder, into continental and sea powers, with Russia and Britain at either end and Germany and France in between.[56] During the War he saw the three world powers of Russia, Germany, and Britain, whom he called 'patrons,' and the others as mere great powers or 'clients' of the world powers.[57] After the war, he foresaw American hegemony and a *Pax Americana*, saw no future in communist Russia, but also could not imagine a proper future for Germany, given her defeat. As is clear, he was heading toward a politics of super power rivalry and was attempting to identify the poles as precisely as he could. America was a constant, Britain was subsiding, and Japan and Germany emerged intermittently.

Kjellén is illuminating for his pan-German and German Grossraum view of the world. He participated fully in Swedish politics as a thoroughly nationalist right-wing member of the Conservative party, was corporativist, and advocated the three-class three-chamber Parliament, and he opposed the independence of Norway, but his global orientation was German. He explained it as necessary to defend and protect his western world from the Russian threat. 'As a Swede and as a bearer of the Swedish cultural tradition and of the Swedish state bourgeoisie I must wish for a powerful Germany as a bulwark against the power from the East, which menaces the culture and state of my country.'[58] He looked to Germany to construct the European alliance that would do so, just as during the thirties and forties so much of the European right did.

Carl Schmitt fastened on to the concept of the Grossraum in the context of the new supranational power structures after Versailles, specifically of the League of Nations, Soviet universalism, and the imminent hegemony of the United States. He focused on four issues: (1) the world being divided into Grossraums over and above sovereign states; (2) multiple Grossraums, rather than just two of them; (3) ideological coherence; and (4) pluralism within the Grossraum. Interestingly, Mackinder's ideas ran parallel to Schmitt's on the first, third, and the fourth; on the second, of multiple Grossraums Mackinder transcended multipolarity in favour of bipolarity leading to unipolarity, which Schmitt deplored as the imperialism of Anglo-Saxon universalism.[59]

Schmitt began by explaining why the supreme arbiters of power in the world were Grossraums rather than sovereign states. He asked who could take a decision unilaterally. In international relations many sovereign states of unequal capacities engaged with each other; but with world wars and global power structures, those forms of sovereignty were clearly limited. Many states banded together under the leadership of one who was sovereign above them all and could take strategic decisions on their behalf. The leader among them was the Reich, the area that it commanded was the Grossraum, and the states within this Grossraum may or may not be sovereign. In his words, 'Reichs are the leading and sustaining powers whose political idea radiates over a specific Grossraum and which on principle exclude intervention by external powers in this Grossraum.'[60] The leader unilaterally defined its own powers of intervention within this area and of exclusion of others from it, a power that Schmitt termed decisionism (*Dezisionismus*). The Grossraum led by its own Reich thus became the decisive actor in world politics, replacing the sovereign state of the European states system, which had in theory played that role from the late fifteenth until the early twentieth century.[61] This form of supersession of sovereign states occurred in Europe after the First World War.

The prime example of such a Grossraum principle in action, according to Schmitt, was the Monroe Doctrine by which the western hemisphere was placed under American strategic protection in 1823. He claimed that it introduced a new doctrine of international law foreclosing outside intervention on the American continent. He noted that as the Doctrine was reiterated in the course of the century, the United States reserved the right to determine what constituted intervention by outsiders. He launched this idea on 1 April 1939 at the University of Kiel, and Hitler likened the principles of the Greater German Reich to the Monroe Doctrine in a speech to the Reichstag on 28 April 1939.[62] Hans Frank promptly telephoned Schmitt to warn him not to claim a patent on the idea lest it offend the Führer, who imagined himself an original thinker.[63] The analogy with the Monroe Doctrine was much favoured by the Nazi leadership, and Haushofer argued that geographical location and isolation from the Eurasian and African landmass (Mackinder's world-island) generated such a 'geopolitics' of a continental bloc led by the United States, which would be emulated by Germany leading the other continental bloc of the world-island. Finally, German theorists were taken up with the idea of American isolation which would be replicated in the new Grossraum to come.

All three propositions have come under severe attack. On the first question of a doctrine of international law, critics have claimed that Schmitt confused law with policy. The United States declared a policy through the Monroe Doctrine but it refused to incorporate it into treaties lest it create obligations, especially of protectorates. Schmitt has answered this objection with the argument that the repeated US practice of constructing treaties has in effect made it into a principle of international law. Similarly, the claim that geographical segregation permitted a geopolitics of isolation from Europe and domination in the Western Hemisphere has been shown to be a mistaken reading of American foreign policy. The Doctrine did not prohibit intervention by European powers on the American continent for it did not object to European colonial powers acting in their colonies in the American continent; it merely objected to further colonisation, to European interference in American states, and any extension of the European political system, for example, the Holy Alliance, to the Western Hemisphere. Third, there was no question of isolation since the United States was always closely aligned with Great Britain. American policy from the 1820s through the two world wars held to the need to keep Britain on the American side and forestall any attempt at domination and unification of Europe lest America be targeted next. As pithily suggested, the Royal Navy enforced the Monroe Doctrine throughout the nineteenth century.[64] Thus, the Monroe Doctrine was not a principle of law, of geopolitics, or of isolation, as various German theorists made out in justification of their drive to domination in Europe.[65]

Schmitt was not alone in seeing the end of the European order of equal sovereign states which had flourished since the sixteenth century. E. H. Carr in Britain, reflecting on the impact of global and total war, saw that this sovereign territorial unit would be superseded in some fashion. It could take the form of race, creed, or class; but he discounted them clearly because race had already been attempted by National Socialism and defeated, class had been similarly broached by the Bolshevik Revolution and had run out of steam, and creed had not been tried at all in modern times. Hence the territorial unit of world politics would remain, but not as the sovereign state.[66] Sovereign states like Poland, Czechoslovakia, or Austria, which had mushroomed after 1919, had collapsed like ninepins along with Belgium, Holland, Denmark, and Norway; and even such a great power and imperial state as France had succumbed. The future international order, he concluded, must consist of groupings of states, which he did not hesitate to term the Grossraum after the German geopoliticians; and he identified three candidates for that role after 1945, the United States, the British Commonwealth, and the Soviet Union.

> Culturally, these units may best be called civilisations: there are distinctively British, American, Russian and Chinese civilisations, none of which stops short at national boundaries in the old sense. Economically, the term *Grossraum* invented by German geo-politicians seems the most appropriate. The Soviet Union is pre-eminently a *Grossraum*, the American continents are the potential *Grossraum* of the United States, though the term is less convenient as applied to the British Commonwealth of Nations or the sterling area which are oceanic rather than continental agglomerations.[67]

Carr had tied the Grossraum to the civilisation: the supra-state and supra-national unit would be economically the Grossraum and culturally the civilisation, as defined by the theorists of the inter-war generation, Oswald Spengler in Germany, the Eurasianists in the Soviet Union and in emigration, and Arnold Toynbee in Britain. However, from the logic of his argument and the entities he identified, the Grossraum was clearly more than economic; it was as much political and strategic, if both the Soviet Union and the United States were to be considered. But he termed it economic perhaps to include the British Commonwealth whose strategic role as a power bloc was vanishing but which might yet display some economic vitality. The Empire and Commonwealth had hollowed, but Britain still had a role to play, according to him. This was to be the Reich to the post-war West European Grossraum, to replace Germany in that position. He foresaw the division of Europe and Soviet supremacy in East Europe after 1945, but Britain could provide symmetrical leadership in West Europe.[68] He based his argument on the history and traditions of Europe and its difference from Soviet state monopolies and American unrestricted competition. The reasoning was free of the abstract universalism of Wilsonian democracy; it was historical, territorial, and particularist in the manner of Schmitt. The suggestion was tentative, but the filiation to Schmitt was evident, if not acknowledged, as has been noted by scholarship on the subject.[69]

Both the absolute sovereignty of the state and the absolute independence of the nation-state were illusory; and these theories from the centres of declining empires were endorsed from the prime centre of optimistic anti-colonial nationalism, Jawaharlal Nehru in India. Drawing, like Schmitt and Carr, on the experience of the inter-war years, he committed himself to international cooperation to overcome the limitations of national independence. He was prepared to surrender part of the newly won independence to some form of supra-national organisation, but he was clear that the British Commonwealth did not qualify.

> When we talked of independence of India it was not in terms of isolation. We realised, perhaps more than many other countries, that the old type of complete national independence was doomed, and there must be a new era of world co-operation. We made it repeatedly clear, therefore, that we were perfectly agreeable to limit that independence, in common with other nations, within some international framework. That framework should preferably cover the world or as large a part of it as possible, or be regional. The British Commonwealth did not fit in with either of these conceptions, though it could be a part of the larger framework.
>
> It is surprising how internationally minded we grew in spite of our intense nationalism. No other nationalist movement of a subject country came anywhere near this, and the general

19

tendency in such other countries was to keep clear of international commitments.[70]

At this point an ambiguity arises. If that supra-national body was to be a power bloc or a Grossraum, he would have none of it, as it would perpetuate global conflict; instead he would steer an independent course through non-alignment which at least would not aggravate such tensions; but the non-aligned powers themselves would not constitute a power bloc of their own. The only higher body that could satisfy him was the United Nations, and he was a fervent believer in its beneficence. But Carr and Schmitt disdained such a single world body above the Grossraum they had foreseen and prescribed. Carr derided it for its 'empty universalism' of demanding that every nation and state must make every concern in the world its own. Thus Albania and Britain would have to meet the same obligations, be it to defend Belgium from Germany or Panama from the United States. Indeed, he claimed, the Monroe Doctrine of exclusion demonstrated how particularism in the Western hemisphere held off universalism.[71] Schmitt on the other hand discounted world government and the perpetual peace that was to ensue on the ground that it implied the extinction of the political from human life. Politics distinguished friend from foe and was inherent in the concept of the state; and one state presupposed another state, as Benedict Anderson was later to claim about nations.[72] A world without war would be devoid of politics; wars were waged for reasons that were not rational, but existential, and economic gain had little to do with them; and even pacifism could be political only if it were ready to wage war against war. Most importantly, he pointed out that the state could posit the internal enemy as much as the external; hence, he seemed to suggest, even the world state would engender internal enemies to vanquish. Ultimately, he argued, the 'political world is a pluriverse, not a universe.'[73] The vision was pessimistic; human nature demanded enemies to feed upon in perpetuity; and politics ingeniously discovered renewable sources of supply of that commodity.[74] World government and the end of power blocs was to Nehru ideal, to Carr impractical, and to the most hard-headed realist of all, Schmitt, meaningless; but all three of them began with realist insights into the illusory nature of sovereignty and the inadequacy of the nation state.

Schmitt's second thesis was an international order composed of multiple Grossraums rather than the impending single one imagined by Mackinder. It took the form of a critique of the abstract universalism and imperialism of Western democracies as embodied in the Versailles system and the Wilsonian programme. Against it he set the historical specificity of the German Reich firmly grounded in a people or *Volk*; and such a Reich would lead a group of peoples in a Grossraum, again understood in particularist terms, against the universalism of the Western democracies. This was a feature he noted with emphasis about the Monroe Doctrine in the nineteenth century: it had been territorial and particularist, limited to the American continent, unlike the British imperial universalism of space, especially with regard to the 'freedom' of the seas. The Monroe Doctrine then altered its principle and veered toward intervention under Theodore Roosevelt and universalism under Woodrow Wilson.[75] Schmitt did consider the possibility of Bolshevism being such a competing universalism; but he seems to have discarded it as a limited Russian Grossraum idea that paralleled the German, not the universalism that the Bolsheviks imagined themselves to embody.[76] He returned to this theme several times, of particularity, historicity, and territorial limits opposed to universalism, abstraction, and imperialism. Universal and abstract principles were deployed to homogenise the world and subject it to a single or imperial centre of power.[77] He nursed a vision of a European Grossraum as one among others; his theory reflected the vulnerable position of Germany after Versailles; but it also expressed the German capacity to lead Europe in the challenge to Versailles and Bolshevism. It proposed an international order that is now called multipolar, which differed from the Mackinderian and eventually American ideal of what is now called the unipolar. It could be one of the reasons for the resurrection of Schmitt after the Cold War.[78]

It could be debated whether he proposed a predatory principle of power blocs stalking the earth, or a defensive one of a German-led Grossraum which would be protected from outside interference, especially from the abstract universalism of 'Anglo-Saxon imperialism.'[79] The one did not exclude the other but he probably inclined toward the latter. The power bloc chalked out a specific territory instead of pretending to universalism; and it ensured ideological coherence and cultural compatibility within this space for effective leadership.[80] The predatory principle melded perfectly with the Third Reich's strategic impulse; but it does not follow that he inspired that outward thrust or approved of the war of conquest beyond the German domination of Central Europe.[81] His purpose was limited; at best, as Schwab has suggested, 'he correctly diagnosed a particular phase in Hitler's foreign policy.'[82] He was disillusioned with the anti-universalist and territorially particularist European Grossraum under Germany mutating into a Nazi racial universalism of its own during the War.[83] He was inclined, as a jurist, to an order, a *nomos*, not to the chaos of endless war, infinite expansion, and serial exterminations, as conducted by the Third Reich. On the defensive premise, however, the regional power bloc would guard the sovereignty of each Grossraum against intervention, oppose the imperialist notion of a single superpower, and would therefore be oriented to a pluralist world politics in spite of its superseding the sovereign state.[84] But it was less a defensive than a realist theory for clearing the board for a limited number of sovereign players and dismissing the absurdity of an infinite number of fictionally equal sovereignties. Its various aspects, realist, defensive, predatory, and pluralist, together corresponded to German strategic policy before total war; more cannot be attributed to it.

Schmitt's third thesis was on ideology, or the political idea as he called it. The Grossraum needs such an idea to hold it together, over and above the raw power of the Reich in question. The Reich or leader of the pack would be the disseminating centre of a 'political idea' which would animate the Grossraum.[85] The content of the idea could not be specified since it must vary from one Grossraum to the next, but he discerned the need for ideological and cultural coherence for the effectiveness of a Grossraum. At the time of the enunciation of the Monroe Doctrine, it was democracy in the Western Hemisphere opposed to the Legitimacy of the Holy Alliance in Europe, to conservatism, and to the anti-democratic crusade. In the twentieth century, the democratic liberalism and abstract universalism of the Allies, operating through such instruments as the League of Nations, was a typical such political idea; opposed to it was the political idea of the Greater German Reich, its historicity, its particularism, and its rejection of the imperialism of the West. A political idea held together this Grossraum, exemplified in Hitler's foreign and security policy as it stood in 1939.

Schmitt's awareness of the importance of ideology was the equal of Mackinder's and far superior to that of Haushofer or even of Kjellén. Kjellén spoke virtually in terms of Realpolitik, the hierarchy of raw power, and of civilisation, of Germany leading the West against Bolshevism, but little more. Haushofer stressed the need for more territory as the population of a state grew, spread a Malthusian veneer on it with dubious calculations of land-to-population ratios, argued the compulsion to expand, and finally linked it to race theory; but he did not cast it as an ideology. Schmitt distanced himself from Haushofer, and distinguished his own Grossraum from the expansionism of Haushofer's

Lebensraum.[86] Mackinder, however, outdid even Schmitt. Schmitt had to satisfy himself with multiple Grossraums and their respective ideologies as roughly equivalent and competing forces in world politics; as such it reverted to, or seemed to revert to, the discredited doctrine of the balance of power, but now between Grossraums rather than sovereign states. But Mackinder was relentless in his logic. As the world united, there would be no room for such competing systems; competition must lead to the elimination of competition, not its perpetuation; and he proposed the universalism of democracy in a postcolonial world which would erase its totalitarian competitors. Schmitt decried such universalism as both a legacy and omen of imperialism. It has been suggested that the 'political idea' was necessarily particularist in principle in opposition to liberal universalism;[87] it may or may not have been so since a liberal universalism is also another 'political idea' or ideology; but it is important that he saw the need for one just as Mackinder did for his 'league of democracies.' On this matter, E. H. Carr's thinking ran parallel to Schmitt's. He discerned the need for ideological coherence and eventually even cultural compatibility to a Grossraum. As he well expressed it, 'If, however, it is utopian to ignore the element of power, it is an unreal kind of realism which ignores the element of morality in any world order.'[88] Such morality amounted to the consent of the governed, and he found, like Mackinder before him, and the polemicists of the Cold War after him, that democracy provided the moral leitmotif to his own western Grossraum.

But there was something more that Mackinder, Schmitt, and Carr shared with respect to the need for coherence within the Grossraum. This was cultural compatibility over and above ideological unity.[89] It is at this point that the concept of Grossraum approaches that of the civilisation. None of them was explicit on the subject and they did not call upon Spengler, Eurasianism, and Toynbee for illustration and reinforcement. Mackinder satisfied himself with rhetoric about German *Kultur*, the cannibalism of their capitalism, their robotic organisation, and chastisement by their scorpions, all accompanied or followed by Russian whips. Schmitt, as he opposed liberal universalism to German particularism, stressed the peculiar historical traditions of the Germans, and therefore presumably its acceptance by the other members of the Grossraum. The argument was civilisational without being explicit. Carr went one step further and tantalisingly linked civilisation to Grossraum, without expanding upon it. He noted that these supranational or multinational entities were often conceived of as civilisations, of which he discerned as leading ones the American,

British, European, Russian, Chinese, Japanese, and possibly Indian, compromised as it was by its colonial mélange.[90] The accuracy or otherwise of the identification need not detain us here; it is significant that he saw civilisation as the cultural analogue of the Grossraum in the manner that Imperial Russian, Soviet, and post-Soviet Russian theorists fuse Russian world power with either pan-Slavic or Eurasian civilisationism, and that Samuel Huntington has posited the West as a civilisational Grossraum to face down the rest of the post-Cold War world.

Schmitt's fourth argument related to the internal pluralism of the Grossraum. He distinguished it from the sovereign state, which imposed its uniform will over the entire territory of the state and would brook no challenge to its authority within that territory. In the Grossraum, on the other hand, the Reich was merely the leader of a group of such states without attempting to substitute for each state. As he explained it, Brazil was part of the Grossraum created by the Monroe Doctrine with the United States as the Reich or the leader; but it was not part of the United States.[91] But he could not explain away an obvious ambiguity. In order to enforce its will as leader, the Reich would need to intervene in or against a member state; the leader would need to use its discretion to do so; to that extent, the subordinate state's sovereignty would be compromised, and the pluralism of the Grossraum would be eroded.[92] The Monroe Doctrine permitted both interpretations, as designed to protect the pluralism of the American hemisphere, but also, as reinterpreted by especially Theodore Roosevelt, Woodrow Wilson, and Franklin Roosevelt, to sanction American unilateralism and intervention.[93] The Reich in such a case had the option to retain the power bloc or to convert it into a new state and the tendency toward the new state was a strong possibility. Hitler's New Order in Europe was such a Grossraum with a remarkable degree of internal pluralism. From the formal independence of Spain, the partitioning of France, and the subordination of all other continental states culminating in the redrawing of the map, deportations, and exterminations in East Europe, Hitler's Grossraum was very plural. But Germany was the undisputed Reich.[94]

These accounts of the emergence of Grossraums anticipated the post-war European submission to America to carry out the same mission of protecting their civilisation from a Russia and communism rearing its double head from the east. It has been suggested that if Germany was to be the leader of the anti-communist Grossraum of the first half of the century, America has assumed that role thereafter. NATO and the European Union, both led by America, embody that purpose. It preserves the sovereignty of the member states, but ultimate sovereignty rests with the American Reich and all the states willingly coordinate their policies with and subordinate themselves to American leadership.[95] Multiple Grossraums have been identified for post–Cold War politics: the European led by a Franco-German partnership, the Latin American under Brazil, the Russian in a shrunken Soviet space, and the East Asian led by China.[96] These are, however, regional power blocs subordinate to the ultimate American one; and Kjellén's hierarchy of the world power superior to the great power must not be forgotten. This search for pluralism to offset American hegemonial impulses, or abstract universalism as Schmitt described them, has led to even the Shanghai Cooperation Organisation being identified as a potential Grossraum; but to elevate such a toothless grouping to that status is to empty the concept of meaning.[97] To repeat, the Grossraum would not only be a grouping of states, or even a power bloc, for it must needs have an unchallenged leader or a Reich, be comparable in power to the other Grossraums if any, and be ready to go to war to assert that position. In effect, Grossraums flourished until 1945; during the Cold War, the Soviet bloc employed the rhetoric but had been emptied of the substance of one; and after the Cold War, no such grouping exists, save those under American leadership. Mackinder was unique for suggesting that the route to unipolarity lay through bipolarity: and Schmitt defensively proposed multipolarity against the prestations of unipolarity. Such was the core of geopolitical theory, a reflection on the nature of the structuring of power in an integrating world.

A number of other concerns were pendant on it, in varying degree secondary, archaic, and even quaint. But they have attracted considerable attention, and it is worth both elaborating them and asking why they have enjoyed such prominence.

The organic state and Lebensraum

These two concepts are so interrelated that they are best considered together. In the work of Friedrich Ratzel from the 1870s states are imagined as organisms: they struggle for survival among other states; they grow and recreate themselves by establishing themselves in new spaces; and they adapt to their environment in the manner of speciation in evolutionary biology. A state is therefore always a project: it remains incomplete, it is perpetually in the making, and it is never made.[98] The adaptation is cultural, and different species both adapt differently and alter themselves constantly in the course of such adaptation.

The growth of the organic state is necessarily territorial, hence its survival required living space or Lebensraum. Ratzel elaborated his version of Lebensraum in three directions: (1) migration stimulating development; (2) the larger the new space, the greater the security; and (3) the new space is demanded and shaped culturally, not merely biologically.

He spoke of migration, settlement, and evolution with disconcerting universality, as if plants, animals, and human beings functioned in the same manner. He could be understood as a biological and geographical determinist, but that might be a misreading of his arguments. He began with Moritz Wagner's decisive insight, that terrestrial space was finite while life forms were infinite and ever varying, and among these forms of life, human life forms were themselves so immensely variable. Given this condition or central contradiction, the struggle for existence is necessarily a struggle for space.[99] While it was applied to individual organisms, Ratzel pointed out that organisms grouped themselves into aggregates like the animal herd. Such an aggregate organism sought space in the same manner as the individual one. While these laws applied to human beings as much as to the animal world, Ratzel isolated the state as the human aggregate organism that would clear and command a space for its existence.[100] Evolutionary theories of the struggle for existence becoming the struggle for space in the Mackinderian 'closed system' moved smoothly into the politics of imperialist rivalry and its zero-sum games.

Security improved with size and creativity grew with space, for it then allowed for a greater range of adaptive strategies and reduced the possibility of decline and of conflict in the species that inhabited or dominated that space. The larger the area, the less there were chances of encountering neighbours and conflicting with them, which brought him to the argument on autarky. He did not pursue this line of argument, but his followers did.[101]

Finally, he argued that space was determined culturally, not merely biologically. It was culture that imagined a space, stimulated the feeling for it, argued the need for it, and eventually shaped it. Cultures that could not imagine in these various ways were necessarily limited to their biological functions and a bit beyond.[102] He summed it up in what was to become or already was a familiar dictum: 'A small Indian tribe in the South American virgin forest has spatial needs and ideas which are very different from those of a European who can see his salvation only in a global context.'[103]

Importantly, he distinguished the state from the nation and distanced himself from the romance of the nation-state. To him the nation was limiting while the state was enabling. The nation was restricted ethnically, and it would reach its limits when all those of that ethnic definition were united or brought together in some fashion. The state on the other hand was not so confined ethnically: it was possessed of a territory, and as it grew, its territory expanded, and all the inhabitants of that piece of the earth's crust would be fused into one people, their linguistic and other differences notwithstanding. He thus provided an intellectual foundation for the infinite expansion of the state beyond a nationality; he broke with the constraints and balance of nation-state politics; and the National Socialist theorists found it productive to appropriate him as their intellectual forbear. Yet, as the foregoing exegesis would suggest, he was no racist; indeed, he believed in equality in the human species and repudiated the racist doctrines of Houston Stewart Chamberlain and Arthur de Gobineau.[104]

Rudolf Kjellén, the political scientist who coined the word 'geopolitics,' complemented Ratzel by arguing the dynamism and perpetually self-transforming nature of the state. While he classified the state's attributes into the natural and the rational, with the rational directing the natural, or the mind the instinct, it revealed a state that was being constantly shaped by its citizens into a dynamic, sometimes volcanic, entity.[105] It did not admit of any determinism. He went on to clarify that the expansion of the state is willed, not natural, and it consists in the effective exploitation of all available resources, human and natural; it is, therefore, a cultural process. Great powers and large states must amalgamate or dominate small ones, but a great power in such circumstances emerges by deliberate choice, and the refusal to do so must lead to its subsidence. States as great powers expand, not out of necessity but by an inner impulse. Indeed, a great power reaches no point of saturation: it must expand endlessly or dissolve.[106] In the inter-war years, Karl Haushofer complemented the organic state and Lebensraum doctrines with elaborate Malthusian arguments on the problem of overpopulation, of food supplies, of the special relation to land and its produce, on the sublime virtues of the cultivator of the soil, and hence of the need for expansion to support a growing population in good health. He compared the population densities of Japan and Europe and suggested the moment when expansion becomes inevitable. But, after much wordy analysis and description, he finally admitted that there was no scientific method of establishing the ideal relation of land to its population. In short, overcrowding is meaningless in conditions of modern technology, trade, and communication.[107] During the Second World War, Nicholas Spykman in the United States made further contributions to the expanding state thesis without being squeamish in the least: a state expands until stopped; every state wants superiority; and the balance of power is a temporary stalemate in a ceaseless struggle. The balance of power is no more than a clever ploy to hinder the expansion of a dangerous rival; it is not a commitment for its own sake; and it may be abandoned at an opportune moment.[108]

The need or the demand for space to develop free of constraint yielded another persistent concern, autarky, implied in Ratzel's claim that greater space allowed for greater security. The experience of British industrial and economic supremacy during the nineteenth century had inspired protectionist advocacy by Alexander Hamilton in the USA in his *The Federalist Papers*, by his admirer Friedrich List in Germany,[109] and through most of the century in Russia. In Germany it culminated in the identification of a territory through which Germany would be both self-sufficient and dominant. List proposed a protected area of German domination stretching from the North Sea to the Adriatic and Black Seas. Friedrich Naumann outlined a geography extending from the North and Baltic Seas to the Adriatic and Black Seas and from Flanders to the frontiers of Russia.[110] Paul Rohrbach followed on by imaginatively carving out the territory of the Middle East, Turkey, and the Caucasus, with the Bagdad railway outflanking the British strategic asset of the Suez Canal. Kjellén was from Sweden but a German in his geopolitical imagination and imagined Germany as the natural leader of Europe.[111] He defined a future Germany that covered most of Europe and took in the Ukraine, parts of Russia, and stretched out into Africa. It was to ensure economic autarky, for which he employed the term *Ekopolitik* to run alongside his successful neologism *Geopolitik*.[112] Such autarky reflected the ultimate moment of independence, of a state beholden to no external presence, capable of satisfying itself from within itself, the pinnacle and embodiment of sovereignty.[113] In Britain, Mackinder's Unionist politics and calls for protection[114] corresponded to these campaigns in Germany for a secure domain beyond mere national sovereignty. These aspirations toward an independent space merged subsequently with strategic planning for global warfare. They were inspired by a search for the ideal condition of self-sufficiency and security to beat off competition. They inspired Haushofer's advocacy of 'space consciousness,' which Germans lacked and which needed to be instilled. Autarky, in this imagination, was not pure self-sufficiency; it was self-sufficiency preparing for expansion.

Lebensraum was an ideal that was undoubtedly expansionist; but that ideal was not a German monopoly. Britain, America, Russia, and

Japan were unabashedly expansionist; their territorial ambitions were comparable to the German; but they did not have recourse to such theorisation. Lebensraum was derived from a theory of the state, as advanced by Ratzel and elaborated by Kjellén, Haushofer, and others, that growth was synonymous with survival, and that it needed expanding territory in addition to other conditions like cultural creativity. On the other hand, economic growth was not premised on territorial expansion, and even Mackinder's vision of global dominion was founded on alliance systems and cultural fusion rather than of territorial conquest. German theorists stressed territory more than other European and American imperialists and they sought support in evolutionary biology, perhaps because, as has often been said, the imperial career of the German state began late, when the world had already become a 'closed system.'

Mobile frontiers

The organic nature of the state and its ineluctable expansion and contraction induced instability on the borders. Theory drew the distinction between a border (boundary) and a frontier. The border was a line demarcated on the ground and drawn on the map; the frontier was an indeterminate zone at the edge of the territory of a settlement or a state; they were 'natural zones of struggle as life shifted back and forth in these spaces.'[115] Ratzel elaborated the difference with finesse and precision;[116] Ellen Semple smudged it not a little in her admiring exegesis on his work;[117] and George Curzon's authoritative pronouncement on the subject in 1907 did not differentiate in theory but described it in fact in considerable detail as he explained the triple frontier of India, especially on the north-west, the administrative, the military, and the strategic.[118] Other geographers followed suit. Thomas Holdich, a former colonial army officer with much experience, like Curzon, of the Indian north-west frontier, and now the vice-president of the Royal Geographical Society, established the difference explicitly in 1916: 'No limit is set to a frontier until an actual line of boundary is defined by treaty; and even then it is generally open to dispute until that boundary is actually demarcated.'[119] Charles Fawcett continued in that vein by defining the frontier as a zone and as a transition between two regions. It was not merely fluid but also differentiated from the interior of the state.[120] The frontier population retained unique features derived from an earlier history of separateness,[121] and they were close to forming or often enough formed a separate community with those beyond.[122] These distinctions became routine as the century wore on.[123] A frontier was indeterminate: it was culturally remote from the centre and the interior; its inhabitants tended to form independent bonds across the frontier; and they were unpredictable and uncertain in their loyalty to the state to which they nominally belonged.

Most observers discerned the uncertainty of frontiers through practical experience, especially on the colonial, Russian, and American frontiers. Ratzel, however, provided the theoretical foundation through the theory of the state as an organism that survived only by growth, which entailed reproducing itself through flourishing diversity on a moving frontier. The frontier participated in every aspect of the state, it absorbed its social energies, and it reflected all its changes and especially its growth.[124] The shifting frontier dissolved the political boundary which political leaders had so painstakingly drawn on maps and demarcated on the ground. To a healthy state, the growing one, the border was deliquescent and the frontier opened out to infinity. Its turbulence was a menace; its creativity was welcome; and the state periodically reconstituted the centre and periphery into a new structure of stability. Turner's paean to the American frontier as a force for perennial renewal, composite nationalism, social mobility, and democracy, expresses this thesis most forcefully.[125] Yet, so does the hosanna to imperial frontiers by Turner's contemporary, Curzon, in his exposition of the Ratzelian thesis of regeneration at the margin: 'I am one of those who hold that in this larger atmosphere, on the outskirts of Empire, where the machine is relatively impotent and the individual is strong, is to be found an ennobling and invigorating stimulus for our youth, saving them alike from the corroding ease and the morbid excitements of Western civilisation.' As he was speaking at Oxford, and as a finished product of Western civilisation, he was diplomatic and inconsistent enough to declare that the English universities were both the equal of the frontier in their capacity to form 'character' and immune to the corruption of civilisation.[126] Mackinder, speaking as a prescient political strategist of the Grossraum and as a professional geographer, pronounced in 1942: 'The Victorian habit of thinking in political frontiers must have been seriously discredited by now!'[127] It was after all the year of the erasure of all boundaries in the bloodlands of East Europe.

These varied reflections on the nature of frontiers and borders were assembled by Karl Haushofer into a number of works, but most of all into his single volume devoted specifically to borders. It was composed immediately after Versailles as a polemic against the settlement, but it advanced his geopolitical thesis with exhausting verbosity and opacity. His frontiers were the theatre of the struggle for survival, they shifted constantly, they were the sites of the renewal of life, and they generated their own forms of life. They were zones of contestation, open spaces that invited the entrepreneur, the explorer, the pioneer, and the conqueror. His accounts of 'wandering frontiers' were buttressed by the realistic insight that during war there were no borders. They were battle zones, subject to dispute; they were regions, not lines; and the jurist's fetish with the abstraction of cartographic delineation fatally ignored the reality of the relations of power at the point of contest. Geography knew natural frontiers, but politics created borders arbitrarily.[128] He resorted to the typically nationalist argument that the political boundary must coincide with the cultural. As a military strategist he demanded that the military boundary must be protected by a glacis. But since a glacis is safe only if settled by a loyal population, in his case the German, it would create a new cultural boundary with which the political one must catch up. It entailed almost an infinite expansion.[129] Borders were supreme products of the human will; all concepts of their being natural, psychological, sociological, or legal, and most of all permanent, were utterly delusional.

But an expanding state no longer had open frontiers as China and Russia suffered with the nomadic frontier, as European settlers discovered in the lands of colonisation, or as colonial empires enjoyed throughout the world in the nineteenth century. With the demarcation of the entire world by the late nineteenth century, an expanding state must encounter another state, and the frontier became a zone of contestation between two states. At this point the political geographer gave way to the political scientist and strategist, Ratzel to Kjellén, Mackinder, Haushofer, and Spykman. The organic theory of the state and of its necessary growth or decline retained its force; but one state would grow at the expense of another at the interstate border, leading into the concepts of Lebensraum and Grossraum.

These doctrines undermined what were then assumed to be an international relations states system of the epoch. It was known, or is now known, as the Westphalian system, so-called after the Peace of Westphalia of 1648 to end the Thirty Years' War. It is credited with having established the principles of the sovereignty of the state within territorial boundaries, legal equality between states, secular politics, nonintervention in the internal affairs of each state, standing diplomacy, international law, and European congresses devoted to maintaining the balance of power between these states while admitting of inter-state anarchy and power politics. It firmly ended the variety of feudal relationships and the claims to universal empire. These assertions have been challenged, and with justification, as exaggerated, since territorial adjustments took place periodically on dynastic principles and many states were no more than agglomerations of hereditary jurisdictions and rights. Europe was plagued by wars until the nineteenth century, and each war ended with major territorial rearrangements. The eighteenth century even witnessed the disappearance of such a major state as the Polish. The revolutionary and Napoleonic wars induced further violent fluctuations of every kind until the Congress of Vienna stabilised the international relations system for the better part of the century.[130] Even so, various parts of East Europe and the Balkans were almost permanently unstable and were a standing mockery of much that was meant by a Westphalian system.

However, one practice held out through all this instability, and that was of borders rather than of frontiers, of the abstraction of cartographic lines over indeterminate frontier zones. International power politics admitted of substantial redistribution of territories and even of altered sovereignties; but borders were nonetheless nearly precise even as each territory was transferred from one state to another. The rest of the world did not know such precision, owing to the retreat of pastoral nomadism and the advance of colonial settlement and colonial conquest, all from the eighteenth century. However, such precision and abstraction as had been established was now to be abandoned in Europe also. The new geopolitical vision conflated the distinction between a border and a frontier: the border would no longer remain a line; it must become a frontier even between states that had been engaging in the making of treaties and the demarcation of boundaries for a couple of centuries or more by then. The mobile border belonged conceptually to the state expanding and contracting as any organic species.

Geopoliticians were not the only ones to discourse on the impermanence of borders. It seemed equally obvious to those who were committed to an international order that transcended the nation-state; and among these was the unlikely figure of Jawaharlal Nehru. His entire reign of seventeen years as prime minister of India was spent on border disputes with Pakistan and China and in an inconclusive struggle to define them permanently. Yet, he periodically reminded his public that borders were impermanent, fluid, and anachronisms to the age of air transport, wireless communication, and high population mobility in an integrating world.[131] But there was an important difference between geopolitical theorising and this form of the global imagination. Geopoliticians spoke of the mobile frontier rather than of its fluidity; they saw it as deriving from their theories of the organic state, a domain of contestation between states, the frontier moving to extend the territory of one state at the expense of that of another, expansion necessary for survival, and therewith Lebensraum. Nehru's globalism understood it as an aspect of subordination to an international order, not of the expansion of a single state and the permanent struggles for survival that must ensue. Both ideals were supranational, but the one was oriented to expansion and conquest, the other to cooperation, confederation, and federation.

Sea power and land power

The opposition between sea power and land power has apparently mesmerised geopolitical theorists from Ratzel in the nineteenth century down to Spykman in the 1940s. This is, however, something of a diversion from the main concern of geopolitics of reflecting on the strategy for a unified global politics determined from one centre and the competition to become that centre. Yet, theorists have devoted so much attention to the subject that it demands more careful scrutiny.

The sudden salience of sea power in analyses of global politics was due the nature of British supremacy and the new challenge to it from Germany, the United States, and Japan, to the extent of Britain accepting its relative decline and entering into an alliance with Japan in 1902. Mackinder's lecture of 1904 reflected anxiety over the disturbing awareness that sea power by itself was insufficient to ensure primacy. The first element of all such analyses was the unique advantages of water communications and of sea power. This was followed by a historical explanation of British leadership, the challenge to Britain from several rivals, and finally the abatement of the relative importance of sea power given the new technologies of rail and air transport. The thrust of the discourse on sea power was not to project a decisive opposition of sea power to land power so much as to argue its subsidence in a world ever more interlocked through new technologies.

In 1890, Alfred Thayer Mahan first drew attention to the specific nature of sea communication and to the British mastery of that medium. The oceans were a single and unbroken mass of water that girdled the globe and surrounded all the continents. Its only boundaries were the land, but it knew no boundaries within itself; land on the other hand was broken into islands and divided into states and their jurisdictions affecting communication in every respect. Movement on the high seas was cheaper and faster, despite its numerous uncertainties and legendary catastrophes, from Antonio's bankruptcy to the fate of the Spanish Armada. Mastery of the seas, therefore, allowed for power to be projected at any corner of the globe at short notice.[132] In 1900 Ratzel elaborated on Mahan's central insights with many deeper reflections on the geography of the seas and the nature of world power. He decreed the end of the old opposition of sea and land power; he noted that sea power could be defeated only by sea power; and he concluded with the dictum that world power must combine sea power with land power, that it must turn in both directions.[133] This was a theme to which all geopolitical theorists returned, as all of them had digested both Mahan and Ratzel.

Mahan went on to explain the rise of Britain. He composed several works on sea power and the most influential of them argued in some detail how Britain had single-mindedly nurtured its sea power from the seventeenth century in repeated contests with first Holland, then France, to master the seas and establish an empire.[134] Britain refused to be drawn into acquiring European territories on land; instead, she organised and financed coalitions against those who attempted to dominate Europe. Her principal target during these two centuries was France. Britain assembled the necessary coalitions to conduct the War of the Grand Alliance or of the League of Augsburg, 1689–1697, and the War of the Spanish Succession, 1701–1714, against Louis XIV, followed in due course by the War of the Austrian Succession, 1740–1748, and especially the Seven Years' War, 1756–1763. In Mahan's argument, France had the option of becoming a naval power like Britain but chose land power instead. The result was twofold. Britain humbled her by organising these coalitions, and in the course of it acquired an empire overseas, in America, the West Indies, and in India, securing along the way all the necessary strategic communication points like Gibraltar, St Helena, the Cape of Good Hope, and others. France was worsted everywhere only because she could not match the British at sea; and she could not do so because she had chosen not to do so. France paid for her strategic choice and Britain reaped all the benefits, with a final moment of glory at Trafalgar. Mackinder added the further historical detail that land power had prevailed until the sixteenth century and had accounted for all the great empires of the world, that the mastery of the seas began only with the age of discoveries and the expansion of Europe in the fifteenth century, and that that phase of human history was drawing to its close with railway technology restoring the balance to land power. Spykman was the last major geopolitical theorist to dwell on this opposition with the usual geographical detail on the nature of the waterways of the world.[135] While the interest in geopolitics has revived somewhat after 1991, the theme of sea power and land power has been passed over.

As may be evident by now, the core of geopolitical theory is not contained in the supposed opposition between sea power and land power. Mackinder has been credited with this contrast as his driving concern, but that was more likely of secondary significance, both for him and the principal geopolitical theorists. He focused attention on sea power as contributing decisively to European expansion (the Columbian epoch) and within it to British supremacy; this led to a global opposition between the continental states of Eurasia and those states that could draw on superior naval power; but this polarity was of declining import in the face of revolutionary technologies of land and air communication. As a consequence, British primacy was fated to settle as a residue of history unless revived through other strategic alliances and further internal revolutions in technology and human resource development. The most important strategic alliance was with the United States; this was to be complemented by possible candidates from among other states, all former or potential rivals, be it France, Germany, Russia, or Japan, with India and China hovering on the margin, not as rivals but as future strategic players. The significance of these powers would be measured, not by their status as naval or continental powers, but by their capacity to act globally by combining their assets optimally. In the course of these reflections over four decades, Mackinder outlined the impending bipolarity of the Cold War with projections possibly even into the post–Cold War condition. That bipolarity consisted in the United States in close association with Britain fashioning a worldwide network of alliances to face down a potential challenger. The only challenger that was discernible was from the Eurasian landmass, which gave rise to the geographical distinctions. If that rival had been located in South America, the logic of the argument may not have altered significantly, but the opposition between land and sea power would have receded ever more into history.

Eclipse

Geopolitical theory mutated into Cold War theory almost imperceptibly, to the extent of the similarities obscuring the differences. The identities are obvious, for once again the Eurasian Heartland and the Atlantic world were led by super states wrestling for the crown, and they seemed to correspond to Mackinder's continental and maritime powers. While in geopolitical theory the power groupings were identified geographically, in Cold War theorisation they were distinguished by ideology, and John Agnew has appropriately enough described the Cold War as 'ideological geopolitics.'[136] Yet, remarkably, the *term* geopolitics fell into disuse during the Cold War, during *les trente glorieuses*, the three decades of Western prosperity, stability, and renewed certitudes until the 1970s.

It has been often suggested that this was due to its association with Nazi strategy. But this is unconvincing given that the fountainhead of geopolitical wisdom was Mackinder and that such ideas had been enthusiastically purveyed to the American public. It has also been seen as a reductionist exercise in geographical determinism that neither explained global politics nor contributed to effective strategy; but again, none of the geopolitical theorists were geographical determinists, whatever the significance they accorded to geography.[137]

The reasons for its atrophy may lie deeper and point to the substantial difference between geopolitics and Cold War. James Burnham, sometimes called the first cold warrior,[138] had argued in 1944–1947 that two centres of power were locked in mortal combat for dominion of the world.[139] He regarded the United States and the Soviet Union as nearly equal powers, and that it was the duty of the United States to lead the rest of the world in extirpating Soviet power. This was geopolitical thinking in the manner of Mackinder. By 1947 however, George Kennan's containment strategy, the one that was successfully deployed throughout the Cold War, saw it differently. He refused to equate the United States and the Soviet Union: his Soviet Union was marooned on the socialist island of its own making, 'the sole truly Socialist regime in a dark and misguided world';[140] it was no more than an obstacle to American leadership and domination and incapable of being an existential threat, for 'Russia, as opposed to the western world in general, is still by far the weaker party,' and that 'This would of itself warrant the United States entering with reasonable confidence upon a policy of firm containment, designed to confront the Russians with unalterable counterforce at every point where they show signs of encroaching upon the interest of a peaceful and stable world.'[141] This was no longer geopolitical strategy, for it was not premised on the struggle for supremacy: the United States had prevailed in that struggle; there were no challengers; there remained only a self-enclosed space called communism and the Soviet Union; and the United States had but to frustrate any attempt at shifting the fence. It was, he reflected nearly four decades later, no more than an 'ideological-political threat,' for in post-war conditions 'there was no way that Russia could appear to me as a military threat.' By the 1980s, even the 'ideological-political threat' had receded in his view; what now remained to be contained was not a Soviet military menace but the danger of an arms race.[142] He did not expect any war between the two states. This reality more than anything else perhaps accounts for the eclipse of geopolitical theory: there was a clear winner by 1945.

But self-confidence faltered on both sides of the great divide from the mid-seventies. It was no longer possible to imagine the contest in such clear ideological terms as the free world versus totalitarianism or capitalism against socialism. Geopolitics as a means to comprehending global politics resurfaced as a default option in multiple reincarnations from the later 1970s, although it does not command the same attention or fascination that it did before 1945. It was resurrected in combative fashion in France in 1976 by Yves Lacoste and his journal *Hérodote*; in the late 1970s by Henry Kissinger and many of the security specialists in the West and in the 1990s in Russia; and most of all in the post-Cold War era by Gearóid Ó Tuathail and others through 'critical geopolitics.'

Lacoste set out to expose the discipline of geography in France as participating in the structuring of power while obfuscating that reality as a purely academic discourse. His journal focused attention on the dilemmas of developing and postcolonial societies, especially of Africa, through a close study of utterly local circumstances, geographical and historical. Its radicalism was a riposte to the imperialism with which geopolitics had been associated until then and for which reason even the word had become anathema. But its readership and influence, though considerable, was confined to the French and Mediterranean world and to South America, bypassing the Anglophone world almost entirely. This may have been due to its valuable articles being highly empirical in nature, regionally specific, and deficient in theory. Ultimately, it was a French geographer's critique of the practice of academic geography in France, a reminder to his colleagues of the manner in which knowledge was complicit with power; it did so by exposing the nature of power in that part of the developing world with which his audience was most familiar; but it did not reach for the skies and analyse the nature of the contest for global dominion. Only in 1997, twenty years after its foundation, did the journal devote a special issue to the United States, and even so only to its domestic fissure of racism, not to globalisation and its implications. Lacoste stoutly resisted Anglo-American academic imperialism by fixing his sights on resistance; and he made French academic geography and the concept of geopolitics sites of such resistance. He dwelt on the nation-state as the principal reality of geopolitics; and he was nationalist, assimilationist, and opposed to multiculturalism. His resort to the nation-state as the instrument to contain Anglo-American domination recalls Carl Schmitt's assigning that task to the Grossraum; Lacoste imparted a new meaning and a radical freshness to the word and the concept; but he did so at the cost of a certain nationalist self-limitation.[143]

Henry Kissinger revived the use of the term more than the concept as late as 1979 to denote equilibrium, permanent national interests, and the balance of power,[144] Metternichian nineteenth-century visions remote from the twentieth-century geopolitical. He was followed by different branches of the security establishments in various countries, including the French L'Institut Internationale de Géopolitique founded in 1981 with its own journal *Géopolitique* and led by American, British, and French security specialists. Russian security analysts followed suit from 1991, with even the Communists led by Gennady Zyuganov freely invoking that proscribed word and equating the concept with Russian state strategy from the early eighteenth century.[145] But none of these innovated theoretically, and geopolitics functioned as a synonym for security and Realpolitik.

Perhaps the most creative form of its renewed usage is 'critical geopolitics,' and Gearóid Ó Tuathail has been its chief exponent. His is a declared postmodernist critique and draws heavily on Foucault. He includes Cold War theory and practice as a continuation of geopolitics; and, while brushing aside much undergrowth, he focuses his attention on the nature of power itself. All those defined structures into which geopolitical thinking was cast, namely territory, boundaries, states and their groupings, their power rivalries, and the binary division of global power: all these must be dispersed, redrawn, and most of all decentred in post–Cold War conditions of deterritorialisation with states no longer the principal or sole agents in the global power play. Power swirls around the globe and flows through states and non-states, agglomerations of states, multilateral entities, transnational corporations, non-governmental organisations, organised crime syndicates, warlords spiritual and temporal, terror groups and networks of every description. It seems to permeate the globe like cosmic energy, apparently without a centre and denuded of an obvious logic to its working. The American state is often assumed to be the centre and beneficiary of the erasure of definitions. But that is to fall victim to the territorial delusion of state power. The American state may indeed be at the centre of this maelstrom, but only as a locus of power detached from the territory and people of the United States. It is a transnationalised entity that moves in and seeks to master this cosmic anarchy, far above the American territorial state with its citizenship and its nationalism.[146] There are periodic attempts to redefine the American role in territorial and cultural and even national terms, but global imperatives and seductions prevail over nationalist and territorial self-denial and self-limitation. The world has been truly globalised, fused into a single space for power, far from united, highly differentiated, yet free of the binaries of the Cold War or the territorial power blocs or Grossraums competing for supremacy. The contestation of the kind witnessed in the two world wars has ended; the world is led from America, but not by the territorially defined American imperial state or a Western civilisation. Such a critique of geopolitics and of its recasting merges it with global power in its most generalised, anarchic, and perplexing forms and seems in effect to dissolve the concept of geopolitics.[147] It is not quite clear why we need continue with it; and Agnew has served notice: 'This may well be an auspicious moment, therefore, to ask whether the modern geopolitical imagination, which lies at the root of all of these scenarios to one degree or another, is not itself overdue for retirement from the global scene.'[148]

Notes

* I am most grateful to Mehrdad Samadzadeh of Toronto University for his considerable help with references.

1 Friedrich Ratzel, *Anthropogeographie*, Part 1, *Grundzüge der Anwendung der Erdkunde auf die Geschichte*, 3rd edn, Stuttgart: Engelhorn, 1909, pp. 148–151.

2 Nicholas J. Spykman, 'Geography and Foreign Policy, I,' *The American Political Science Review*, 1938, 32(1): 28–50; Nicholas J. Spykman, 'Geography and Foreign Policy, II,' *The American Political Science Review*, 1938, 32(2): 213–236; Nicholas John Spykman, *America's Strategy in World Politics: The United States and the Balance of Power*, New York: Harcourt, Brace, 1942; Nicholas John Spykman, *The Geography of the Peace*, edited by Helen R. Nicholl, New York: Harcourt, Brace, 1944.

3 See, among others, Karl Haushofer, *Weltpolitik von Heute*, Berlin: Zeitgeshichte, 1935.

4   Halford J. Mackinder, 'The Geographical Pivot of History,' *The Geographical Journal*, 1904, 23(4): 421–437.

5   André-Louis Sanguin, 'L'évolution et le renouveau de la géographie politique,' *Annales de Géographie*, 1975, 84(463): 275–296, especially pp. 275–278.

6   Carl Schmitt, *Völkerrechtiche Großraumordnung mit Interventionsverbot für raumfremde Mächte. Ein Beitrag zum Reichsbegriff im Völkerrecht*, Berlin – Wien: Deutscher Rechtsverlag, 1939.

7   Joseph W. Bendersky, *Carl Schmitt: Theorist for the Reich*, Princeton, NJ: Princeton University Press, 1983, pp. 252–253, 259.

8   Carl Schmitt, *Land and Sea*, translated by Simona Draghici, Washington, DC: Plutarch Press, 1997, (original German edn 1954), pp. 54–57.

9   Francis P. Sempa, *Geopolitics: From the Cold War to the 21st Century*, New Brunswick and London: Transaction Publishers, 2002, pp. 41–42.

10 Rudolf Kjellén, *Die Grossmächte der Gegenwart*, translated from the Swedish by C. Koch, 7th edn, Leipzig and Berlin: B. G. Teubner, 1915; but adumbrated in 1897, see Sven Holdar, 'The Ideal State and the Power of Geography: The Life-Work of Rudolf Kjellén,' *Political Geography*, 1992, 11(3): 307–323, here p. 314.

11 His confidential assessment for the Office of Strategic Studies (later the CIA), was prepared in 1944 and its ideas published mainly in James Burnham, *The Struggle for the World*, New York: John Day, 1947, but preceded by two short articles: James Burnham, 'The Sixth Turn of the Communist Screw,' *Partisan Review*, 1944, 11(3): 364–366; James Burnham, 'Lenin's Heir,' *Partisan Review*, 1945, 12(1): 61–72. See Sempa, *Geopolitics*, pp. 43–44.

12 Maurice Matloff, *Strategic Planning for Coalition Warfare 1943–1944*, Washington, DC: Center of Military History, United States Army, 1994, pp. 523–524; Paul Kennedy, *The Rise and Fall of the Great Powers: Economic Change and Military Conflict from 1500 to 2000*, New York: Random House, 1987, p. 357.

13 Paul Vidal de la Blache, 'Le principe de la géographie générale,' *Annales de Géographie*, 1896, 5(20): 129–142.

14 See, for example, John McCannon, 'By the Shores of White Waters: The Altai and Its Place in the Spiritual Geopolitics of Nicholas Roerich,' *Sibirica: Journal of Siberian Studies*, 2002, 2(2): 166–189.

15 Friedrich Ratzel, 'Die Gesetze des räumlichen Wachstums der Staaten. Ein Beitrag zur Wissenschaftlichen politischen Geographie,' *Petermanns Geographische Mitteilungen*, 1896, 5: 97–107, here pp. 106–107.

16 Robert Strausz-Hupé, *Geopolitcs: The Struggle for Space and Power*, New York: Arno Press, 1972 (reprint of 1942 Putnam edn), p. 31.

17 Kjellén, *Die Grossmächte*, pp. 3, 207.

18 Kjellén, *Die Grossmächte*, pp. 1–2; Holdar, 'The Ideal State,' pp. 310–311.

19 George Nathaniel Curzon [Lord Curzon of Kedleston], *Frontiers* (The Romanes Lecture, 1907), Oxford: Clarendon Press, 1907, pp. 7–8.

20 Frederick Jackson Turner, *The Frontier in American History*, New York: Henry Holt, 1921, pp. 311–315.

21 Mackinder, 'The Geographical Pivot of History,' p. 422.

22 Halford J. Mackinder, 'The Teaching of Geography from an Imperial Point of View, and the Use Which Could and Should Be Made of Visual Instruction,' *The Geographical Teacher*, 1911, 6(2): 79–86.
23 R. Mayhew, 'Halford Mackinder's "New" Political Geography and the Geographical Tradition,' *Political Geography*, 2000, 19: 771–791, here pp. 776–781.
24 Halford J. Mackinder, 'Geography, an Art and a Philosophy,' *Geography*, 1942, 27(4): 122–130, here p. 126.
25 William Wordsworth, '*The Prelude*, Book Twelfth, Lines 128–129,' in Ernest de Selincourt, (ed), *The Poetical Works of Wordsworth*, London: Oxford University Press, 1936.
26 Mackinder, 'The Teaching of Geography,' p. 83.
27 Edward W. Soja, *Postmodern Geographies: The Reassertion of Space in Critical Social Theory*, London: Verso, 1989, pp. 16–21.
28 See Gearóid Ó. Tuathail, *Critical Geopolitics: The Politics of Writing Global Space*, London: Routledge, 1996, chapter 4; Gerry Kearns, *Geopolitics and Empire: The Legacy of Halford Mackinder*, Oxford: Oxford University Press, 2009, p. 15.
29 Strausz-Hupé, *Geopolitcs*, p. 3.
30 Andreas Dorpalen, *The World of General Haushofer: Geopolitics in Action*, New York: Ferrar and Rinehart, 1942, p. 55.
31 Andrew Gyorgy, *Geopolitics: The New German Science*, Berkeley: University of California Press, 1944, p. 155.
32 Spykman, *The Geography of the Peace*, p. 35.
33 John Agnew, *Re-Visioning World Politics*, 2nd edn, London and New York: Routledge, 2003, p. 5.
34 Tuathail, *Critical Geopolitics*, pp. 53–54, 5, 12, 22–23.
35 Soja, *Postmodern Geographies*, p. 2.
36 Agnew, *Re-Visioning World Politics*, chapter 6.
37 See Dierk Walter, '*Grossraum* (Large Space) Concepts and Imperial Expansion: Some Remarks on a Familiar Theme,' *Geopolitics*, 2002, 7(3): 61–74.
38 Curzon, *Frontiers*, pp. 7–8.
39 Mackinder, 'The Teaching of Geography,' p. 80.
40 Mackinder, 'The Geographical Pivot,' p. 441.
41 *War in the Air*. It was written in 1907 and published in serial form in 1908.
42 Kjellén, *Die Grossmächte*, chapters 5 and 6.
43 Mackinder, 'The Geographical Pivot,' pp. 433, 436, 437.
44 Halford J. Mackinder, M.P., *Democratic Ideals and Reality: A Study in the Politics of Reconstruction*, New York: Henry Holt and Company, 1919.
45 Mackinder, *Democratic Ideals*, pp. 93, 141.
46 Mackinder, *Democratic Ideals*, pp. 194, 195, 212.
47 See Kearns, *Geopolitics and Empire*, pp. 43–50.
48 Mackinder, 'The Teaching of Geography,' pp. 79–80.
49 Gerry Kearns, 'The Political Pivot of Geography,' *The Geographical Journal*, 2004, 170(4): 337–346, here p. 342.
50 Mackinder, *Democratic Ideals*, p. 4.
51 Kearns, *Geopolitics and Empire*, p. 10, n. 51.

52 Kearns has stressed the contrast at the expense of what they might have had in common, see Kearns, 'The Political Pivot of Geography,' pp. 337–346.

53 Mackinder, *Democratic Ideals*, p. 176.

54 'The Prussians decided that if, in the end, men must come to man-eating in order to survive, they, at any rate, would be the cannibals!' Mackinder, *Democratic Ideals*, p. 222.

55 Mackinder, *Democratic Ideals*, p. 171.

56 Holdar, 'The Ideal State,' p. 314.

57 Rudolf Kjellén, *Die politisichen Probleme des Weltkrieges*, translated from the Swedish by Friedrich Stieve, Leipzig and Berlin: Teubner, 1916, pp. 9–10.

58 Rudolf Kjellén, *Studien zur Weltkrise*, translated from the Swedish by Friedrich Stieve, München: Bruckmann, 1917, p. vii.

59 Schmitt, *Völkerrechtiche Großraumordnung*, p. 88.

60 Schmitt, *Völkerrechtiche Großraumordnung*, p. 69; for a slightly different translation, see George Schwab, 'Contextualising Carl Schmitt's Concept of *Grossraum*,' *History of European Ideas*, 1994, 19(1–3): 185–190, here p. 188.

61 See Carl Schmitt, *The Nomos of the Earth in the International Law of the Jus Publicum Europaeum*, translated and annotated by G. L. Ulmen, New York: Telos, 2006 (written in 1942–1945).

62 Schwab, 'Contextualising Carl Schmitt's Concept of *Grossraum*,' p. 185.

63 Bendersky, *Carl Schmitt*, p. 257; Hooker, *Carl Schmitt's International Thought*, p. 34, n. 26.

64 See Sempa, *Geopolitics*, p. 93.

65 See Lothar Gruchmann, *Nationalsozialistische Großraumordnung. Die Konstruktion einer 'deutschen Monroe-Doktrin*,' Stuttgart: Deutsche Verlags-Anstalt, 1962, especially pp. 30–31, 50–51, 64–65, and chapter 4.

66 Edward Hallett Carr, *The Twenty Years' Crisis 1919–1939: An Introduction to the Study of International Relations*, 2nd edn, London: Macmillan, 1946, chapter 14.

67 Edward Hallett Carr, *Nationalism and after*, London: Macmillan, 1945, p. 52.

68 Carr, *Nationalism and after*, pp. 71–74.

69 Mika Luoma-Aho, 'From Carl Schmitt to E. H. Carr and James Burnham,' in Louiza Odysseos and Fabio Petito, (eds), *The International Political Thought of Carl Schmitt: Terror, Liberal Order, and the Crisis of Global Order*, London and New York: Routledge, 2007, pp. 36–54, especially pp. 41–42 and 51.

70 Jawaharlal Nehru, *The Discovery of India*, New Delhi: Jawaharlal Nehru Memorial Fund, 1981, (original edition, 1946), p. 421.

71 Carr, *Nationalism and after*, pp. 44–45.

72 Benedict Anderson, *Imagined Communities: Reflections on the Origin and Spread of Nationalism*, rev edn, London: Verso, 2006 (1st edition, 1983), p. 7.

73 Carl Schmitt, *The Concept of the Political*, translated from the German by George Schwab, expanded edn, (based on the 1932 edition of *Der Begriff des Politischen*), Chicago: The University of Chicago Press, 1996.

74 Richard J. Bernstein, 'The Aporias of Carl Schmitt,' *Constellations*, 2011, 18(3): 403–430, especially pp. 409–413.
75 Hooker, *Carl Schmitt's International Thought*, p. 135.
76 Gruchmann, *Nationalsozialistische Großraumordnung*, pp. 51–52.
77 Schmitt, *Völkerrechtiche Großraumordnung*, pp. 70–71. See also Schwab, 'Contextualising Carl Schmitt's Concept of *Großraum*,' p. 188; Hooker, *Carl Schmitt's International Thought*, p. 133.
78 Chantal Mouffe, 'Carl Schmitt's Warning on the Dangers of a Unipolar World,' in Louiza Odysseos and Fabio Petito, (eds), *The International Political Thought of Carl Schmitt*, pp. 147–153.
79 Patricia Chiantera-Stutte, 'Space *Grossraum* and *Mitteleuropa* in Some Debates of the Early Twentieth Century,' *European Journal of Social Theory*, 2008, 11(2): 185–201, here p. 196.
80 William Hooker, *Carl Schmitt's International Thought: Order and Orientation*, Cambridge: Cambridge University Press, 2009, pp. 35–37, and chapter 6 generally.
81 Andrea Gattini, 'Sense and Quasisense of Schmitt's *Grossraum* Theory in International Law – a Rejoinder to Carty's "Carl Schmitt's Critique of Liberal International Legal Order,"' *Leiden Journal of International Law*, 2002, 15: 53–68.
82 Schwab, 'Contextualising Carl Schmitt's Concept of *Großraum*,' p. 189.
83 Hooker, *Carl Schmitt's International Thought*, p. 148.
84 Michael Salter, 'Law, Power and International Politics with Special Reference to East Asia: Carl Schmitt's *Grossraum* Analysis,' *Chinese Journal of International Law*, 2012: 393–427, here pp. 402, 420, 424–426.
85 Hooker, *Carl Schmitt's International Thought*, pp. 137–141.
86 Bendersky, *Carl Schmitt*, pp. 252–253.
87 Hooker, *Carl Schmitt's International Thought*, pp. 137–141.
88 Carr, *The Twenty Years' Crisis 1919–1939*, pp. 235–236.
89 Hooker, *Carl Schmitt's International Thought*, p. 128, referring to Schmitt specifically.
90 Carr, *Nationalism and after*, pp. 45–53. His uncertainty about India clearly was due to having to cope with both Gandhi and Nehru: 'India in one sense is a multi-national civilisation, in another sense a part of the British unit: her political thought in one sense is a baffling amalgam of traditional Indian and modern English.' Carr, *Nationalism and after*, p. 53.
91 Schmitt, *Völkerrechtiche Großraumordnung*, p. 69.
92 Schmitt, *Völkerrechtiche Großraumordnung*, p. 71.
93 Salter, 'Law, Power and International Politics,' pp. 412–413.
94 For the variety of regimes, see Yves Durand, *Le nouvel ordre européen nazi. La collaboration dans l'Europe allemande (1938–1945)*, Paris: Editions Complexe, 1990; Mark Mazower, *Hitler's Empire: How the Nazis Ruled Europe*, New York: Penguin, 2008; Gruchmann, *Nationalsozialistische Großraumordnung*, chapter 3.
95 See the following exchanges: Ola Tunander, 'The Uneasy Imbrication of Nation-State and NATO: The Case of Sweden,' *Cooperation and Conflict*, 1999, 34(2): 169–203; Ola Tunander, 'Swedish-German Geopolitics for a New Century. Rudolf Kjellén's "The State as a Living Organism,"'

Review of International Studies, 2001, 27(3): 451–463, here pp. 459–463; Ola Tunander, 'Geopolitical Traditions: Swedish Geopolitics: From Rudolf Kjellén to a Swedish "Dual State,"' *Geopolitics*, 2005, 10: 546–566; the critique by Olof Kronvall, Magnus Petersson, Charles Silva, and Kjetil Skogrand, 'Comments on Ola Tunander's article "The Uneasy Imbrication of Nation-State and NATO: The Case of Sweden,"' *Cooperation and Conflict*, 2000, 35(4): 417–429; and the response Ola Tunander, 'A Criticism of Court Chroniclers: A Response from Tunander,' *Cooperation and Conflict*, 2000, 35(4): 431–440.

96 Salter, 'Law, Power and International Politics,' pp. 395, 411–412.

97 Michael Salter and Yinan Yin, 'Analysing Regionalism within International Law and Relations: The Shanghai Cooperation Organisation as a *Grossraum?*,' *Chinese Journal of International Law*, 2014: 819–877.

98 A declaration in the introduction to both his major works, see Ratzel, *Anthropogeographie*, Part 1, pp. 1–6; Friedrich Ratzel, *Politische Geographie*, München and Leipzig: R. Oldenbourg, 1897, pp. 9–12.

99 Friedrich Ratzel, 'Der Lebensraum. Eine biogeographische Studie,' in K. Bücher et al., (eds), *Festgaben für Albert Schäffle zur siebenzigsten Wiederkehr seines Geburtstages am 24. Februar 1901*, Tübingen: Verlag der Laupp'schen Buchhandlung, 1901, pp. 101–189, here, p. 153.

100 Mark Bassin, 'Imperialism and the Nation State in Friedrich Ratzel's Political Geography,' *Progress in Human Geography*, September 1987, 11(4): 473–495, especially pp. 477–478.

101 Ratzel, 'Der Lebensraum,' pp. 169–170.

102 Friedrich Ratzel, *Politische Geographie oder die Geographie der Staaten, des Verkehres und des Krieges*, 2nd edn, München and Berlin: Oldenburg, 1903, pp. 217–224.

103 Ratzel, 'Der Lebensraum,' p. 147.

104 Friedrich Ratzel, 'Nationalitäten und Rassen (1903),' in Friedrich Ratzel, (ed), *Kleine Schriften*, Vol. 2, München and Berlin: R. Oldenbourg, 1906, pp. 462–487, especially 485–487; Bassin, 'Imperialism and the Nation State in Friedrich Ratzel's Political Geography,' p. 489, n. 12.

105 Tunander, 'Swedish-German Geopolitics for a New Century,' pp. 451–463.

106 Kjellén, *Die Grossmächte*, pp. 199–200.

107 Strausz-Hupé, *Geopolitcs*, pp. 93–100.

108 Spykman, *America's Strategy in World Politics*, chapter 2.

109 Frederick List, *National System of Political Economy*, translated from the German by G. A. Matile, Philadelphia: Lippincott, 1856, (original German edition, 1841), book 2, chapter 5.

110 Friedrich Naumann, *Central Europe*, translated from the German by Christabel M. Meredith, London: P. S. King & Son, 1916.

111 Kjellén, *Die Grossmächte*, p. 205.

112 Kjellén, *Die Grossmächte*, pp. 79–83; Holdar, 'The Ideal State,' pp. 313–314.

113 Siegfried Marck, 'Rudolf Kjelléns Theorie des Staates,' *Kant-Studien*, 1919, 23: 77–100, here p. 83; Kjellén, *Die Grossmächte*, p. 202.

114 Mayhew, 'Halford Mackinder's "New" Political Geography,' pp. 782–787.

115 Ratzel, 'Der Lebensraum,' p. 165, and generally, pp. 164–169.

116 Ratzel, *Anthropogeographie*, Part 1, chapter 12.

117 Ellen Churchill Semple, *Influences of Geographic Environment on the Basis of Ratzel's System of Anthropo-Geography*, New York: Henry Holt, 1911, chapter 7.

118 George Nathaniel Curzon [Lord Curzon of Kedleston], *Frontiers* (The Romanes Lecture, 1907), Oxford: Clarendon Press, 1907, p. 41.

119 See Thomas H. Holdich [Col. Sir Thomas H. Holdich], *Political Frontiers and Boundary Making*, London: Macmillan, 1916, p. 76 and chapter 5 generally.

120 C[harles] B[ungay] Fawcett, *Frontiers: A Study in Political Geography*, Oxford: Clarendon Press, 1918, p. 24, and chapter 2 generally.

121 Ratzel, 'Die Gesetze des räumlichen Wachstums der Staaten,' pp. 102–103.

122 Owen Lattimore, 'The Inland Crossroads of Asia,' (1944) in Owen Lattimore, (ed), *Studies in Frontier History: Collected Papers 1928–1958*, Paris: Mouton, 1962, pp. 118–133, here pp. 127–128; Ratzel, *Anthropogeographie*, Part 1, p. 171.

123 Owen Lattimore, 'The Frontier in History,' (1955) in Owen Lattimore, (ed), *Studies in Frontier History*, pp. 469–491, here pp. 469–470.

124 Ratzel, 'Die Gesetze des räumlichen Wachstums der Staaten,' pp. 102–103.

125 Turner, *The Frontier in American History*, especially chapter 1.

126 Curzon, *Frontiers*, pp. 56–57. There is no evidence that Curzon had read Ratzel; but such ideas had been in circulation for some time, and had become a Victorian commonplace.

127 Mackinder, 'Geography, an Art and a Philosophy,' p. 125.

128 Karl Haushofer, *Grenzen in ihrer geographischen und politischen Bedeutung*, 2nd rev edn, Heidelberg-Berlin-Magdeburg: Kurt Vowinckel Verlag, 1939, (1st edn, written 1924, published 1927), chapters 1–3 generally, but especially the Introduction and p. 18; Dorpalen, *The World of General Haushofer*, p. 62.

129 Dorpalen, *The World of General Haushofer*, p. 65.

130 See Benno Teschke, *The Myth of 1648: Class, Geopolitics and the Making of International Relations*, London: Verso, 2003, chapter 7; see also Hans J. Morgenthau, *Politics among Nations: The Struggle for Power and Peace*, New York: Knopf, 1948, chapters 9 and 12.

131 For example:
      'We talk of countries, of Pakistan and India and a frontier between the two and yet in these days of jet travel and various types of missiles, a frontier has no meaning. You cross a number of frontiers in the course of an hour or two. You cannot even delimit it quite clearly where one frontier in the air ends and where the other begins, broadly you may know that underneath is some other country. You cannot draw a line in the air. In other words, the growth of science and technology and communications has really rather made the idea of national frontiers out of date, precise national frontiers they do not just fit in, you are crossing them, all the time, and I have little doubt, that unless some catastrophe intervenes, we shall have to outgrow completely this idea of national frontiers.' Madhavan K. Palat (ed), Inaugural speech to the India Pakistan Cultural Conference, 31 March 1961, *Selected Works of Jawaharlal Nehru*, series 2, Vol. 67, New Delhi: Jawaharlal Nehru Memorial Fund, 2015, p. 484.

132 A. T. Mahan, *The Influence of Sea Power upon History, 1660–1783*, 5th edn, Boston: Little, Brown, and Company, 1894, chapter 1.
133 Friedrich Ratzel, *Das Meer als Quelle der Völkergrosse. Eine politisch-geografische Studie*, 2nd enlarged edn, München and Berlin: R. Oldenburg, 1911, (1st edn 1900), *passim*, especially pp. 71–73.
134 See Mahan, *The Influence of Sea Power upon History*.
135 Spykman, 'Geography and Foreign Policy, I,' pp. 28–40; Spykman, 'Geography and Foreign Policy, II,' pp. 213–236; Spykman, *America's Strategy in World Politics*.
136 Agnew, *Re-Visioning World Politics*, pp. 102–112.
137 See Carl T. Dahlman, 'Geopolitics,' in Carolyn Gallaher et al., (eds), *Key Concepts in Political Geography*, London: Sage, 2009, chapter 7; Klaus Dodds, *Geopolitics: A Very Short Introduction*, Oxford: Oxford University Press, 2007, pp. 22–24.
138 See Sempa, *Geopolitics*, chapter 4, entitled 'The First Cold Warrior.'
139 Throughout his work, Burnham, *The Struggle for the World*. On the initiative of M. R. Masani, Burnham's two books, *The Struggle for the World*, and *The Coming Defeat of Communism*, New York: John Day, 1950, were edited by Max Eastman into one book for an Indian edition, but with the same title as the latter one: *The Coming Defeat of Communism*, Bombay: The National Information and Publications, 1951.
140 George Kennan [X], 'The Sources of Soviet Conduct,' *Foreign Affairs*, 1987, 65(4): 852–868, (reprinted from *Foreign Affairs*, July 1947), here p. 858.
141 Kennan, 'The Sources of Soviet Conduct,' p. 867.
142 George Kennan, 'Containment Then and Now,' *Foreign Affairs*, 1987, 65(4): 885–890, here pp. 886, 888–889.
143 See Paul Claval, '*Hérodote* and the French Left,' and Leslie W. Hepple, 'Géopolitique de gauche: Yves Lacoste, *Hérodote* and French Radical Geopolitics,' in Klaus Dodds and David Atkinson, (eds), *Geopolitical Traditions: A Century of Geopolitical Thought*, London and New York: Routledge, 2000, pp. 239–267 and 268–301, respectively.
144 Geoffrey Sloan and Colin S. Gray, 'Why Geopolitics?,' in Colin S. Gray and Geoffrey Sloan, (eds), *Geopolitics, Geography and Strategy*, London and New York: Routledge, 2013, (first published 1999), pp. 1–11, here p. 1; Dodds, *Geopolitics*, pp. 38–39.
145 John Erickson, '"Russia Will Not be Trifled with": Geopolitical Facts and Fantasies,' in Colin S. Gray and Geoffrey Sloan, (eds), *Geopolitics, Geography and Strategy*, London and New York: Routledge, 2013, (first published 1999), pp. 241–268.
146 Tuathail, *Critical Geopolitics*, chapter 7, especially p. 188.
147 See Gearóid Ó Tuathail and Simon Dalby, 'Introduction: Rethinking Geopolitics: Towards a Critical Geopolitics,' in Gearóid Ó Tuathail and Simon Dalby, (eds), *Rethinking Geopolitics*, Routledge: London and New York, 1998, pp. 1–15.
148 Agnew, *Re-Visioning World Politics*, p. 125.

2

THE IMPERIALISM OF ANTI-IMPERIALISM

The United States and India in the Second World War

Srinath Raghavan

The historiography of the United States' involvement in South Asia is all but exclusively focused on the Cold War era. This is perhaps unsurprising. After all, the onset of the Cold War coincided with the British withdrawal from the subcontinent accompanied by its partition into the new states of India and Pakistan. Over the following decades, the confrontation with the Soviet Union played a major role in shaping American attitudes and policies in South Asia. In particular the United States' military alliance with Pakistan cast a long shadow over its involvement in the subcontinent during the Cold War and, indeed, after it ended.

Thus, we have some fine historical accounts of the United States' bilateral ties with India and Pakistan, the triangular relationship between these countries, and the Anglo-American relationship in South Asia during the first two decades of the Cold War.[1] The historiography of the period after 1970 has not been covered as exhaustively, though the pivotal moment of 1971 has received some attention.[2]

While this literature has transformed our understanding of American involvement in South Asia, it has also skewed our historical imagination. On the one hand, it tempts us to read the more recent past primarily through a 'post–Cold War' lens. On the other hand, it neglects the period before the Cold War and so obscures the larger pattern of American engagement with this part of the world. We lack historical accounts that look behind and beyond the Cold War, so tracing the longer arc American involvement in the region. Indeed, much of the best recent work on the Cold War attempts to place it against

47

the backcloth of the wider currents of the twentieth century's international history – in particular, globalisation and decolonisation. Within this broader historiography, there is renewed emphasis on understanding the trajectory of America's global dominance, which predates and succeeds the Cold War.[3]

This essay attempts to turn the historiographical tiller in these directions. It examines American involvement in South Asia during the Second World War. Unlike existing accounts of the subject, I am not interested merely in probing whether the United States under President Franklin D. Roosevelt was supportive of India's quest for freedom.[4] Rather I am interested in examining American policy towards India against the background of U.S. grand strategy during the war. The Second World War marked America's rise to preponderance. By examining its approach to South Asia during this period, I hope to cast into relief some of the longer-term determinants of America's engagement with the subcontinent.

II

The mid-1930s was the high-water mark of American 'isolationism.' As a doctrine, isolationism was composed of many strands that commanded varying degrees of public assent. Ruthlessly simplified, it amounted to the belief that the United States, shielded adequately by two oceans, should avoid getting embroiled in external alliances or wars; that it should retain the freedom to act without binding commitments; that the nation's economic interests overseas were small in comparison with the domestic market; and that the United States should promote liberal values by demonstration rather than imposition. The Roosevelt administration was sensitive to the currents of isolationism swirling through the American populace. Yet by the time the United States was pulled into the war, public opinion had begun to shift away from isolationism. And the United States began to plan not just to win the world war, but for world order after the war.

'We are not isolationists,' President Roosevelt had declared in 1936, 'except insofar as we seek to isolate ourselves completely from war.' At the same time, he had held that it was a 'vital interest . . . that the sanctity of international treaties and the maintenance of international morality be restored.'[5] Once the United States entered the war, Roosevelt sought to create – after the defeat of Germany and Japan – an international security organisation capable of deterring or defeating any country that challenged the international order so created.

48

An essential complement to this vision of a liberal, law-governed world order was thriving international commerce. Although the United States had pulled out of the London Economic Conference of 1933 and embarked on an attempt to reflate the American economy via the New Deal, Roosevelt and his colleagues – especially Secretary of State Cordell Hull – remained committed to reducing tariff barriers by the extension of the 'most favored nation' principle. In particular they sought to push this agenda forward in bilateral settings through the Reciprocal Trade Agreements Act of 1934.

This policy was not shaped by a straightforward drive to secure foreign markets as part of a renewed 'Open Door' policy. Rather, economic, strategic, and ideological concerns were entwined in various ways in this vision of a liberal, capitalist world order. As the global economy fragmented into autarkic zones and as Japan and Germany went on the offensive in Asia and Europe, Roosevelt was convinced that the war was a consequence of the closing of the world economy. After the war, he declared, 'the United States must use its influence to open up trade channels of the world in order that no nation need feel compelled in later days to seek by force of arms what it can gain by peaceful conference.' Business internationalists were worried whether 'the American capitalist system could continue to function if most of Europe and Asia should abolish free enterprise.' A variant of this concern about the feasibility of capitalism in one country was that access to foreign markets was essential to reduce government intervention in the American economy to harmonise domestic production and consumption. Hull emphasised both these aspects when he told a Senate committee in February 1940: 'The question of survival or disappearance of free enterprise is bound up with the continuation or abandonment of the trade agreements program.'[6]

A State Department report in December 1943 briskly summarised the many reasons for which the Roosevelt administration aimed at promoting a liberal, capitalist world order: 'A great expansion in the volume of international trade after the war will be essential to the attainment of full and effective employment in the United States and elsewhere, to the preservation of private enterprise, and to the success of an international security system to prevent future wars.'[7] The desire for full employment indicated that the capitalist order aimed at by post-war planners would differ as much from that of the Gold Standard era as would the international security order from the old balance of power or the League of Nations.

From the outset, the Americans were confident of imposing their design on the post-war world. Their confidence stemmed from an awareness of the extraordinary margin of power that the United States could command over its rivals and friends. As the Nazis punched their way into Western Europe in the spring of 1940, *Life* observed: 'the German victories brought shock and deep fear into the United States, but they brought also a consciousness of national strength. The old nations of Europe may fall before the conqueror but the young, strong giant of the West will meet any challenge that Adolf Hitler dares to make.'[8] A few months later, Adolf Berle Jr., assistant secretary of state and long-time advisor to Roosevelt, wrote in his diary: 'I have been saying to myself and other people that the only possible effect of this war would be that the United States would emerge with an imperial power greater than the world had ever seen.'[9]

In attaining the purposes of such preponderant power, the Roosevelt administration perceived the British Empire as a major stumbling block. The imperial preference system instituted at the Ottawa Conference of 1932, erected a high tariff wall around the entire British Commonwealth but allowed low duties on goods traded between countries of the empire. Not only did American exporters find their largest export market ring-fenced by higher tariff rates, but the Americans believed that the continuation of imperial preference after the war would encourage others to follow suit, and so keep the world economy divided in blocs. Dismantling this system became a key American objective.

The negotiation of a master lend-lease agreement in early 1941 gave the United States an opportunity to lean on Britain to open up the Ottawa system. The British delegation led by John Maynard Keynes refused to hold out any such commitment. The Anglophile assistant secretary of state, Dean Acheson, tartly observed that after obtaining such vast quantities of American aid, the British must 'not regard themselves as free to take any measures they chose directed against the trade of this country.' After almost a year of wrangling the British signed up to a generic clause agreeing to cooperate in securing the 'elimination of forms of discriminatory treatment in international commerce.' Then, too, Prime Minister Winston Churchill clarified that this was not tantamount to an advance commitment to repeal imperial preferences.[10]

Colonial monopolies were also one reason why Roosevelt and his advisors sought to prepare the ground for gradual decolonisation in Asia and Africa. The continued exploitation of colonial peoples, they worried, could touch off a wave of revolutionary violence leading to further wars. 'The colonial system means war,' said Roosevelt to his son in 1943. 'Exploit the resources of an India, a Burma, a Java; take all the wealth out of these countries, but never put anything back into them, things like education, decent standards of living, minimum health requirements – all you're doing is storing up the kind of trouble that leads to war.'[11] The Americans were also concerned that British, French, and Dutch imperial subjects in Asia would be susceptible to the sirens of Pan-Asiatic ideas that had already emanated from Tokyo. In consequence, the new 'imperial power' envisaged by Berle that stood ready to dislodge the older ones was self-consciously anti-imperial: 'the imperialism of anti-imperialism,' as Niall Ferguson wittily calls it.

But as with imperial preferences, the American stance on decolonisation had to triangulate between the wartime imperative of defeating Germany and Japan, and post-war objectives of creating a new international order buttressed by America's unexampled hegemony. All these considerations shaped US policy towards India during these years.

III

Before the Second World War began, the United States evinced no strategic interest in India. To most Americans, India was a land of fantasy and faith. Popular perceptions of India were heavily shaped by the adventure tales of Rudyard Kipling and exotic Hollywood productions featuring magnificent maharajas and cool colonial officials. Among the cognoscenti, it was religion that served as a vestibule to India. Religion was also the conduit for the transmission of negative images of India. American missionaries, active in India since the early nineteenth century, were appalled at practices such as self-mutilation and torture, immolation of widows and female infanticide. The influence of such perceptions lingered in popular imagination well in to the next century. Commercial exchanges were meagre. American investment in India in the late 1930s amounted to less than $50 million with over half of this in missionary schools, hospitals, and other non-commercial activities.[12] All this would change rapidly with the onset of the war.

On 3 September 1939, the viceroy, Lord Linlithgow declared war on India's behalf without any consultation with Indian opinion. Although the provinces of the Raj were run by Indian political parties, the viceroy did not deem it fit to sound anyone out. Piqued by his refusal to make any commitment on India's political future after the war, the ministries of the Indian National Congress resigned in October 1939. Thereafter the viceroy and the Congress remained at loggerheads.

No sooner had war broken out in September 1939, than desk-level officials in the state department began insisting that 'the Indian attitude towards the War is of great importance.' Assistant Secretary of State Berle, head of the near eastern division dealing with India, was told that there were 'large American interests in India.' Meanwhile, American officials in India took a sympathetic stance towards the Indian National Congress's protests against the unilateral declaration of war by the viceroy as well as his subsequent refusal to carry the nationalists along. By May 1941, the US consul general, Thomas Wilson, had concluded that the situation in India was 'very serious indeed'. The viceroy was a man of 'small vision' and too hidebound to handle the crisis.[13]

The American press reflected these views. The viceroy's response to the nationalists was criticised as inadequate by such prominent magazines as *The New Republic*, *The Nation*, and *Time*. The editorials in traditionally pro-British papers like the *New York Times* and *Christian Science Monitor* as well as others like *Los Angeles Times* were sceptical of the British stance. Even the conservative *Reader's Digest* carried a favourable profile of Jawaharlal Nehru written by John and Frances Gunther. American journals also offered considerable column-inches for supporters of Indian nationalism to expound their views. Nehru himself availed of these opportunities to present the Congress' case at strategic points in April 1940 in the *Atlantic*, and in November 1940 in the *Asia*.[14]

Even before sections of the American press grew censorious, the British cabinet was alert to American opinion on India. Indeed, hardly any major decision on India was taken without reference to its impact on public opinion in the United States. With a view to keeping a closer tab on American opinion as well as shaping it, the British government proposed to the state department in April 1941 the appointment of a senior Indian official to its embassy in Washington. The state department expressed no objection to the proposed 'Agent-General of India', but sought and obtained the reciprocal appointment of its own "Commissioner" in New Delhi.[15]

The state department's demand stemmed from its growing realisation of the strategic importance of India. India had recently become a member of the Lend-Lease system, which was approved by the US Congress in March 1941. The Roosevelt administration was aware of

India's contribution to the war effort. India, the US treasury noted in May 1941, had already raised over 300,000 men and could 'greatly increase' the number. India had sent 'important forces' to fight in North and East Africa and supplied garrison troops for the Far East. The Allied operations in Iraq and the Persian Gulf were entirely based on India. Further, from the beginning of the war, India had made a 'most important contribution' to war supplies. If India were to fully mobilise its 'enormous basic internal resources,' it needed to be able to 'import finished and semi-finished manufactures and certain materials' for which the United States was the sole source.[16]

Simultaneously, the state department grew concerned about the situation in the Middle East. And this brought to the fore the political problem of India. Berle believed that if the political impasse were not resolved, India could become an 'active danger' to the war effort in the Middle East. The British seemed to be doing 'nothing' about it. Berle recommended sending a formal note to the British government underlining India's 'vast influence' on the Middle East and the need to convert India into an 'active, rather than a passive, partner' in the war. They should pointedly ask Britain to 'promptly explore' the possibility of granting India equal membership in the British Commonwealth. Berle conceded that this may seem 'sensational,' but added that 'this is no time for half measures.'[17]

At his suggestion, Secretary of State Hull met the British ambassador and former viceroy of India, Lord Halifax. When Hull queried him about the possibility of further 'liberalizing' moves towards India, Halifax claimed that conditions in India were 'really very good.' Indians had self-government in provinces and has been offered berths in the viceroy's council. Despite Gandhi's opposition, the sentiment towards Britain was very strong. Halifax concluded that his government did not deem it 'feasible or even necessary now to make further liberalising concessions.'[18]

There the matter rested until three months later when the Americans grew concerned about Japanese strategic moves in the Far East. The US ambassador in London, John Winant, felt that India had a 'large' role to play in securing the Far East. In the rapidly evolving context, it may be wise for the United States to raise the question of India with Britain. The British, he observed, had emphasised the Hindu-Muslim divide as the main stumbling block towards a settlement. Winant, however, believed that the absence of a settlement 'handicaps the support of war in India itself.' It might be possible, he argued, at least to get the British to announce dominion status for India within a stated period after the end of the war. Among other advantages, such a move would have 'a sobering effect upon the Japanese.'[19]

Berle supported Winant. He suggested to Under Secretary of State Sumner Welles that they point out to the British government that this was a 'more opportune time' than ever for such a declaration. It would be 'very helpful' from the standpoint of American public opinion. Besides, India could become the 'nucleus of a Far Eastern alliance,' which included China, Australia, and New Zealand, and which could hold its own against Japan or possibly even Germany. Welles disagreed. He wrote to Hull that in his judgement the United States was 'not warranted' in suggesting a status for India to Britain. But if the president was disposed to take up the matter, he might wish to discuss it 'in a very personal and confidential way directly with Mr. Churchill.'[20]

Three days later, Franklin Roosevelt and Winston Churchill met secretly off the coast of Newfoundland. While the principal objective of the meeting was to cement the Anglo-American alliance and discuss grand strategy, a statement of war aims – the Atlantic Charter – attracted attention the world over. In fact, the Charter had emerged without much deliberation.[21] Over dinner on 9 August, Churchill and Roosevelt talked about the possibility of a joint statement. The next morning the British advanced the draft of a five-point declaration. The third point originally read: 'they respect the right of all people to choose the form of government under which they will live; they are concerned only to defend the rights of freedom of speech and of thought without which such choosing must be illusory.' Welles, however, was dubious of Congress and public support to such a sweeping pledge to defend human rights – rights that had been abolished by the Axis countries. Roosevelt accordingly suggested removing the second clause and substituting it with: 'and they hope that self-government may be restored to those from whom it has been forcibly removed.' Churchill agreed, only suggesting adding 'sovereign-rights and' before self-government. Obviously all this was in the context of European countries under enemy occupation.

The Atlantic Charter took a life of its own and sent ripples of excitement through the colonial world. The Burmese premier asked if it applied to his country and dashed off to London to obtain an answer. The leader of the Hindu Mahasabha V.D. Savarkar wrote to Roosevelt urging him to state whether the Atlantic Charter applied to India and whether the United States guaranteed freedom to India within a year of the war's end. If the United States failed to affirmatively respond,

'India cannot but construe this as another stunt like the War aims of the last Anglo-German war.'[22] Indeed, the response to the Atlantic Charter was comparable in enthusiasm to that evoked among colonial subjects by Woodrow Wilson's fourteen points after the First World War.[23] But Churchill scotched any such suggestion. On 9 September, he told the Commons that article three applied only to countries under Nazi occupation and that it did 'not qualify in any way' the various statements made about India from time to time.

In India, the reaction to Churchill's comment was uniformly critical. Even such loyalists as the Punjab premier, Sikander Hayat Khan, termed it the strongest rebuff ever received by India.[24] Gandhi was characteristically witty and incisive in his comments:

> What is the Atlantic Charter? It went down the ocean as soon as it was born! I do not understand it. Mr. Amery denies that India is fit for democracy, while Mr. Churchill states the Charter could not apply to India. Force of circumstances will falsify their declarations.[25]

Consul-General Wilson cabled the state department that Churchill's statement was a 'most unfortunate pronouncement,' which went 'far towards banishing perhaps forever' any goodwill towards him in India. As for the Indian government, he wrote dyspeptically, there was 'no leadership worthy of the name anywhere to be found.'[26]

Churchill had, in fact, shared in advance the text of his speech with Ambassador Winant, especially since it had referred to a statement issued jointly with the United States. Winant felt that Churchill's references to the inapplicability of article three to countries like India was unwise. It ran 'counter to the general public interpretation' of the article. It would intensify charges of imperialism and leave Britain with 'a do nothing policy' towards India. Minutes before Churchill left for the Commons, Winant urged Churchill to omit the offending paragraph in his speech. The prime minister was determined to press ahead. He told Winant that this position was approved by the cabinet and, in any case, was a matter of internal British politics.[27]

Desk-level officials at the state department urged that the matter be brought to the president's notice. Since Churchill had offered an interpretation of the joint declaration, it was an opportune moment to raise with the British government the question of Indian politics and to do so along the lines suggested earlier by Winant. The political situation in India, it was felt, was 'deteriorating rapidly' owing to the stalemate between the government and the nationalists. This in turn was preventing India from doing its best to help win the war. Welles yet again threw a wet blanket on the idea. Interestingly, he now held that if article three had 'any real meaning, it should be regarded as all-inclusive' and in consequence applicable to India. Yet the United States, at least for the present, was 'facing a question of expediency.' He had been told by Halifax – the 'most liberal viceroy India has ever had' – that British officials were unanimous that an immediate grant of dominion status would trigger 'internal dissension in India on a very wide scale' and render it thoroughly useless for the war effort. US officials were not familiar with the problems of India. Nor did the issue mean 'very much to public opinion' at home. Above all, Churchill would feel that the administration was taking advantage of British dependence on America to force its hand against its considered judgement.[28]

In the wake of Pearl Harbor, thinking within the administration underwent important changes. Apart from advocates in the state department, intelligence assessments by the Office of Coordination of Information held that the United States had to help arrest the downward political slide in India.[29] Thus when Churchill came to Washington two weeks after Pearl Harbor, Roosevelt gingerly broached the question of India. The only available account of this meeting is in Churchill's memoir. The prime minister claimed to have 'reacted so strongly and at such length that he [Roosevelt] never raised it verbally again.' Towards the end of his trip, Churchill confidently cabled his colleagues that they would not have 'any trouble with American opinion.'[30] This judgement would prove premature.

IV

On 11 November 1941, President Roosevelt had decided that the defence of India was of vital importance to the United States and hence India could directly receive Lend-Lease supplies from America. While welcoming the decision, British officials realised that it was pregnant with problems for them. The US proposal to negotiate Lend-Lease supplies directly with the British-Indian mission in Washington was seen as 'something of a bombshell,' for it threatened to displace Britain's economic pre-eminence in India. The United States' economic importance for India was already growing. India's imports from the US had increased from 9% of its total imports in 1939–40 to 20% in 1940–1941, while over the same period imports from Britain had fallen to 21.2% from 25.2%. Similarly, Indian exports to the US had risen from 12% to 19.6% while exports to Britain had fallen to 32.3% from 35.5%.[31]

British officials were also aware of the Americans' proclivity for driving a hard bargain. Earlier in the year, while negotiating a treaty of commerce, navigation, and consular rights between the United States and India, the Americans had sought a clause that would give private companies from both sides the right to undertake mineral and oil exploration in the other country. They were interested in securing rights for exploration in Balochistan. The government of India resisted this clause, claiming that its rights would only be theoretical as no Indian company had the requisite capital to extract minerals or oil in the United States. American officials argued that they had a similar treaty with Britain, which too was only notional since Britain had no deposits of oil or minerals. An agreement with India would amount to actual reciprocity on the part of Britain.

The Americans also demanded a most-favoured nation clause explicitly clarifying that the it would mean 'the most favored third nation, *including the Kingdom of Great Britain and Northern Ireland.*' The Indian negotiator, Sir Feroz Khan Noon, argued that this would contravene the agreement on imperial preferences between India and Britain. He also observed that the deletion of this clause would exclude the other Dominions from the definition of most-favoured nation. State department officials, however, felt that removing the clause would have deleterious consequences for America's longer-term plans: it 'would accord recognition in a treaty to preferential tariff treatment now accorded certain British and Colonial products.' Although the United States had recognised imperial tariffs in a trade agreement signed with Britain in 1938, it did so in exchange for a substantial reduction in the tariff. 'The recognition of imperial preferences in a treaty is a recognition of a more formal character and the initial compulsory period is for a much longer time.' The Indians, however, continued to plead their inability to sign on to this clause but requested a speedy conclusion of the agreement in the light of the war. Eventually the Roosevelt administration forbore from pressing its demand. Britain and India were informed that though the United States had hoped that the treaty would 'embody the most liberal principles of international trade,' it would refrain from raising this question owing to the 'unsettled world conditions.'[32] Evidently once conditions were more settled, the United States would take up this issue.

With the onset of Lend-Lease, British Indian officials grew concerned that this might become the thin of the wedge with which to prise open the system of imperial preferences. These concerns were stoked during the negotiations on the master agreement for lend-lease. When negotiations began for a similar agreement between Washington and India, the Americans pressed for the inclusion of a similar clause. On this occasion, it was the Indian member for commerce in the viceroy's executive council who demurred, arguing strenuously that it would be detrimental to India's fledgling industries. The Roosevelt administration refused to relent. And the negotiations had to be shelved – though the United States reluctantly agreed to continue with existing arrangements.[33]

The fact however remained that India's plans for the expansion of its war effort were heavily reliant on American economic assistance. Indeed by 1944–1945, the United States would account for 25.7% of India's total imports, while Britain would lag behind at 19.8%. None realised this more clearly than the Indian agent-general in Washington, Sir Girja Shankar Bajpai. A senior official of the Indian Civil Service, Bajpai had previously served at the League of Nations and had been a member of the viceroy's executive council until 1940. Although he epitomised the 'Steel Frame' of the Raj, Bajpai – by his own account – did not regard India under British rule as 'the best of possible worlds.' Indeed, in private conversations with US officials Bajpai forthrightly disagreed with the stance espoused by Halifax.[34] At the same time, he was keen to leverage American assistance for India's war.

Soon after Pearl Harbor, Bajpai shared with Berle a report on India's war effort. The report observed that while India had 'modernized and expanded' its ordnance factories, it would continue to rely on Britain and the United States for 'some key items of supply.' What is more, despite the increased flow of more modern equipment from Britain, 'the releases have never been and cannot be equalled to India's needs.' Indeed, these could only be met by a 'generous flow of help' from the United States. India was similarly dependent on America for general engineering equipment, especially power generation sets, motor and machine tools as well as motor vehicles which were entirely procured from the United States. The report also stated that India planned to raise 124 Indian infantry battalions, taking the total strength of the Indian army to 1.5 million.

Following the meeting with Bajpai, Berle felt that for a considerable time transportation of cargo from the United States to the Far East would be 'limited, difficult and dangerous.' In consequence, it was in America's interest to promote production in the region rather than shipping it from home. In this scheme, India bulked large. If, by providing 'technical assistance' alongside supplies, the Indian army could be strengthened, then the United States would achieve 'considerable economy' in the war effort, would make 'more effective use' of India's man-power, and would be building up 'defensive and offensive striking power in a region where it is vitally necessary.' Berle recommended sending to India a suitable representative to survey the possibility of increasing India's war effort.[35]

When there was no movement for a month, Bajpai met Berle and impressed upon him the gravity of the situation in the Far East. While China had put up a splendid resistance, India was more accessible to the Allies and had a highly developed system of internal communications. Underlining India's potential, Bajpai trotted out a series of figures: 64,000 miles of railways; steel production capacity of over a million tons a year; an industrial base that already produced 85% of the 60,000 items required for the war; and 'almost unlimited manpower' for the army, which had already proved its mettle in modern warfare. When Japanese submarines closed the port of Rangoon, Bajpai yet again impressed upon Berle to consider India's needs with 'very great speed.' He also wrote to the viceroy recommending an American technical mission to assess India's potential and requirements. Berle was sufficiently impressed to write directly to the president urging him to send a technical mission to India. Should things 'go badly in Singapore and Burma,' he added, India's role might be of 'crucial importance.' On 2 February, President Roosevelt gave his approval.[36]

IV

The fall of Singapore in mid-February 1942 alarmed the state department. Above all, it brought to the fore the latent yet lingering concerns about the political situation in India. Berle argued that they must 'immediately get to work' and the 'first item on the list ought to be tackle the Indian problem in a large way.' The technical mission had already been approved by the president, but India's war effort would not go very far 'unless the political situation is handled with extreme vigor.' He called for a joint Anglo-American announcement that India would be brought in 'as a full partner in the United Nations.' In other words, the Atlantic Charter would apply to India. Not only should Churchill make such an announcement, but the viceroy should be directed to convene a 'constitutional conference' in India. Even if the Congress did not come in at this stage, its stance would determine whether India cooperated in waging the war, or whether there was 'more or less passive resistance' which would be exploited by Japan 'to the limit.'[37]

Interestingly, Berle noted that President Roosevelt had 'indicated his sympathy' for the view that Britain must promptly recognise India's aspiration to 'a freer existence and a full membership in the British family of nations.' For a range of reasons, the president's sentiment would be strengthened in the days ahead. To begin with, the American press turned sharply critical of Britain. Renowned columnists like Walter Lippmann and John Thompson as well as editorials in a series of newspapers and journals argued that Britain's imperial policy must change. *The New York Times* witheringly wrote that countries like India were no longer 'suppliants at the white man's door. Not all the faded trappings of imperialism, not all the pomp of viceroys . . . has much meaning for them now.'[38]

These feelings were reflected in political debates. The US Senate's Foreign Relations Committee commenced hearings on the situation in the Far East. There was a 'serious undercurrent of anti-British feeling' among the senators, who argued that having done 'so much' for Britain by Lend-Lease the United States was well positioned to 'dictate to England' political changes in the British empire. One senator went so far as to declare that 'Gandhi's leadership in India became part of America's military equipment.' India's contribution could only be secured by accepting 'Gandhi's political objective.'[39]

The president's views also seem to have been sharpened by a gloomy letter written to Eleanor Roosevelt by the writer and Nobel Laureate Pearl S. Buck, which the first lady shared with the president. The letter expressed deep concern at the prospect of the Allies planning a stand against Japan in India. Buck argued that there was a serious rift between Hindus and Muslims in India – 'fostered by the British divide-and-rule policy.' Jinnah, in particular, was 'a demagogue of the most dangerous type.' He had no love for his country and was the 'perfect tool for the Axis.' It was a 'fallacy' to think that Indians could defend their country as the Chinese had done. They were 'so filled with bitterness' towards the British that there would be 'revengeful massacres' on a large scale – massacres in which American soldiers might well be caught up.[40]

Finally, the president's thinking was influenced by intelligence and strategic assessments. The Office of Coordination of Information now believed that India 'might well be the decisive element in the war in southeast Asia.' Arguing that India 'lights a gleam in the eye of the German and the Japanese,' the assessment concluded that the 'Allied cause *requires* that India should cooperate more vigorously in the war than heretofore.'[41]

A worried Roosevelt ordered a detailed report on the military situation from the combined chiefs of staff. On 15 February, the president himself drafted a tough missive to Churchill. After commenting generally on Britain's attitude towards its colonies – out of date by a decade or two – and contrasting it with America's record on the Philippines, Roosevelt wrote that the Indians felt that 'delay follows delay and therefore that there is no real desire in Britain to recognize a world change which has taken deep root in India as well as in other countries.' There was, he concluded, 'too much suspicion and dissatisfaction in India.' In consequence, the resistance to Japan was not whole-hearted.[42]

Roosevelt turned the letter over in his mind until late that night. He hesitated to send it because he felt that 'in a strict sense, it is not our business.' At the same time, India was of 'great interest' from the standpoint of conducting the war. Eventually, the president decided against sending the letter to Churchill. Instead he asked his representatives in London, John Winant and Averell Harriman, to send him an assessment of Churchill's thoughts on India.[43]

Meanwhile the president received a message from Marshal Chiang Kai-shek of China who had recently visited India to drum up support from the nationalists. Chiang claimed that if the Indian problem was not 'immediately and urgently solved, the danger will be daily increasing.' If the British government waited until the Japanese bombed India and Indian morale collapsed, or if they waited until the Japanese army invaded India, 'it will certainly be too late.' The danger was 'extreme.' If Britain did not 'fundamentally change' its policy towards India, it would amount to 'presenting India to enemy and inviting them to quickly occupy India.'[44]

Even as Roosevelt read Chiang's cable, the British cabinet had stormy meetings about how to deal with the situation in India. At the insistence of Clement Attlee, Churchill reluctantly agreed to send Stafford Cripps to negotiate a settlement for India. The viceroy was aghast and threatened to resign. In explaining the decision to him, the secretary of state for India stressed the 'pressure [from] outside, upon Winston from Roosevelt' as a prime factor.[45] The Cripps mission was clearly intended to head off further American intrusion into Indian affairs. It was impeccably timed. Hours after the mission was approved, the Roosevelt administration announced the appointment of an American advisory mission to assist the war effort in India. The head of the mission, Louis Johnson, was appointed as the president's special representative.[46]

The next day Roosevelt wrote directly to Churchill. Expressing 'much diffidence,' he suggested for India lessons from the history of the United States. Between 1783 and 1789, the thirteen states had formed a 'stop-gap government' by joining the articles of confederation – an arrangement that was replaced by the union under the US constitution. Roosevelt suggested setting up a 'temporary Dominion Government' in India, headed by 'a small representative group, covering different castes, occupations, religions and geographies.' This government would have executive and administrative powers over finances, railways, telegraph, and other 'public services.' It could also be charged with setting up a body to consider a more permanent government for India. Having put forth these radical ideas, Roosevelt wrote: 'For the love of Heaven don't bring me into this, though I do want to be of help. It is strictly speaking, none of my business, except insofar as it is a part and parcel of the successful fight that you and I are making.'[47]

By the time Roosevelt's special representative, Louis Johnson, reached Delhi on 3 April 1942, the Cripps mission was on the brink of collapse. In his first cable, Johnson requested the president to intercede with Churchill to prevent the failure of Cripps's mission. Although Roosevelt refused to intervene, he wished to be kept informed of developments. Thereafter, Johnson worked hectically with Cripps and Nehru to try and hammer out an arrangement satisfactory to both sides. But to no avail.

Churchill was all along concerned about influencing American opinion. As soon as he received Cripps cable claiming that the Congress had rejected his proposals on the 'widest grounds,' Churchill passed it on to Roosevelt. The prime minister also sent a copy of his cable to Cripps wherein he observed that the effect of the mission on Britain and the United States was 'wholly favourable.' However, Louis Johnson had already written to the president that the Congress's rejection was 'a masterpiece and will appeal to free men everywhere.' Johnson pinned the blame squarely on Churchill's chest. Cripps and Nehru could overcome the problem 'in 5 minutes if Cripps had any freedom or authority.' London, he wrote, 'wanted a Congress refusal.'[48]

On the afternoon of 11 April, Roosevelt sent a private message to Churchill urging him to postpone Cripps's departure from India and ask him to make 'a final effort.' The president observed that Churchill had misread the mood in America. 'The feeling is almost universally held here' that Britain was unwilling to go the distance despite concessions by the Congress party. Roosevelt warned that if the negotiations were allowed to collapse and India was invaded by Japan, 'prejudicial reaction on American public opinion can hardly be over-estimated.' Cripps was already on his way home and Churchill sent an emollient reply to Roosevelt: 'Anything like a serious difference between you and me would break my heart and surely deeply injure both our countries at the height of this terrible struggle.'[49]

Although Roosevelt refrained from bearing down upon Churchill, the prime minister took note of his warning about public perception in America. The British embassy in Washington swung into action. Even while Cripps was in India, Halifax had argued in a nationally broadcast speech that the Congress party was not prepared to assume responsibility for defending India, nor indeed for maintaining law and order. After Cripps had thrown in the towel, the British embassy persisted with this line of propaganda, adding for good measure that the communal divisions in India were another reason for the failure. These arguments were faithfully reflected in prominent pro-British newspapers like the *New York Times* and the *Washington Post* in the immediate aftermath of the mission.[50] American newspapers also picked up on statements by Amery and Cripps in the House of Commons, which pointed to the Congress and the communal problem for the failure of the mission.

The Congress too was struggling to get its version heard in America. At Louis Johnson's urging, Nehru had written directly to Roosevelt, expressing the Congress's continued eagerness 'to do our utmost for the defence of India and to associate ourselves for the larger causes of freedom and democracy.'[51] Following his exchange with Churchill, Roosevelt did not reply to Nehru. Matters were made worse by Gandhi's obiter dicta on the United States. In May, he told the press that the United States should have stayed out of the war. Criticising racial policies in the US, he added that Americans were 'worshippers of Mammon.' The following month, he called the presence of American soldiers in India a 'bad job' and the country itself a 'partner in Britain's guilt.'[52] Gandhi's subsequent calls for Britain to leave India were spun by the British embassy in Washington as indicative of his alleged sympathy for Japan.

In this contest over American opinion, the Congress eventually found some worthy allies: American journalists who had descended on India in the summer of 1942. To be sure, not all of them were sympathetic to the Congress's stance. But at least two influential voices weighed in on their behalf. Louis Fischer of the *Nation* landed in India just as Cripps was on his way out. Fischer had spent long years in Moscow, during which time he had got to know Cripps. He had also met Nehru a few times in Europe in the 1930s. Fischer had returned to the US in 1941 and had plunged into a lecture tour where he made the case for a post-war world without imperialism. India naturally bulked large in his arguments. Fischer knew senior state department officials, including Cordell Hull and Sumner Welles. His trip to India had, in fact, been facilitated by Welles.[53]

Fischer's stint in India overlapped with that of another influential journalist, Edgar Snow. Although junior to Fischer by a decade, Snow too had spent many years outside the United States – in his case, in China where he made a name for himself with his book *Red Star Over China* published in 1937. In February 1942, he met President Roosevelt and discussed whether India 'might soon become an American problem.' Roosevelt asked him to write from India if he learnt of anything interesting and to report to him on returning from India. The president also asked Snow to tell Nehru to write to him.[54]

On returning home, Fischer and Snow wrote important articles drawing on numerous conversations with Indian and British leaders. These articles at once punched holes into British propaganda about the Cripps mission and presented a sympathetic account of the Congress's predicament. Fischer published a two-part article, 'Why Cripps Failed,' in the *Nation* in September 1942. Fischer's forensic pieces were laced with polemical verve.[55]

Snow focused on the consequences of the failure of Cripps's mission. His article 'Must Britain Give Up India?' appeared in the *Saturday Evening Post* a week before Fischer's first piece was published. Cripps' failure, Snow wrote, had exacerbated the considerable mistrust of the British government harboured by Indians. Taking a broader view, Snow added that the humiliating defeat and withdrawal of British forces from Malaya, Singapore, and Burma had made a hefty dent in the prestige of the Raj. India, he concluded, was the Allies' last bastion. If it fell, China and the Middle East would be endangered.[56]

These views were echoed elsewhere in the American press. The well-known *Washington Post* columnist Ernest Lindley wrote that the Roosevelt administration would be 'remiss in its duty' if it failed to 'assert its influence on behalf of the treatment of the Indian which will best serve to win the war.' Halifax was troubled at this turn of opinion. Unless they did something to counteract this trend, he advised London, the American press would 'rapidly and perhaps completely change its attitude much to the detriment of Anglo-American relations.' The problem was not just the press. Senior officials like Harry Hopkins had spoken to him about the 'strong pressure now being exerted on the President from both official and unofficial quarters to do something.'[57]

Halifax would have been still more alarmed had he known of the attempt by Gandhi to reach out to Roosevelt. Prior to Fischer's departure from Wardha, Gandhi had asked him to carry a letter as well as conveying a verbal message to President Roosevelt. 'I hate all war,' wrote Gandhi. But he also knew that his countrymen did not share his abiding faith in non-violence in the midst of the raging war. Gandhi advanced a straightforward suggestion. India should be declared independent and the Allies should sign a treaty with the free government of India which would allow their troops to stay on in India for 'preventing Japanese aggression and defending China.'[58]

On returning to America in early August, Fischer sought a meeting with the president to share a message from Gandhi as well as his impressions of the situation in India. Roosevelt was busy so Fischer was asked to brief the secretary of state. Fischer, however, wrote again to Roosevelt, emphasizing that the Congress might lurch towards civil disobedience. 'A terrible disaster may be impending in India.' Gandhi had explicitly said to him: 'Tell your president that I wish to be dissuaded [from civil disobedience].' The viceroy, Fischer added, was hardly inclined to do so.[59]

By this time, however, the Roosevelt administration was not open to intervening on India. The president had no desire to break with Churchill, especially when the Congress seemed set on civil disobedience. A few weeks later, Hull pointed out to the president that they had expressed to Britain their 'unequivocal attitude' about the need for change in India on the basis of agreement between the government and the Congress. 'Our attitude,' he added, 'has not been one of partisanship toward either contender.' It was not clear that they could do more.[60] The president agreed. This was not surprising: the Quit India revolt had just begun.

V

Even as Indian politics juddered to a halt, the United States had to focus on the demands of the war. In early March 1942, the United States despatched a technical mission to assess the needs of Indian industry in supporting the war effort. Led by Henry Grady, a former assistant secretary of state, the mission stayed in India for five weeks and produced its report towards the end of May. The report stated that 'India is of great strategic importance to the cause of the United Nations . . . because India can be utilised as a base for an offensive against the Japanese in Burma, because India and Burma are essential links in the efforts of the United Nations to supply China with war materials, and, finally, because India possesses great natural resources which . . . must be fully developed for the benefit of the United Nations.'[61]

The remainder of the report was at once a sweeping survey of Indian industry and a sharp indictment of the Indian government. 'The Government of India and the industries of India, with few exceptions,' the report noted, 'were not organized on a war basis.' No single official or group of officials were charged with coordinating the entire industrial war effort. A large number of industrial plants were 'mere jobbing shops.' The seriously congested railways plied goods with 'little regard for their importance or ultimate use.' Despite a shortage of electric power, no attempt was being made to curtail consumption for non-essential uses. There was no method for prioritising projects and allocating resources. Prices were rising but there was no mechanism for their control. The lack of coordination and inefficiency in the war economy was epitomised in a ship repair plant in Bombay which produced shoe-nails for the army and railway switch gear, while 'more than 100 ships waited in the harbor for major and minor repairs.'[62]

The report made specific recommendations to revitalise all major industries: transportation and communication, petroleum and minerals, iron and steel, shipping and armaments, motor vehicles and machine tools. The mission insisted that Indian workers had the mechanical aptitude to become 'skilled craftsmen after a short period of training.' In conclusion, the report emphasised 'India's great potentialities for industrial production because of its vast natural and human resources.'[63]

The Grady Mission's recommendations and plan came with a price-tag of $212 million. The Joint Chiefs felt, however, that the programme would throw an enormous burden on American shipping, machine tools, and raw materials. Economic concerns were overlaid with strategic ones. Admiral King reacted to the mission's conclusion that 'the value . . . of an India strengthened by a program of this magnitude will be very great' by scribbling on the margins: 'especially to England after the war.'[64]

Economic assistance apart, there were differences with the Indian and British governments on the strategy to be adopted in Burma and the resources to be devoted to it. These strategic, operational, and logistical discussions were overlaid by sharp political differences. As earlier, the Americans were disinclined to shore up British rule in India or elsewhere, while the British led by Churchill were determined to restore the prestige of their empire. Papering over these cracks proved almost as taxing as preparing to take on the Japanese.

The loss of Burma heightened American concerns about China's continued determination to resist the Japanese. The War Department's policy paper was tellingly titled 'Keeping China in the War.' Tangible support would have to be offered to Chiang in order to buttress his position. It was imperative to reopen the Burma Road; for airlifts alone could not deliver enough supplies over the 'Hump' to China. The strategic responsibility for an offensive into Burma had to rest with Britain and India – supported by the American Tenth Air Force and lend-lease supplies.[65] Meanwhile, General Joseph Stilwell – the American commander of Chinese soldiers who had retreated from Burma to India – wanted to train his troops in India.

Some 10,000 Chinese soldiers had escaped overland to India from Burma. Most of them were in a terrible physical condition, having had little access to food, water, or medicines during the 200-mile trek. The Indian government decided to host them at a capacious camp in the town of Ramgarh in Bihar. The location was originally a prisoner-of-war camp, with several thousand German and Italian internees from North Africa. From early June 1942, Stilwell designated it the Ramgarh Training Center. Soon American supplies and trainers trickled into Ramgarh. In July 1942, the first train-load of Chinese troops arrived, followed by the rest in the next couple of months.

Chiang was prepared to fly more troops to India for training. Stilwell initially proposed to bring in an additional 8,000 troops. Soon he raised the number to 13,000, bringing the total at Ramgarh to 23,000. The Indian government, however, baulked at the prospect of having more Chinese soldiers on its territory. The viceroy felt Chiang had more than an eye on the future. The greater the Chinese participation in an attack on Burma, the greater their influence in deciding its future after the war. Further, Linlithgow was wary of Chiang's dalliance with the Congress leadership and felt that the presence of large Chinese forces in Ramgarh might allow Chiang to meddle in Indian politics.[66]

'So they are determined to bitch it,' thought Stilwell in early October. '"Can't have the dirty Chinks"; Long-range policy: fear of Chinese-Indian co-operation; fear of independent operation; or what not.' 'Limeys getting nasty about Ramgarh,' he noted a few days on. 'How many [Chinese] troops, and what for. WHAT FOR? My God! I told them to help our allies retake Burma. They are making it difficult; they don't want to be beholden to the Chinese for anything. Same old stuff, like closing the Burma Road and refusing troops. They appear to learn nothing.'[67]

Wavell was inclined to accede to the request but sought to cap the numbers at Ramgarh at 20,000. Yet Linlithgow wrote to the secretary of state for India outlining his concerns. The British cabinet agreed with these. Accordingly, London requested Washington to withdraw the proposal. It was argued that there was no immediate military advantage in training such large numbers of Chinese in India. Besides, there were considerable administrative and logistical difficulties in hosting them. The Americans not only persisted with their demand but increased the numbers. General George C. Marshall said that they envisaged bringing the Chinese force in India to anywhere between 30,000 to 40,000 troops. Even as Delhi and London engaged in another round of deliberations, President Roosevelt floated a figure of 45,000. The Commander-in-Chief in India, Field Marshal Wavell, thought this absurd; but it was clear that further stone-walling would not work. Eventually, Wavell and Stilwell struck a bargain at 30,000 troops: a corps with two divisions. Stilwell confirmed this – only to ask for an additional 4,000. Delhi and London had little choice but to acquiesce.

In February 1943, Chiang and Stilwell wanted to send another division worth of troops to train in India. Linlithgow yet again demurred:

> The presence of Chinese troops may cause the Chinese government to meddle in Indian politics. They have already shown an embarrassing tendency in that direction. . . . There may even be a danger of Chinese troops assisting the Congress Party . . . in the event of really serious civil disorders breaking out in India . . . [And] the greater the part which Chinese troops play in the reconquest or subsequent garrisoning of Burma, the greater the voice China will expect to have in the settlement of Burma's future.'[68]

The viceroy, however, gave in to London on the assurance that the number of Chinese troops was firmly and finally fixed at 42,000. Four months on, Stilwell returned with a demand to allow more Chinese troops: he wanted a total of 100,000. The additional 58,000, he informed Delhi, would arrive from August to December 1943.

The Americans, Wavell wrote to the chiefs of staff, had been 'tiresome' on this matter. They were continually asking for more, insisting each time that this was their last requirement: 'it is rather like Hitler's last territorial demand.' There was no question of accommodating 100,000 Chinese troops. Administratively, it would impose an enormous administrative burden – not least in having to find another location apart from Ramgarh. Strategically, it was not possible to employ and support so many soldiers in Assam for operations into Burma. Politically, the issue was 'even more complicated.' India was staunchly opposed to taking in more Chinese troops: 'there are obvious objections to a large Chinese force in India or to the Chinese being able to claim that they played a preponderant part in the recapture of Burma.' Moreover, an increase in Chinese troops 'undoubtedly means an increase of American influence and of American claims to run the campaign from Assam.' Ultimately, Wavell and Stilwell settled on 15,000 more troops from China.[69]

An agreement on the strategy for Burma proved still more elusive. Stilwell's staff felt that the British 'have no intention of attempting to retake Burma in the foreseeable future.' This stance stemmed from 'a British conviction that no Asiatic possession is worth any appreciable diversion of strength from the British Isles; that the war will be won in Europe; and that lost possessions will at the Peace Conference revert with clear title to the British if those colonies remain upon termination of hostilities under enemy occupation, whereas if those possessions are reoccupied with Chinese and American assistance, British title may be compromised.'[70] This was a shrewd assessment of some of the impulses behind British attitude towards Burma. Yet the Americans were wrong in believing that in the summer of 1942 the British had no desire to take back Burma.

Even before the evacuation from Burma, Wavell had been thinking of its reconquest. Churchill wrote to Wavell that the proposed operations were 'very nice and useful nibbling,' but his real interest lay in the recapture of Rangoon and Moulmein, followed by an advance on Bangkok. Following their recent losses, the Japanese navy would be cautious; so Wavell should plan to strike across the Bay of Bengal into southern Burma and thence Malaya. Wavell accordingly instructed his commanders and staff to undertake detailed planning for the limited operations in north Burma and to consider the question of launching a major offensive with Rangoon as its objective. The latter was given the code name 'Anakim.'[71]

In early December, Roosevelt approved of Anakim and directed that the requisite resources be placed at Stilwell's disposal. But Wavell's doubts about the enterprise were deepening. A major offensive on

Burma in spring 1943 was out of the question. Even limited operations in north Burma could not be undertaken then. The problem was not of getting troops into the area but of maintaining them there during the monsoon of 1943. The British chiefs backed Wavell, insisting that Burma was a British theatre of war and India was operationally responsible.[72] On 7 December, Wavell formally told Stilwell that Anakim would have to wait until autumn or winter of 1943. Operations in upper Burma in the spring of 1943 would also be premature.[73]

Plans for Burma were picked up in mid-January 1943 at the Anglo-American conference in Casablanca. The conference was convened to arrive at definite decisions on grand strategy for the year. American and British joint planners submitted separate plans for Burma. The Americans emphatically called for Anakim, 'with a view to keeping China in the war, keeping pressure on the Japanese in this area.' The British felt that the operations 'certainly required in 1943' were recapturing Akyab, establishing bridgeheads in the Chindwin Valley, and covering the construction of a road from Ledo via Mytikyina to Lungling. While plans for Anakim should be made for the winter of 1943–1944, they were not sure if the requisite naval and amphibious forces could be found. Diversion of these to Anakim 'cannot but react adversely on the early defeat of Germany.'[74]

The Americans felt that the British were exaggerating the problem of resources. Marshall came down heavily on them: 'unless operation ANAKIM could be undertaken he [Marshall] felt that a situation might arise in the Pacific at any time that would necessitate the United States regretfully withdrawing from the commitments in the European theatre.' The carrot accompanying the stick was an American commitment to make up any deficiency in landing craft and naval forces. It was eventually agreed that all plans and preparations should be made to mount Anakim by 15 November 1943; though the actual decision to attack would be taken in the summer of 1943.[75]

Although Wavell had swallowed the idea of Anakim, he strained at the requirements of the plan. The Americans in the delegation thought that his outline plan really consisted of 'several pages of well written paragraphs, telling why the mission could not be accomplished.'[76] Indeed, Wavell's qualms about Anakim deepened with every passing day. Wavell now felt that it might be better altogether to avoid a major offensive on Burma. For one thing, they could not hope to surprise the Japanese by an attack there: 'this is an obvious move and must be expected by the enemy.' For another, they could 'only progress very slowly and at considerable cost.' Instead, Wavell felt that they should undertake an offensive to capture the Sunda Straits between Sumatra and Java. This would catch the Japanese off-guard and threaten Japanese control of Singapore and the Netherlands East Indies. Such an operation, he argued, would be 'no more formidable than the capture of Burma.' The problem, of course, was in reneging from the plan agreed with the Chinese: 'it will be necessary to conceal our intentions from the Chinese who are naturally anxious to see the reconquest of Burma . . . we can continue preparations and discussions with the Chinese on an offensive into Burma . . . We shall in fact make a limited offensive into Upper Burma, with the object of confirming the Japanese of our intentions to attack in Burma.'[77]

Anakim, in short, should be abandoned. Wavell, however, reckoned without the resources for this ambitious new plan – as well as with the providers of these resources, the Americans. By early April, he was complaining to the chiefs that the actual allotment of shipping to India fell far short of the monthly requirements agreed for Anakim. The target date of 15 November, he declared, was already impossible to meet. Wavell was right: decisions at Casablanca to press ahead with Anakim had been taken on a total misconception of the amount of shipping that would be available over the next six months. And the chiefs recognised that they had erred.

Later that month Wavell travelled to London to confer with the chiefs of staff. After some days of discussion, it was agreed that Anakim could not be attempted in the dry season of 1943–1944. Apart from operational and logistical problems, it was felt that launching Anakim would commit British forces to a major operation not essential for the ultimate defeat of Japan. Only minor land operations should be undertaken from Assam in the coming campaign season.[78] The challenge, of course, was to convince the Americans. Opinion in Washington was divided. President Roosevelt seemed ready to drop the idea: ' "Anakim out." Keep China going by air,' he had scribbled in a note. But the joint chiefs wanted to take 'vigorous steps' to launch Anakim.[79]

In early May, Churchill and the chiefs travelled to Washington for the Trident conference. The prime minister had never been enthusiastic about an overland invasion of Burma – an undertaking that he likened to munching a porcupine quill by quill. Churchill favoured a landing at some unexpected point in the crescent stretching from Moulmein to Timor. This slotted smoothly with Wavell's thinking about alternatives to Anakim.

At the conference, the British delegation expressed their inability to take on Anakim. The reconquest of Burma, however desirable, was not 'indispensable from the military point of view.' Even if Anakim were successful, the Burma Road was unlikely to be open until mid-1945. After considering alternatives such as Sumatra, the joint planners recommended concentrating Allied efforts on increasing the airlift to China and operations in northern Burma. Wavell and the British chiefs sought to whittle down the latter, but Stilwell insisted that abandoning Anakim would devastate Chinese morale. Roosevelt eventually came round to the view that operations should be undertaken to clear north Burma and open a road from Ledo to Yunnan.

At the next Allied conference in Quebec in August 1943, the Americans were insistent on sticking to the earlier agreement. They maintained that reopening the Burma Road, and indeed the eventual recapture of the whole of Burma, was imperative. Churchill's suggestion on Sumatra was shot down by Roosevelt. The president argued that the Japanese could only be defeated by an advance across the Pacific towards Formosa and an advance from Burma into China proper. Ultimately, it was agreed that northern Burma should receive priority for the coming campaign season.[80]

In any event, the Americans felt that the British were reluctant to use their resources in India to retake Burma and reopen the road to China. The British seemed far more interested in harbouring their strength for a strike at Singapore.[81] Their desire to establish a new South East Asia Command (SEAC) under a British supreme commander was seen as a move in the same direction: to recover the prestige of the British empire. As Stilwell's political adviser, John Davies, trenchantly noted in October 1943: 'We have chosen to bring a third-class island kingdom back to its anachronistic position as a first-class empire. We are rejecting the opportunity to move boldly forward with the historical tide.'[82]

SEAC was soon dubbed 'Save England's Asiatic Colonies.' Stilwell's staff sang: 'The Limeys make policy, Yank fights the Jap, And one gets its Empire and one takes the rap.'[83] Davies pointed out in December that by participating in SEAC operations, 'we become involved in the politically explosive colonial problems . . . we compromise ourselves not only with the colonial peoples of Asia but also the free peoples of Asia, including the Chinese.' It would, therefore, be best to restrict involvement in SEAC: 'after the recapture of North Burma there comes a parting of ways. The British will wish to throw their main weight southward for the repossession of colonial empire.'[84]

The SEAC commander-in-chief, Lord Louis Mountbatten, had his own ideas about the best way to implement the decisions of Quebec.

On 1 November, he informed the combined chiefs of staff that the best objective for the amphibious operation would be the Andaman Islands.[85] Affirming his amphibious orientation, Mountbatten shifted his headquarters from India to Ceylon, though the botanical gardens of Kandy were rather removed from the island's coastline. Much discussion ensued between SEAC, India, London, and Washington on whether the land operations in north Burma (Tarzan) should be braided with an amphibious operation for the capture of the Andamans (Buccaneer) or one aimed at Akyab (Bullfrog). Stilwell was soon disenchanted with the supreme commander: 'The Glamour Boy is just that. He doesn't wear well and I begin to wonder if he knows his stuff. Enormous staff, endless walla-walla, but damned little fighting.'[86]

By the time the Allies met next in Tehran in late November 1943, no agreement had been reached on the capture of Andamans. Churchill felt that the operation was best postponed until the Allied landings on Western Europe had been successfully completed. After some consideration, Roosevelt sent a laconic message to Churchill: 'Buccaneer is off.' In mid-January, Mountbatten realised that it was too late to put into motion any amphibious operation for that year. So, the supreme commander issued a directive rescinding all previous orders for operations in 1944. The only operations that would now be undertaken were an overland advance on Arakan, a limited probe from Imphal-Tamu, an advance on the northern front to cover the construction of the Ledo road, and operations by Long Range Patrol groups.[87]

Stilwell and the American chiefs made one more attempt to persuade the British to launch a serious offensive on Myitkyina. Roosevelt gave his go ahead and a telegram was sent to Churchill. But the prime minister refused to consent.[88] And so the Allies remained deadlocked on Burma. The impasse would only be overcome when the Japanese launched their own offensive on India on 7 March 1944 and pulled the Allied forces back into Burma.

VII

The contours of American involvement in South Asia during the Second World War are best grasped against the backdrop of the larger wartime and post-war policies and plans drawn up in Washington. The former entailed keeping Chiang Kai-shek's forces in play and helping rollback the Japanese from South-East Asia. The latter called for prying India loose from the system of imperial tariffs with Britain. More importantly, the United States had to encourage the British to promise

India political freedom in exchange for full-fledged participation by the nationalists in the war effort. The tensions between the immediate demands of the war and the more distant plans for the aftermath ensured that the United States was unable to pursue these objectives in a single-minded fashion. Moreover, South Asia was not a theatre of high priority for the United States during the war.

In the immediate aftermath of the war, the Truman administration's grand strategy went well with Britain's own plans for India. The Labour government led by Clement Attlee wished to rid itself of the incubus of governing India (and Palestine) and to refashion the imperial system. Whitehall's policies on South Asia were mainly influenced by strategic considerations. The large standing army; the vast reservoir of military manpower; India's importance in defending the Middle and Far East: all of these mandated preserving Indian unity and ensuring India's continued presence in the Commonwealth.[89]

South Asia did not rank high in Washington's priorities in the emerging Cold War. It was neither industrially advanced nor a producer of key commodities like oil or rubber. It was a supplier of certain raw materials – mainly cotton and jute – to Japan and was potentially a large market for Japanese goods. It was also seen as 'a major source of raw materials, investment income, and carrying charges for the UK, thus strengthening the UK's and Western Europe's effort towards economic recovery essential to US security.'[90] In American eyes, too, the subcontinent mattered primarily because of its military manpower and its geographic location between the Middle East and South-East Asia. In this context, it is not surprising that the Truman administration supported Britain's efforts to ensure the emergence of a united, independent India and a stable transfer of power. But these hopes proved unfounded. By the summer of 1947 it was clear that India would be partitioned. The conjunction of the Cold War and the Partition of India created several new imperatives for American policy towards the subcontinent in the decades ahead.

That said, American approach and policy during the war set the tone for much that was to follow in the subsequent years. To be sure, wartime planners ended up confronting a world that was very different from what they had imagined. Their thinking was shaped by the inter-war years whereas the strategic, economic, and ideological contexts of the Cold War were rather different. Nevertheless, the keynotes of American policy in South Asia had already been sounded during the war: the qualified acceptance of the importance of the subcontinent; the divergent views on free trade and economic policy; the challenges of dealing with South Asian nationalisms; and above all, the ambivalences in the 'imperialism of anti-imperialism.' These themes would form the warp and weft of the United States' relationship with South Asia for the remainder of the twentieth century.

Notes

1 Rudra Chaudhuri, *Forged in Crisis: India and the United States Since 1947*, New York: Oxford University Press, 2014; Andrew Rotter, *Comrades at Odds: The United States and India, 1947–64*, Ithaca: Cornell University Press, 2000; Dennis Kux, *Estranged Democracies: India and the United States*, Fort McNair: National Defense University Press, 1992; Dennis Kux, *Disenchanted Allies: The United States and Pakistan*, Baltimore: Johns Hopkins University Press, 2001; Robert McMahon, *Cold War on the Periphery: The United States, India and Pakistan*, New York: Columbia University Press, 1994; Anita Inder Singh, *The Limits of British Influence: South Asia and the Anglo-American Relationship 1947*, London: Continuum, 1990; Paul McGarr, *The Cold War in South Asia: Britain the United States and the Indian Subcontinent, 1945–1965*, Cambridge: Cambridge University Press, 2013.
2 Gary Bass, *The Blood Telegram: Nixon, Kissinger and a Forgotten Genocide*, New York: Knopf, 2013; Srinath Raghavan, *1971: The Global History of the Creation of Bangladesh*, Cambridge, MA: Harvard University Press, 2013.
3 From a vast literature, see, Charles Maier, *Among Empires: American Ascendancy and its Predecessors*, Cambridge, MA: Harvard University Press, 2006; Michael Hunt, *The American Ascendancy: How the United States Gained and Wielded Global Dominance*, Chapel Hill: North Carolina University Press, 2007; Bruce Cummings, *Dominion from Sea to Sea: Pacific Ascendancy and American Power*, New Haven: Yale University Press, 2009; Adam Tooze, *The Deluge: The Great War and the Remaking of the Global Order 1916–1931*, London: Allen Lane, 2014; Frank Ninkovich, *The Global Republic: America's Inadvertent Rise to World Power*, Chicago: University of Chicago Press, 2014; John Thompson, *A Sense of Power: The Roots of America's Global Role*, Ithaca: Cornell University Press, 2015.
4 For contrasting views, see, M. S. Venkataramani and B. K. Shrivastava, *Roosevelt Gandhi Churchill: America and the Last Phase of India's Freedom Struggle*, New Delhi: Radiant Publishers, 1983; Guy Hope, *America and Swaraj: The U.S. Role in Indian Independence*, Washington, DC: Public Affairs Press, 1968; Gary Hess, *America Encounters India, 1941–1947*, Baltimore: Johns Hopkins University Press, 1971; Kenton Clymer, *Quest for Freedom: The United States and India's Independence*, New York: Columbia University Press, 1995. In *India's War: The Making of Modern South Asia*, London: Allen Lane, 2016, I take a broader view of America's role in India during these years. This essay builds on the treatment in the book.
5 Cited in Thompson, *A Sense of Power*, pp. 142, 146.

6 Cited in Patrick Hearden, *Architects of Globalism: Building a New World Order during World War II*, Fayetteville: University of Arkansas Press, 2002, pp. 14–16. See also Ninkovich, *Global Republic*, pp. 160–168.

7 Cited in Hearden, *Architects of Globalism*, p. 41.

8 John A. Thompson, *A Sense of Power: The Roots of America's Global Role*, Ithaca: Cornell University Press, 2015, p. 142, 146.

9 Cited in Thompson, *A Sense of Power*, p. 183.

10 Hearden, *Architects of Globalism*, pp. 29–33, 42–43.

11 Cited in Niall Ferguson, *Colossus: The Rise and Fall of the American Empire*, London: Penguin Books, 2005, p. 67.

12 Harold R. Isaacs, *Scratches on Our Minds: American Images of China and India*, New York: John Day, 1958, pp. 259–267.

13 Cited in Clymer, *Quest for Freedom*, pp. 14–19.

14 Hess, *America Encounters India*, pp. 18–21.

15 British aide mémoire, 17 April 1941; Hull to Halifax, 28 May 1941; press release, 21 July 1941. *Foreign Relations of the United States* (hereafter *FRUS*), 1941, 3: 170–174.

16 Memorandum on 'India and the Lend Lease Act,' 14 May 1941, File no. 2, Roosevelt Library Papers. Nehru Memorial Museum and Library (hereafter NMML).

17 Memorandum by Berle, 5 May 1941, *FRUS* 1941, 3: 176–177.

18 Memorandum by Hull, 7 May 1941, *FRUS* 1941, 3: 178.

19 Winant to Hull, 1 August 1941, *FRUS* 1941, 3: 178–179.

20 Berle to Welles, 5 August 1941; Welles to Hull, 6 August 1941, *FRUS* 1941, 3: 179–181.

21 William Roger Louis, *Imperialism at Bay: The United States and the Decolonization of the British Empire, 1941–1945*, Oxford: Oxford University Press, 1978.

22 Cited in Dhananjay Keer, *Savarkar*, Bombay: Popular Prakashan, 1966, p. 297.

23 Erez Manela, *The Wilsonian Moment: Self-Determination and the International of Origins of Anti-Colonial Nationalism*, New York: Oxford University Press, 2007.

24 Indian reactions to the Atlantic Charter can be sampled in Amit Gupta and Arjan Dev (eds), *Towards Freedom: Documents on the Movement for Freedom in India 1941*, Part 1, New Delhi: Oxford University Press, 2012, pp. 60–75.

25 Interview to Evelyn Wrench, December 1941, *Collected Works of Mahatma Gandhi*, www.gandhiserve.org/e/cwmg/cwmg.htm, 81: 348. Accessed on 7 September 2017.

26 Cited in Clymer, *Quest for Freedom*, p. 35.

27 Winant to Hull, 4 November 1941, *FRUS* 1941, 3: 181–182.

28 Memorandum by Murray, 7 November 1941; Welles to Hull, 15 November 1941, *FRUS* 1941, 3: 184–187.

29 Clymer, *Quest for Freedom*, p. 44.

30 Churchill, *Hinge of Fate*, p. 209; Churchill to Attlee, 7 January, 1942, in N. Mansergh et al. (eds), *Transfer of Power* (hereafter *TP*), Vol. 1, p. 14.

31 Johannes H. Voigt, *India in the Second World War*, New Delhi: Arnold-Heinemann, 1987, pp. 98–99.

32 These negotiations can be followed in *FRUS* 1941, 3: 192–199.
33 Voigt, *India in the Second World War*, 99.
34 Cited in memorandum by Murray, 24 April 1942, *FRUS*, 1942, 1: 640.
35 Memorandum of conversation by Berle, 23 January 1942, *FRUS*, 1942, 1: 593–595.
36 Memoranda of conversations by Berle, 23 January and 28 January 1942, Memorandum to President, 29 January 1942, *FRUS*, 1942, 1: 595–599.
37 Memorandum by Berle, 17 February 1942, *FRUS*, 1942, 1: 602–604.
38 Cited in Clymer, *Quest for Freedom*, 41; Hess, *America Encounters India*, 35.
39 Long to Welles, 25 February 1942, *FRUS*, 1942, 1: 606.
40 Pearl Buck to Eleanor Roosevelt, 7 March 1942; President to Eleanor Roosevelt, 11 March 1942, File no. 12, Roosevelt Library Papers. NMML.
41 Cited in Klymer, Quest for Freedom, 45.
42 Roosevelt to Churchill (draft), 25 February 1942, Warren Kimball (ed), *Churchill and Roosevelt: The Complete Correspondence*, Vol. 1, pp. 400–401.
43 Message to Winant, 25 February 1942, *FRUS*, 1942, 1: 604.
44 T.V. Soong to Roosevelt, 25 February 1942, *FRUS*, 1942, 1: 604–606.
45 Amery to Linlithgow, 10 March 1942, *TP*, 1: 396–397, 404.
46 *FRUS* 1942: 613, 617.
47 *FRUS* 1942: 615–617.
48 Johnson to Roosevelt, 11 April 1942, *FRUS* 1942, part 1: 631–632.
49 Roosevelt to Churchill, 11 April 1942; Churchill to Roosevelt, 12 April 1942, *FRUS* 1942, part 1: 633–635.
50 Auriol Weigold, *Churchill, Roosevelt and India: Propaganda during World War II*, New Delhi: Routledge, 2009, 112.
51 Nehru to Roosevelt, *Selected Works of Jawaharlal Nehru* (hereafter *SWJN*), New Delhi: Jawaharlal Nehru Memorial Fund, series 1, 12 pp. 212–213.
52 Cited in Clymer, *Quest for Freedom*, p. 82.
53 Auriol Weigold, 'Cripps' Offer and the Nationalist Response: Constructing Propaganda in the United States,' *South Asia*, 2000, 23(2): 69–70.
54 Weigold, 'Cripps' Offer,' pp. 67–68.
55 Louis Fischer, 'Why Cripps Failed,' *The Nation*, 19 and 26 September 1942.
56 Edgar Snow, 'Must Britain Give up India?,' *Saturday Evening Post*, 12 September 1942.
57 Halifax to Eden, 16 September 1942, *TP*, 2: 969–970.
58 Gandhi to Roosevelt, 1 July 1942, File No. 12, Roosevelt Library Papers. NMML.
59 Fischer telegram and letter to Roosevelt, 5 and 7 August 1942, File No. 12, Roosevelt Library Papers: NMML.
60 Memorandum by Hull, 15 August 1942, File No. 12, Roosevelt Library Papers, NMML.
61 Report of the American Technical Mission to India, WO 32/10269, The National Archives, Kew, London (hereafter TNA).
62 Report of the American Technical Mission to India, WO 32/10269, TNA.
63 Ibid.

64 Cited in Ehrman, 'Ways of War,' p. 49.
65 Charles F. Romanus and Riley Sunderland, *Stilwell's Mission to China*, Washington, DC: Office of the Chief of Military History, 1953, p. 151.
66 Exchanges between Delhi and London over Chinese troops in Ramgarh can be followed in WO 106/3547. TNA.
67 Theodore H. White (ed), *The Stilwell Papers*, London: MacDonald, 1949, pp. 161, 163.
68 Linlithgow to Amery, 25 February 1943, cited in Thorne, *Allies of a Kind*, p. 310.
69 Wavell to CoS, 3 June 1943; Minutes of CoS Meeting, 23 July 1943, WO 106/3547. TNA.
70 Memorandum by Davies in Gauss to SS, 12 August 1942, *FRUS* China 1942: 129.
71 S. Woodburn Kirby, *The War against Japan: Volume II: India's Most Dangerous Hour*, London: HMSO, 1958, pp. 235–236.
72 Kirby, *India's Most Dangerous Hour*, p. 294.
73 Romanus and Sunderland, *Stilwell's Mission*, pp. 247–249.
74 Michael Howard, *Grand Strategy: Volume IV: August 1942–September 1943*, London: HMSO, 1970, pp. 248–249.
75 Romanus and Sunderland, *Stilwell's Mission*, pp. 270–271.
76 Tuchman, *Stilwell*, p. 356.
77 Kirby, *India's Most Dangerous Hour*, pp. 362–363.
78 Kirby, *India's Most Dangerous Hour*, pp. 368–369.
79 Howard, *Grand Strategy*, pp. 397–404.
80 Howard, *Grand Strategy*, pp. 573–574; Kirby, *India's Most Dangerous Hour*, pp. 419–422.
81 Romanus and Sunderland, *Stilwell's Mission*, p. 359.
82 Memorandum by Davies, 21 October 1943, cited in Voigt, *India in the Second World War*, p. 222; Merrell to SS, 23 October 1943, *FRUS* China 1943: 879–880.
83 Thorne, *Allies of a Kind*, p. 337.
84 Memorandum by Davies, December 1943, *FRUS* China 1943: 188–189.
85 S. Woodburn Kirby, *The War against Japan Volume II: The Decisive Battles* London: HMSO, 1961, 14–15.
86 White, *Stilwell Papers*, pp. 277–278.
87 Kirby, *Decisive Battles*, pp. 58–66.
88 Tuchman, *Stilwell*, p. 431.
89 John Darwin, *Britain and Decolonisation: The Retreat from Empire in the Post-War World*, Basingstoke: Palgrave Macmillan, 1988; R. J. Moore, *Escape from Empire: The Attlee Government and the Indian Problem*, Oxford: Clarendon Press, 1983.
90 Cited in Robert J. McMahon, *Cold War on the Periphery: The United States, India and Pakistan*, New York: Columbia University Press, 1994, p. 13.

3

WAR AND THE WORLD

Tagore's praxis of the global from the
1890s to the 1920s

Pradip Kumar Datta[1]

When the Great War of 1914 broke out in Europe, Rabindranath
Tagore was far away, in what was still a small educational colony
in Santiniketan, located about 100 miles from Calcutta. Despite the
distance, his response to the war was prompt and passionate. On
5 August, the day after Germany declared war on England – after it
had done the same in the preceding days against Russia and France –
Tagore delivered his regular *upasana* (sermon) in school. These upasa-
nas were normally delivered on broad spiritual and ethical issues, but
this one was specifically on the war. He followed this up with another
address on the fall of Belgium that had been invaded by Germany
although it had declared its neutrality. Later, he wrote at least three
poems – and possibly one powerful song – that were inspired by his
anguish at the war.[2] His letters also testify to his disturbance. In one
of these Tagore writes of the 'chained barbarism at the heart of the
Western Civilisation, fed in secret with the life-blood of alien races'
that had now snapped its chains and begun to attack its own master.[3]

The Reverend C. F. Andrews was a close friend of Tagore as he was
of Gandhi and tied to them through personal bonds and shared public
campaigns in India and South Africa. Of English extraction, Andrews
can be described as a freewheeling public intellectual with global concerns. He was in Santiniketan with Tagore when the news of the war
reached them. He remembers Tagore feeling depressed for some time
before the war, intuiting a looming tragedy. In the words of Andrews,
Tagore 'was entirely preoccupied with the foreboding of some disaster
which was about to overwhelm mankind.'[4] Tagore even wrote a poem

called "The Destroyer" that, in an act of ironic perversity, asked the reader to give all she possessed to the 'chariot crowned by Death' as tribute.[5] We do not know from Tagore's own words if what Andrews reported is true. Nevertheless it is remarkable that Andrews should explain Tagore's mood in these terms. If nothing else, it testifies to an intuitive knowledge of one global intellectual of another, the awareness that one's deepest emotions and involvements may not only be with what is conventionally regarded as intimate, whether it's with immediate relationships or with a conventionally felt collective like the nation. It was already possible in the early decades of the twentieth century to be so involved with global events that it shaped one's state of mind and emotional orientation.[6]

The deep belonging to the global exceeds what is often posited in cosmopolitan belonging. Even in Nussbaum's skilful defence of cosmopolitanism, it is apparent that the relationship with the world cannot exceed the scope of a mediated experience, such as the sympathy one feels for a fictional character with which one is not culturally or affectively familiar.[7] The kind of involvement that Tagore – and by extension, Andrews – has with the world is of a far more direct and unmediated kind: they live in it. Deep global belonging is obviously opposed to the critical readings of cosmopolitanism that tend to dismiss it as something that boils down to non-belonging. Incidentally Tagore himself dismissed cosmopolitanism as 'colourless.'[8] At the same time, deep belonging is different from what preoccupies commentaries on globalisation, for these address issues of social, economic, and cultural change that bring regionally diverse times and spaces closer than ever before. Tagore's global belonging is closer to cosmopolitanism in that it is about affiliations and commitments. But as I have said, it exceeds cosmopolitanism as it has been imagined in the current debate by a sense of direct affective contact. I hope to show further that this translates itself into a corresponding language by which Tagore explains global events. And finally, that all of this betrays an involvement that is customarily associated with the nation. If the testaments to the depth of feeling for the nation are that its definition becomes a site of passionate debate that can involve violence and the risk of imprisonment on the one hand and the command over the power of death for its sake on the other hand – then we have in Tagore's commitment to the global a similar depth of belonging but one directed to the global. He too engages in a critique of the existing modes in which the global is being produced and posits other possibilities of inhabiting and making it. At the same time there is a big difference. If the ultimate test of nationalism is that of sacrificing life in its cause, global commitment demands the necessity to avert death. In other words, the global, too, is an intensely contested imaginary in Tagore and springs from his commitment to life.

The idiom that Tagore deploys in the poems arising from the war is an important testimony. Significantly these poems were published in English in journals that came out in England, indicating Tagore's attempt to expand and reach out to a global public that tended to be concentrated in Europe. These poems use and reverse the idiom of elemental nature, a feature that is an essential part of Tagore's poetic self. If elemental nature is one that is embodied in harmonious correspondence with the self in the *Gitanjali* poems, these poems invert the fusion of man and nature. Man's destruction infects the state of nature. In "The Oarsmen," published in *The Times* in 1916, the same year as the *Nationalism* lectures, the distance between the poet and the war is bridged through images of aerial warfare that convulses the basic structure of nature: 'Do you hear the roar of death through the listening hush of distance. / And that awful all amidst fire – floods and poison clouds and the wrestle of earth and sky in mortal combat.'[9] Similarly Tagore enacts the perversion of another conception that is as fundamental to this thought as the belief in harmony. This is of the concept of love as something which defines the relationship between the creator and creation. There is a poem given by Tagore to Andrews on Christmas 1914, which was translated as "The Judgment".[10] Here Tagore envisages a figure which carries resonances of the Semitic God of Judgment as well as the lover God of *Vaishnavism* while its judgment seat is reserved within the bower of nature. From here this God-lover is asked to judge the 'revelry' of thieves and of the 'reckless greed' that has violated the relationship with creation. There is anger expressed in a vicarious identification with divine violence. If the grammar of Christianity marks a distance between the birth of peace and the violence of punishment, Tagore's poem collapses that separation. The poem rains down images of retributive nature in the form of storms, thunderstone, 'shower of blood,' and the 'angry red of sunset.'

These images testify to a nascent hope that there is a principle of justice operating through the self-inflicted violence of men. However, by counterposing the violence of man with the counterviolence of an apocalypse, the poem compromises the basic spirit of hope and rebirth in the peace of Christmas. There is, in other poems of this time, a desperate casting around for other sources of hope, but what shape this will take remains uncertain. The metaphysical recedes into the background in "The Trumpet" which gives to the poet the opportunity to rouse up from despair: 'Strike my drowsy heart with thy spell of youth! / Let my joy in life blaze up in fire.'[11] The image of the trumpet holds out cross-cultural resonances; it doubles up as the trumpet (the title of the English translation) that rings out the Judgement Day as well as the *sankha* (conch shell) which Vishnu blows in mythology and which is sounded for prayers in Hindu ceremonies (the first line of the Bengali original [*Balaka*, No.4] translates as 'Your sankha lies in dust'). But the important point is that it rests in dust: it simply acts as a passive sign that produces a rush of re-commitment in the poet.[12] The stress on human agency – qualified by the sense of present hopelessness – is more clearly presented in "The Oarsmen" *The Oarsmen* which envisions a ship that will greet the dawn in a new land. Incidentally this search for a new space is one that marks some of the Bengali poems of *Balaka* (Flight of the Wild Geese) published in 1916.

It is instructive to compare the expressionistic landscape of these poems with one that was also published during the Great War. Entitled "The Sunset of the Century," this poem provided the epilogue to *Nationalism*, his volume of lectures released in 1916. While this was presented as a single poem in English, it was actually culled from a number of poems originally published in the Bengali volume called *Naibedya*. The structure of the poem is polemical and depends on 'tradition and narrowness of patriotic pride.'[13] It operates on what Naoki Sakai calls a co-figurative space. Commenting on some of the philosophical trends in modern Japan, Sakai argues that these work on a mutually homogenizing binary of the West versus the Nation/East.[14] Co-figuration lends itself to a polemical structure and the poems of *Naibedya* revolve on a stark contrast between the self-destructive greed of the West and the peaceful, meditative space of the East. Here the poem's structure of despair and hope is clearly plotted on a geo-moral space that identifies a known and stable place of alterity in the East. In contrast, the space of hope in "The Oarsmen" and in the *Balaka* poems is unknown and uncharted even if its presence is not doubted. Interestingly, the contrast between the two sets of poems also corresponds to the different occasions for the writing of these poems. The *Naibedya* poems arose in the context of the Anglo-Boer War and the Opium War in which the machinery of colonial expansion was clearly visible in the non-West. On the other hand, the glossary to the *Balaka* poems indicates recognition of fractures within the West. Tagore tells us that those lines were inspired by the dissent of pacifists like Bertrand Russell and Romain Rolland, many of whom faced public opprobrium and state repression for protesting against involvement in the war.[15] These two sets of events also correspond in Tagore, to a changing critique of the possibilities of violence that complicates the co-figurative relationship of East and West, even as they raise fairly different resources of global hope. In the next sections I will turn to this area.

II

In his review of the Gandhi-Tagore relationship, Bhikhu Parekh notes that Gandhi kept referring to Tagore as 'The Poet.' Parekh shrewdly observes that Gandhi may have done this partly to marginalise Tagore's criticism of him by relegating it to the realm of the aesthetic. By implication it projected Gandhi as a practical realist.[16] The binary between Gandhi/pragmatism and Tagore/poetic may be popular but its significance is overstated. This simple opposition overlooks the fact that although Tagore may not have engaged in a grand enterprise of leading a movement for national liberation, he did set up and run a pedagogic institution that exceeded the scope of a conventional university. A critical component of this institution was dedicated to practical training for villagers that would transform the rural hinterlands of Santiniketan. More germane for us here is the fact that Tagore was also a poet who was deeply involved in the quotidian world of political events. His involvement with the early part of the *Swadeshi* movement is well known but we are less familiar with his keen perusal of newspapers and publications that dealt with global events. In his encyclopaedic biography of Tagore, Prosanto Pal relates how Tagore read English newspapers and journals of a liberal orientation. Many of their reports impacted on English newspapers in India and these also probably provided another channel of information.[17]

In general it may be observed that while newspapers have been regarded as formative for nationalism, their contribution to the growth of a sense of global belonging has been less emphasised. After all, in colonial times, it was only by tracking the activities of self-governing nations (that were also the colonising ones) that the sense of one's own nationhood could come into being by underlining its lack. But, besides the power of this co-figuring schema, the news of global events could establish a more direct involvement. Tagore's relationship with newspapers is an instance. In one of his sermons delivered in the context of the Great War, Tagore told his boys that each item of news in the papers held grief, the sorrow of mothers and children, of daughters, sons, sisters, and wives who had lost their near and dear ones.[18] The identification with grief is stitched to an ethical frame. In the same passage Tagore goes on to say that grief is deepest where love is at its softest and most deeply manifest. Loss is not felt in the calculations of politicians or the bravehearts in the battlefield, all of whom can unleash bloodbaths. It's the women who experience loss most deeply. This insight allows Tagore to deploy women as tropes to embody the condition of all those who have been targeted by the war. Hence Tagore's poem features a 'woman in the silent courtyard' that Tagore glossed as a reference to Belgium which had to bear an invasion from Germany, despite declaring its neutrality. The figure of the woman becomes a metonymic extension to indicate the ethical act of non-participation in war.[19] The feminisation of the war points to the necessity for an ethical response to the logistical assumptions of political and military events. It is the attempt to reinscribe the language of politics in affective and ethical responses that marks Tagore's involvement with newspapers and the understanding of the global.

I should say here that there appears to be two sources for the development of Tagore's global vision. One of these derives from his revisionist Vedantism which is fairly complex and therefore, of which, I will mention two elements. The first is something he talks about in *Viswabodh*,[20] an early sermon in which he described his global vision. Tagore told his boys that the ideal of India was the Rishi (sage) who was able to recognise the *paramatma* (oversoul) in his *atman* (soul). The *paramatma* was premised on *juktatma* (joined soul), that involved recognition of union with everyone. And this was contrasted to a commitment of the self to grasp and acquire the possession of others. Further, he differentiates this from the *mayabadis* (those who believed in Shankara's doctrine of *maya* or of the world as an inferior reality) who he says privilege a single truth over other truths. It's in this category that he places European imperialism which seeks to impose its universalism. As against this universalism he posits the idea of *viswabodh*, or global consciousness. This detaches universalism from the singularity of a law and instead upholds the softer but equally effective ethic of foregrounding the consciousness of a shared condition of humanity.

The second element of Tagore's religious philosophy was that of love. While Tagore believed in a Creator, he also argued that the creator was dependent on his creation. This is possibly an idea he inherited from his father Debendranath Tagore and further developed on his own. As Collins describes it, Debendranath modified Rammohon Roy's monist idea of the Brahman by asserting that any act of worship needed the worshipper: man too was necessary for the existence of the Brahman.[21] Tagore refashions the dualist notion to talk about the interdependence of the creator and creation. He does this in a letter in which he tries to comfort Andrews who is struck by the random cruelty of creation. Love, for Tagore, was a theological principle in which the creator could not be complete in infinitude. The creator needed the finite to realise Himself and this was a process that was premised on both joy and pain.[22] Human beings engaged in an analogous action when they exceeded the needs of their individual ego's and interests. It is this doctrine of love that provides a sub-text to the feminisation of war that I have noted above. The figure of the woman is embedded in the love of others and hence can experience their loss in war. I must add that this love is privileged not only because of the depth of suffering that war inflicts. It is also because love is the principle of creation and war distorts it by giving a free run to the will to expand the empire of the self and dominate the other – just as it overturns the logic of nature that we had observed in his poetry above.

Tagore's philosophical orientation sets the frame for the way he understood the logic of global events as it unfolded in his life. This brings me to something that has been latent in my presentation so far. Tagore's empirical engagement with global events is one that tends to respond most intensely to instances of conflict and war. While he was aware of the depredations on the natives of Australia and America, what hit him immediately were the theatres of conflict in China and Southern Africa. It was in the 1880s that Tagore read a tract written by a missionary which indicted the Opium trade in China. Tagore reacted by writing a condemnation of the brute power of the British in controlling territory and trade by which they could change the dispositions of a whole people. The ferocity of colonial power was something that he also noted in the war against the Zulus. Nearly two decades later, the suppression of the Boxer Rebellion together with the Anglo-Boer War was something that occasioned a more developed and elaborate critique of colonial power as representing a new kind of global power formation. He was to later write about it as Imperialism and, even later, fully elaborate it as the global phenomenon of Nationalism. But in between, he was moved and angered by the war against the Matebellis.

As I have hinted above, his philosophical orientation was just that, an orientation. Clearly it was his commitment to global consciousness as the substance of the *paramatma* together with his doctrine of love as the logic of creation that shaped the intensity of his reactions to conflict. The violation of these basic principles of existence moved

Tagore to write out his critiques that were anchored in the global. However, it must not be thought that his reaction to global events was a simple extension of his philosophical frame. The involvement with the conflicts of the world opened up another avenue of thinking about the logic of events and of the global condition in general. Indeed it was this analysis of the global condition that was operatively more productive in shaping the substance of his thought. It raised the basic question that motivated his conception of the global in his essays on Nationalism. The issue is formulated thus: they lived in a world that was coming together – a world that he felt was a blessing for them to live in since it was something that allowed *viswabodh* to manifest itself in practical reality. But the cruel irony was that it was also a world that could not live with itself. The art of living together, of developing relationships of mutuality between the self and its others, had not kept pace with the universalisation of the global that scientific and other developments had initiated. While this predicament was clearly posed by Tagore in the second decade of the century, it retrospectively throws light on the kinds of questions that shaped Tagore's mental condition in the previous decade.

One of the outstanding features of Tagore's global vision in the years preceding and immediately succeeding the turn of the century is his sense of solidarity with the objects of colonial wars. Tagore quite clearly held colonialism – specifically British colonialism – responsible for the conflicts that serrated the world. While I have mentioned China, what I wish to focus on here is his concern with Africa. The exceptional status of this involvement can be appreciated when we compare it with another Indian who is closely associated with Africa, that is, Mahatma Gandhi. Studies of Gandhi in South Africa have established his imperial map of races in which Africans were placed in a position inferior to that of Africans. The recent work by Desai and Vahed has more fully elaborated the hierarchical nature of Gandhi's conceptual and practical relationships with Africans. Interestingly Tagore's comments on the Matebellis were made in 1893, a year before Gandhi stepped on to African shores at Natal, a state where 85% of the population was Zulu.

A little background here is necessary. Desai and Vahed have shown how the subjugation of the Zulus was the critical element in the establishment and consolidation of colonial power in South Africa. Zulu power established by Chief Shaka had already crumbled by 1877 when diamonds were discovered in Kimberley. The economic exploitation of these mines required a stable environment which, the British felt, was not available because of (what was effectively the marginal) assertions of independence by the Zulus. This led to the war against the Zulus. The logic of the British Empire was nowhere better displayed, as Ferguson points out, than in the conquest of the territory of the Matebellis in what is now Zimbabwe.[23] It was the De Beers mining interest led by Cecil Rhodes who also aspired to be a conqueror and empire builder with the backing of the Rothschild banking establishment that fine-tuned the operation. Acting on reports that there were fabulous stashes of gold in Chief Lobengula's territory, Rhodes negotiated a deal by which he hoodwinked Lobengula into signing away more than just the mineral rights. Lobengula had no choice but to declare war. But the ensuing conflict was technologically overdetermined. The deployment of water-cooled, rapid-fire Maxim guns simply mowed down the warriors before they could even come close to the British troops.[24] The new land was appropriately named Rhodesia.

As may be presumed from the date of Gandhi's arrival in South Africa in the early 1890s, his social and political battles against mounting discrimination against Asians occurred at a time when Black Africans were being rendered powerless and dispossessed of their land. His focus on the struggles of Asians to the detriment of any alliances with the Africans was partly a product of the vulnerable state of Indians. As I have pointed out in an earlier essay, unlike Africans who could claim a native relationship with the land and the Europeans who could dictate events from the position of mastery, Asians had limited rights to residence and faced a real possibility of 'ethnic cleansing.' It was from this desperate position that Gandhi claimed the privileges of an imperial subject and tried to placate and earn recognition of this status from the British. Together with his helpers, Gandhi underwent severe hardships as stretcher-bearer, first in the Anglo-Boer War in 1899–1901 and then in the British war against Zulus in 1906. But Gandhi's disregard for Africans was also based on a notion of civilisational hierarchy which placed Africans at the bottom with Europeans marking the upper limits and Indians occupying a mobile position that could aspire to a degree of symmetry with the Europeans on account of customs and cultural achievements. Both set of factors produced a fear of being classed with the Africans by the colonial administration.[25] The apprehension was continuously couched in (viscerally) negative terms. Thus, in a speech in Bombay delivered in 1896, Gandhi criticised the whites who tried to 'degrade us to the level of the raw Kaffir [black Africans] whose occupation is hunting . . . and then, pass his life in indolence and nakedness.'[26] Even in *Hind Swaraj* where Gandhi moves towards a moral definition of civilisation, the African is missed out from the grand map of civilisations.

Gandhi's conceptual categories are constantly negotiated by his politically pragmatic objectives. But it's also true that – at least in the case of Africans – his conceptual categories remain largely unshaken, although he does change his understanding of the Zulus by 1939.[27] Gandhi's early understanding was not an individual failing: a great deal of public media back home in India also shared the same views about Africans.[28] It's this context that defines the extraordinary nature of Tagore's understanding of Africans. Possibly the most startling stand taken by Tagore – and hence the most clearly definitive – is one he expressed in 1928, a few decades after the pacification of the Africans by the colonial order. An Indian in South Africa had written a letter to the British authorities in 1927 to protest against Indians being invited to attend Fort Hare Natevi College for university education. His grounds echoed Gandhi's: the letter writer claimed that it was 'humiliating to Indian sentiment, and to the Indian National Honour and Civilisation' to be asked to attend classes with blacks. In response Tagore observed that colour prejudice from an Indian who was himself is a victim of racism was 'revoking [sic] in the extreme' and was not in accord with either sentiment or civilisation. Tagore continued, 'Our only right to be in South Africa at all is that the native Africans, to whom the soil belongs, wish us to be there.'[29] Clearly Tagore's premise was moral and ethical. The Africans – and not the Europeans – had the moral right to land since they were its original inhabitants, regardless of the claims established by violence and conquest. Flowing from this is a corresponding understanding of the position of Indians in South Africa. That is, that Indians were dependent on the hospitality of the Africans for their continued stay. This assertion needs to be glossed by his observations made three decades earlier on the Matebelli war. In it he related the story of the war as one in which Lobengula had offered his hospitality to the British. But motivated as they were by the greed for minerals, the latter repaid the generosity by proceeding to wage war against Lobengula and decimating the Matebellis.[30]

While Tagore's conception of civilisation appears to be more inclusively ethical than that of Gandhi's, it was not entirely free from equivocation. Behind his assertion that the British showed themselves as more naked (in a moral sense) than the actually naked natives, there is a sense of the uncivilised being more civilised than those who were regarded as civilised. A trace of the popular, teleological historicism that held Western civilisation as the end of history clings to this statement. In the poem popularly known as "Africa" – written in response to the Italian invasion of Ethiopia in 1935 – Tagore ambivalently uses the sub-text of the dark continent to characterise Africans themselves. They are seen to be severed from the historical developments of the East and deposited in a brooding, mysterious darkness where they hid themselves behind a 'black veil.' However, Tagore's use of the grammar of historicism and Orientalism is counteracted by the more deeply felt emotion of anger against colonial greed. This takes the form of a condemnation of British civilisation in the *Rajnitir Didha* essay. The British are seen to preserve their basic historical tendency that developed in their origins in piracy and which is made respectable by adopting new justifications for the forceful dispossession of others. In an essay written about the same time as Gandhi was helping the British troops to quell the Bambatha rebellion of 1906 with a heavy and bloody hand, Tagore wrote an indictment of the imperial subject. He argued that the British first proclaim the Empire as an ideal and then seek to persuade those whom they oppress to become its part.[31] What the will to piracy has done in modernity is to detach the ethical from the political. The effect of this, Tagore notes, is played out in the way in which Boer families had been targeted by British troops together with the burning down of Boer villages.[32] "Africa" goes beyond this to contain a denunciation of the hypocrisies of the Church that underwrites the savagery of the slave trade while benevolently ringing out its bells in western lands. The poem ends with calling upon 'the poet of the fatal hour' that has struck the 'diseased Continent' of Europe, to ask forgiveness of the 'ravished' woman who embodies the humiliated history of Africa.[33]

But there is yet another strand. Tagore's observation that the Matebellis had shown a much greater sense of civilisation by their liberalness to the British was something that was to be developed later into a fundamental element of the global itself. A story – culled from the newspapers – which Tagore often repeated was that of a British pilot who had been part of the saturation bombing of Afghanistan. The bomber had come down and the British survivors were rescued by a girl and were guarded by a 'Malik' who dissuaded other Afghans from killing them.[34] The culture of hospitality trumped revenge. Hospitality did not seek anything from the other or a stranger, and this allowed it to work on a level that was different from the logic of aggression and retribution that was, after all, a product of the violence of self-aggrandisement. Hospitality, for Tagore, became a key consideration for it represented a constant openness to the other. The value of hospitality was derived from Tagore's ethical conception of the self–other relationship. Tagore's core belief was that the self could gain its selfhood only amongst many others. In his essays entitled *Vishwab-harati*, he argued that till now this maxim had worked within limited boundaries but now history had opened up the prospect of establishing this relationship globally.[35] The degree to which a mode of life privileged a non-instrumental relationship with the other pointed to the extent to which an ethic of inter-relationship or what he called, co-operation, had developed. It was this entire ethical edifice that lay behind the short, angry outburst against the racist South African Indian, as previously cited.

The notion of co-operation involves a sense of familiarity with the other. Tagore's notion of hospitality stretches co-operation to its limits where it becomes a mechanism for making the unfamiliar – that is, the stranger – a part of the familiar. Co-operation in this sense allows itself to be stretched outside its assumed boundaries and can become a principle of global inter-relationship which has to assume unfamiliarity. It is possibly this global reach that is responsible for the degree to which Tagore privileges it. While Tagore's notion of hospitality resonates with Kant's definition of it as a 'right of temporary sojourn,'[36] he goes further than Kant in not assuming its dependence on the toleration of the State, an assumption that qualifies its reach.[37] Although Tagore's idea of hospitality may not have been as unqualified in practice, it retains a normative claim that exceeds Kant's conception. It corresponds to a different version of the global, namely one that was not premised on the system of nation-states.

III

It was in a series of lectures given at the two ends of the world – Japan and the United States – in 1916 that Tagore defined a phenomenon that was truly global in its spread. This was nationalism. Tagore's use of the category of Nationalism extended his critique of what was mainly the working of British colonialism, although it was often used as a synecdoche of the West. The Great War was, of course, a fight of nationalisms even though its footprints affected the entire world because the nations involved were also colonial powers. The structural cause of the war was arguably the contest over the share of colonies. I have also described Tagore's extraordinary sensitivity to the onset of the conflict. The war confirmed the sort of prophetic language of his poetry that was written at the turn of the century – which is why he added a transcreation of those poems from *Naibedya* as an appendage to his lectures on nationalism. His lectures on nationalism conceptualise the nation as a global, social imaginary that is indissociable from the machinery of the state. The nation – which is seen to be Western phenomenon – arises from the privileging of competitive accumulation as the primary feature of social organisation. This reproduces society on the principles of efficiency to accumulate the greatest amount of resources over rival societies. The progress of social life on these lines leads to the invention of the nation as the most efficient mode of competitive organisation. This is especially because the nation acquires a transcendental power that commands the devotion of the lives of its subjects. The formation of the nation as a compact unit of competition also involves the exercise of mastery over the conquered, as for instance the native Americans – or the Zulus. This drive to mastery leads to a situation in which the other is either marginalised or suppressed. At the same time, the competition with the external others, that is, other nation-states, produces a logic of violence that is uncontrollably self-destructive. The Great War is its logical consequence.[38] Tagore produces, through the global conception of nationalism, what I have earlier called critical cosmopolitanism.[39] Given the intensity of the critique, I think it would be better to revise the characterisation of nationalism as one of negative cosmopolitanism.

While nationalism was seen by Tagore as a foreign word and relevant for the West, what made it a global explanation was Tagore's prescience about its power over the newly emerging world of the non-West. He was already seized of Japanese imperialism that demonstrated, in its assault on China, that the East was not impervious to the seductions of nationalism. More penetrating was his critique of nationalism in its heroic, anti-colonial form that was presented in a fictive mode. The novel *Ghare Baire* (Home and the World) was published serially in 1915, which was roughly the same period of his critique of Nationalism. This suggests that Tagore was including home-grown nationalism within his global critique of it. Among other stories, *Ghare Baire* revolves around the conflict between two friends, Nikhilesh and Sandip, who conduct a great number of debates on their opposed ideas of nationalism. Their conflict is resolved by tragedy: Sandip's nationalist mobilisation alienates the low castes and the Muslims and the latter retaliate through a riot against Hindus. Sandip's nationalism opens up Tagore's critique of the general phenomenon of anti-colonial nationalism as one that also suppresses and marginalises its minorities and internal others. Further, it is a structure that tends

91

to produce, through unquestioning devotion, loyalty to a nation that actually centralises power within its leadership.[40] At the same time the tragedy of *Ghare Baire* is also that a rival conception of the country articulated by Nikhilesh, that is, of slow, gradual improvement of people's lives, does not have a larger frame of reference. It represents simply his efforts. It lacks the force to change people. This is not so much because of a lack of passion in Nikhilesh but something that is not presented as a possibility in the novel but which is to supplement Nikhilesh's vision by Tagore's own life. This is the insertion – and redefinition of the country by the needs of the global. I will return to this soon.

But, for now, let me recapitulate my argument. I have, in the introductory section, shown how Tagore was embedded in a global structure of feeling. I then went on to show how his involvement with the global was also one of developing critical conceptions of its contemporary condition. What I now wish to touch on in the concluding part is the acts of intervention in which Tagore engaged. Actually he deployed language in a performative manner, and this was not just restricted to his enactment of the prophetic to denounce colonial violence through his poetry. His lectures on nationalism in two extremities of the East and the West, in Japan and the United States, can be seen as a brave attempt to mobilise a global public that would be committed to peace. While this intervention held shades of the quixotic, it resonated with the efforts of the anti-war movement that was going on in Europe at the same time. As I have stated, the anti-conscription movement in 1916 had alienated the movement from the patriotic public: consequently, peace activists in England, among whom Bertrand Russell was one, had to face police suppression and public humiliation. For Tagore this confirmed the desperate isolation of pacifists even as it, in the same action, raised hope. To recall what I have mentioned earlier, Tagore included about four poems (nos 2, 4, 36, and 37) in *Balaka*, a volume of verse released at this time, that evoked the condition of violent upheaval of the war. But these also held out the need to migrate with the birds figured in the title, away to another land that held the silent promise of re-founding another habitation. Five years later, in 1921, Tagore glossed the desperate longing of these lines by the protest movement of Russell, Rolland, and the peace activists that, to him, had offered hope of a better life.[41]

The end of the Great War brought no relief to Tagore. While many leaders in the national movement in India congratulated allies on the peace treaty,[42] Tagore was unrelentingly critical. He saw the Versailles negotiations as simply the attempt by the victors to reap the fruits of their conquest. Indeed, the re-slicing up of the world by England and France was presaged by the war waged by England in China that divided up its provinces for the benefit of the coloniser.[43] This recalls Tagore's assertion made on the colonial impulses of the Great War in the letter that I cited in the introductory paragraph. But there was a new, positive development as well. And this was a fresh initiative by Romain Rolland and others to consolidate the peace movement. Coming after the war, when the large majority of intellectuals had sided with their respective governments, Rolland and others circulated a *Declaration of the Independence of the Spirit*. This pacifist manifesto aimed to bring together anti-war intellectuals on a common platform. Tagore was one of the signatories, and he was requested by Rolland to act as bridge to bring together other intellectuals of the 'East' (including those of Japan and China) with those of the 'West,' so that a truly shared worldview of the global intelligentsia could be forged. The *Declaration* appealed to the 'Toilers of the Spirit' who were companions separated by 'armies, censorship and hate of nations at war' to come together to 're-form your fraternal union.' It went on to say that it would serve only 'Truth' free from frontiers, from boundaries of race and caste. It declared that it did not recognise nations but the 'interests of Humanity,' which it identified with the 'People.' The elaboration of the People is significant. It talked of those who marched and fell and raised themselves again 'drenched with their sweat and their blood.'[44]

The *Declaration* was issued in April 1919. The Third International (Comintern) had been formed a month earlier, in March. Nepal Mazumdar draws attention to the conjunction of these events and the link is justified by the very language of the appeal that smuggles in the idealist claims of universal Humanity into the world of working people. Indeed Rolland entertained the ambition of bringing together the intelligentsia with the working class. There would be a division of labour with intellectuals fighting for intellectual independence while workers would struggle for social revolution.[45] It is, of course, interesting that the signatories included leftist thinkers like Henri Barbusse and Upton Sinclair along with others like Albert Einstein and Benedetto Croce. But Rolland's aspiration was not to be. The limitation of this project is underlined by the parallel desire of Rolland to produce a new enclave of intellectuals that would separate themselves out from the rest of the world. Indeed, Rolland appears to be radically uncertain of the constituency to which he was related. Thus, for instance, in his exile in Switzerland, he at last found himself able to relate to universal humanity in the empty expanse,[46] an identification that underlines the actual groundlessness of the human in Rolland's praxis. To observe these dissonant features in Rolland – that resonated with other pacifists including Tagore – is to register the complexity of their condition of engagement rather than to patronise their quixotic aspirations. It is to also register the minor and often suppressed element in the grand narratives of modernity that neglect to understand the losers of modernity who are embedded in it and work through its difficult pathways.

The *Declaration* initiative did not succeed. At any rate, Tagore was already possessed by another idea that would gather together the desire for another world by training up his contemporary world for the future. Moreover, Tagore combined the two imperatives that Rolland strove to unite in his notion of Humanity/People but gave it a more effective and practical shape. Tagore was a firm believer in the importance of individual cultural actors who could affect social change; but he also believed in social action that would not be directed to elite interests. It is this kind of patriotism that Tagore advanced during the Swadeshi movement[47] and which Nikhilesh in *Ghare Baire* represents, wedded as he is to the idea of making the peasants change their own circumstances. But there was a more institutionally mature and ambitious project that Tagore had up his sleeve in the period that *Declaration* was circulating. This was the project of starting a 'world university' in Viswa-Bharati that aspired to shape the future through a mix of education, creativity, and practical experimentation.

Tagore – presciently for the public debate on education today – desisted from calling Viswa-Bharati an university since the very word brought to mind negative comparisons with Oxford, Cambridge, and other European universities – and hence the disposition to imitate these.[48] But Viswa-Bharati was also different from other universities that sprang up in the early decades of the twentieth century such as Benares Hindu University (1916), Osmania University (1918), Jamia Millia Islamia (1920), all of which were impelled by the need of providing national centres of higher learning.[49] The difference with established universities lay in the ambition that Viswa-Bharati attached to the conventional functions of knowledge production and dissemination. Tagore conceived knowledges as cultures and on that basis sought to produce a cultural selfhood for the country and initiate a civilisational process of global interactions. While he aimed at making it a 'Centre of Indian Culture' (as the title of his essay on Viswa-Bharati reads), its motto aspired to also make it a 'nest' of the world. Further, Viswa-Bharati did not concentrate on higher education alone. It consisted of three basic units. Besides the college and research branch that was dedicated to knowledge production, artistic creation, and dissemination, there was the school wing that had already been established in 1901; in addition, there was a rural development centre at Sriniketan located next to Santiniketan, that taught village children, carried out experiments in agrarian production, and disseminated these to surrounding villagers while establishing institutions such as credit and artisanal co-operatives. Viswa-Bharati addressed itself to the task of nurturing a possible future of the country that would not just open it up to the rest of the world but reinvent its selfhood within the global. At its heart was an idea of India-in-the-world. This was not an internationalist vision in the sense of different nations making up a global organisation. Instead it was a notion of a country that would be a coherent cultural entity, materially self-sustaining, relating to other cultures without hard, policed boundaries – whether of a cultural, social, or territorial nature. Bharat/India was premised on the imaginary of a cultural collective being made through processes of exchange.

Tagore's conception of an educational institution was rooted in the idea with which he had started his boys' school in 1901. This was something that resonated with John Dewey's notion of education being co-extensive with life instead of being a preparation for it. The conversion of the school into a university expanded this notion into the idea of a national and global 'nest' that would produce a new culture of selfhood and exchange. While the idea of the country was based on bringing together its different knowledge cultures, the understanding of culture was shaped by ethical considerations and not by a belief that culture is the possession of a national territory and/or the people. The ethical imperative is one that I have already mentioned, namely the need to reach selfhood through relationships with others. This belief prompts the imagining of a collective that would be continuously processual and that would blur boundaries even as it produced a coherent sense of itself. This framework led Tagore to first identify the different cultural elements of the country which he felt had not been amalgamated in the course of history. These elements were defined in terms of religious traditions of knowledge – Hindu, Buddhist, Jain, Islamic, and so on. But Tagore also included the European and English pool of ideas for he believed that these needed to be incorporated in the dynamic entity that would produce a new conception of the country.[50] The scope of this ambition was backed up by recruiting students from provinces outside Bengal.[51]

The production of a self for the country also drew on locating the 'foreign' as an important element in making up the self. Tagore said that foreignness produces shock that stimulates the 'native' culture. European culture was itself produced by Christianity, a religion of the East, which ran counter to the basic assumptions of the West. Likewise, European culture had introduced dynamism in India that had shaken its formalism.[52] One of the ways in which 'foreign' perspectives were embedded in Viswa-Bharati was the practice of inviting scholars who would bring to bear different perspectives on the (dominantly) Orientalist modes of learning that Viswa-Bharati pursued. Hence there was a procession of such scholars such a Sylvan Levi, Maurice Winternitz, Stella Kamrisch, and so on. The hope was that they would interact with resident scholars such as Kshitimohon Sen to produce a new conception of the cultural entity of India. In short this was one of the ways in which Viswa-Bharati sought to make an India/Bharat-in-the-world.

Another element of Viswa-Bharati was that of rural development. If the heart of Santiniketan was to generate original cultural conceptions through research, Sriniketan was designed to conduct experiments in rural production and modes of living. Experimentation with new techniques and resources such as imported seeds and livestock or the use of machinery and so on were devised in Sriniketan to be tested out in the fields of the surrounding villages. It may be noted that this highly localised initiative was actually conducted by a Leonard Elmhirst, an Englishman, while it was financed by his wife Dorothy, who was American and inspired by the ideas of Tagore on rural transformation. Sriniketan sought to integrate activists with their different practices of work and new technologies from all over the world. This process was not without its own share of 'shocks' from a foreign culture. But the net effect was to cosmopolitanise the local through the production of new technologies of production and of self-formation of peasants, artisans, and adivasis.

The localised cosmopolitanism corresponded to the intersectional design of Viswa-Bharati itself. As a habitation it was connected to Calcutta which was about a hundred kilometres by railroad. Calcutta was then the second capital of the most globalised empire in the world and was thus connected with the other metropolitan centres of the world. On the other hand, from Santiniketan, a traveller could traverse a swathe of about 400 kilometres of rural life on which Viswa-Bharati – through Sriniketan, its rural development branch – exerted its influence on production, finance, and, in many cases, the reshaping of village life.[53] In short, Viswa-Bharati was located in a continuum between the rural interiors and the global habitations of metropolitan centres. At the same time Viswa-Bharati – especially Santiniketan – produced itself as a distinct habitation that was marked by its own customs, rituals, festivals, and modes of working and teaching. Although these had a Hindu character, they were novel and innovative, qualities that detached them from invoking an immovable tradition. Also, it was Hindu without a proclamation of its Hinduness and in many registers recognised that Hinduness was imbricated in non-Hindu elements.[54] It aspired to be a boundaryless entity, and it embodied this in a special relationship with nature. Viswa-Bharati was – unlike the way it looks today – located in an unwalled and open space that embodied its openness to the shared entity of nature – even as it sought to make this openness intimate through various modes such as hosting classes in Santiniketan under trees. Innovativeness also contributed to an attempt to produce universalist features such as the *halchalan* festival that Tagore invented around the celebration of agrarian labour in Sriniketan. In this form Viswa-Bharati provided a modern embeddedness as it inhabited the intersection of the global, metropolitan, and rural.

In conclusion, let me restate some obvious points that have been made in this chapter. The first is that modern conceptions of the global have also sprung from the modern non-West and possess a deep and productive belonging that is different from the recognised modes of internationalism, cosmopolitanism, and globalisation with which we conventionally frame the global. Further, studying Tagore allows us to understand a global conception that is both a constitutive part of modernity (and hence arises in other parts of the world) as well as a series of specific conjunctures. This global idea arises from the ever extending reach of global wars. The violence of war raises more generally the prospect of global survival even if this is glimpsed in apocalyptic metaphors in the age of Tagore. The prospect of unlimited violence is also the crucible which gives birth to passionate thought about the global, raising questions about what are the alternative ways of relating to it and the kinds of action needed for the world to survive. These are admittedly large and ambitious challenges but in Tagore we have the most sophisticated and pragmatic attempts to work these out. The significance of Tagore is that he is not just a simple cosmopolitan in the sense of pitting the global against the national or vice versa. What he does is to frame the country – and with it, other collective forms of life such as local, rural, urban, regional, and so on – by the needs of the global. This allows him to rethink all these collectives while reinventing them and their mutual relationships within a distinctive habitation. In doing this Tagore opens the possibility of exceeding the frames of modernity, even as he produces this pathway from the grounds of the modern itself.

Notes

1 I am grateful to Ashok Bhattacharya and Isabel Hofmeyer for their criticisms and suggestions.
2 Prosantokumar Pal, *Rabijiboni, Vol. VII, 1914–1920*, Calcutta: Ananda Publishers Private Limited, 1997, pp. 25–28.
3 'Letter to Ms Semru,' *Rabijiboni, Vol. VII, 1914–1920*, Calcutta: Ananda Publishers Private Limited, 1997, p. 32.
4 C. F. Andrews, 'Letters to a Friend,' in Sisir Kumar Das, (ed), *The English Writings of Rabindranath Tagore, Vol. III: A Miscellany*, New Delhi: Sahitya Akademi, 2002 (first published 1996), pp. 231–232.
5 Andrews, *The English Writings*, Vol. 3, p. 231.
6 Krishna Kripalani, a close co-worker of Tagore and his biographer, hit the right note when he observed that Tagore was a citizen of the world because he felt with the world. Pal, Vol. 7, p. 6.
7 Martha C. Nussbaum, *For Love of Country?*, edited by Joshua Cohen, Boston, MA: Beacon Press, 1996, pp. 139–143. Nussbaum also cites the instance of child learning in which she develops the capacity for imagining things faraway. While this is apposite for Tagore, the point remains that this is not just the Romantic idea of imagination that afflicts Tagore with the sufferings of the faraway.
8 Tagore's description anticipates the criticisms of Nussbaum in the present debate but discounts the possibilities that are raised by her reply to this objection. See Nussbaum, *Reply, for Love*, pp. 131–144.
9 Andrews, *The English Writings*, Vol. 1, p. 607.
10 Andrews, *The English Writings*, Vol. 3, pp. 240–241.
11 Andrews, *The English Writings*, Vol. 1, pp. 606–607.
12 Andrews, 'Letters to a Friend,' *The English Writings*, Vol. 3, pp. 240–241.
13 Abu Sayeed Ayyub, *Modernism and Tagore*, New Delhi: Sahitya Akademi, 1995, p. 60.
14 See Naoki Sakai, *Translation and Subjectivity: On 'Japan' and Cultural Nationalism*, Minneapolis: University of Minnesota Press, 1997, pp. 15–17.
15 See his explanatory lines on poem no. 4 (later translated as *The Trumpet*, see above), Rabindranath Tagore, *Balaka*, Calcutta: Viswa-Bharati, 1405 [1998], (first published 1916), p. 119.
16 Bhikhu Parekh, *Debating India*, New Delhi: Oxford University Press, 2016, pp. 61–62.
17 Tagore read a great many English papers for news on Europe and the United States. He would relay the contents of these to Bengali readers through the columns of *Samayik Saarsangrahain Sadhana*, the journal he edited. Prosantokumar Pal, *Rabijiboni, Vol. III, 1292–1300*, Kolkata: Ananda Publishers Private Limited, 2009 (first published 1990), pp. 291–292.

Tagore was so deeply acquainted with media that he was aware of the role that the English media played in controlling representations of events such as the anodyne reportage of the Matebelli war; something which *Truth*, the English newspaper, had disturbed by providing detailed reports on the outrages perpetrated by the British forces. 'Rajnitir Didha,' 1300 [1893], in *Rabindra Rachnabali*, Vol. 5, Kolkata: Viswa-Bharati, 1415 [2009] (first published in revised form, 1394 [1987]), p. 639.

18 'Paaper Marjana' (09 bhadra, 1321), in *Santiniketan*, Vol. 2, Calcutta: Viswa-Bharati, 1401 [1994] (first published 1909–16), pp. 497–499.

19 'the woman in the silent courtyard . . . represented Belgium,' Tagore to Andrews, cited in Pal, *Rabindrajiboni*, Vol. 7, p. 28.

20 11 Magh, 1316, *Santiniketan*, Vol. 1, pp. 282–293.

21 Michael Collins, *Empire, Nationalism and the Post-Colonial World: Rabindranath Tagore's Writings on History, Politics and Society*, London, New York: Routledge, 2012, pp. 30–31.

22 Andrews, 'Letters to a Friend,' *The English Writings*, Vol. 3, p. 247.

23 Ashwin Desai and Goolam Vahed, *The South African Gandhi: Stretcher Bearer of Empire*, New Delhi: Navanya, 2015, pp. 31–32.

24 Only 4 invaders were killed while 1,500 Matebellis died. Niall Fergusson, *Empire: How Britain Made the Modern World*, London: Penguin Books, 2007, pp. 222–225.

25 Pradip Kumar Datta, 'The Inter-Locking Worlds of the Anglo-Boer War in South Africa / India,' *South African Historical Journal*, 2003, 57(1): 35–59.

26 Desai and Vahed, *The South African Gandhi*, p. 37.

27 In an interview in 1939, Gandhi described black Africans as 'indigenous inhabitants' whose rights could trump those of the Indians while the Europeans were 'usurpers.' Cited in Ajay Skaria, *Unconditional Equality: Gandhi's Religion of Resistance*, Ranikhet: Permanent Black and Ashoka University, 2016, p. 51. It would be interesting to speculate if Gandhi's attitudes developed in a dialogic response to Tagore and Nehru.

28 Africans were routinely regarded as savages in the Indian press during the Boer War. Reacting to a news item, the *Bangabasi*, an orthodox Hindu newspaper, departed from its loyalism to criticise the British for using Zulus and Basutos in the army, something which privileged the 'uncivilised' over the 'civilised' Indians who were not allowed to serve in the British force against Boers. See Datta, *Inter-Locking Worlds*, p. 58.

29 In *The Modern Review*, April 1928, *The English Writings*, Vol. 3, p. 785.

30 'Rajnitir Didha.'

31 'Imperialism,' *Rachanabali*, Vol. 5, pp. 655–657.

32 'Poth o Patheyo,' *Rachanabali*, Vol. 5, p. 667.

33 I have drawn on Tagore's translation. Poem No. 102, 'Poems,' *The English Writings*, 1: 376–377.

34 'Supreme Man, Man,' *The English Writings*, 3: 207.

35 Rabindranath Tagore, 'Viswabharati No. 5,' *Rachanabali*, 11: 759.

36 Immanuel Kant, 'Third Definitive Article for a Perpetual Peace,' *Perpetual Peace: A Philosophical Sketch*, www.mtholyoke.edu/acad/intrel/kant/kant1.htm (accessed on 21 February 2017).

37 See the critique of Kant's conception on these lines in Jacques Derrida, 'On Cosmopolitanism,' in Garreth Wallace Brown and David Held, (eds), *The Cosmopolitanism Reader*, Cambridge: Polity Press, 2010, pp. 419–421.

38 This is a summary of some of the key elements of the argument in Pradip Kumar Datta, *Revisiting Rabindranath, Thinking the Global: Some Questions on Identity Formation, Heterogeneities: Identity Formations in Modern India*, New Delhi: Tulika Books, 2010, pp. 214–258.

39 Swati Ganguly and Abhijit Sen (eds), *Rabindranath Tagore and the Nation: Essays in Politics, Society and Culture*, Kolkata: Punascha and Visva-Bharati, 2011, pp. 36–48.

40 See P. K. Datta (ed), *Rabindranath Tagore's Home and the World: A Companion*, Delhi: Permanent Black, 2000, especially the essays by Sumit Sarkar and Malini Bhattacharya, and the editor's introduction.

41 The account is drawn from Pradip Kumar Datta, *Prothom Mahayuddha, Rabindrik 'Nation' o Rabindranather Antarjatikata, Baromash*, Saradiyo, 2006.

42 Madan Mohan Malaviya, for instance, in his presidential speech at the Congress of 1918, profusely congratulated the Allies for their victory and their magnanimity in accepting peace proposals. Nepal Mazumdar, *Bharatey Jatiyata*, 1988 f.pub.1966, Vol. 2, Calcutta: Dey's Publishing, pp. 19–20.

43 Mazumdar, *Bharatey Jatiyata*, Vol. 2, p. 187.

44 Mazumdar, *Bharatey Jatiyata*, Vol. 2, pp. 50–51.

45 Mazumdar, *Bharatey Jatiyata*, Vol. 2, pp. 52–53.

46 Letter of Romain Rolland to Rabindranath Tagore, dated 07.05.1922 translated by Indira Debi Chaudhrani, cited in Alex Aronson and Krishna Kripalani (eds), *Rolland and Tagore*, Calcutta: Viswa-Bharati, 1945, p. 31.

47 Sumit Sarkar felicitiously names and elaborates this as Constructive Swadeshi. See his discussion in *Swadeshi Movement in Bengal 1903–08*, new edn, Ranikhet: Permanent Black, 2010, pp. 43–48.

48 He argued that the word *university* indicated a model that was sought to be transplanted to India without considering the social and historical milieu in which universities had grown in Europe. This urge to model higher education on a university was present in the National Education movement. Hence he did not wish to call Viswa-Bharati a university. See 'The Centre of Indian Culture,' *The English Writings* of Rabindranath Tagore (ed) Sisir Kumar Das, 2004, 2, Delhi: Sahitya Akademi, pp. 471, 482. This formulation indicates the genealogy of our present fetish of examining international rankings of universities and bemoaning the fate of 'our' universities – and then seeking to alter them to fit a standardised version; all the while ignoring the distinctive evolution of our universities and their strengths in relation to a clear understanding of their nagging problems.

49 Apropos of national schools, in 'Dharmasiksha,' *Santiniketan Patrika*, 1990, 1326: 4–5, Tagore observed that these had been Hindu institutions. Instead of removing divisions, they simply exacerbated them. Tagore himself was not purely secular but made a distinction between religious imaginaries based on pride, supremacism, and hard boundaries and those that opened out to other streams of thought and belief. He believed the

Upanishads contained invocations of such universal value that no religion could have any objection to these. Nepal Mazumdar, *Bharatey Jatiyata O Antarjatikataebong Rabindranath*, Vol. 2, Kolkata: Deys Publishing, 1988, p. 65.

50 For instance, courses taught at Vidya Bhavan in 1928 included Tibetan, Prakrit, Pali, Medieval Indian Religions, Avesta, Comparative Philology, French, German, Jaina Logic, Nyaya – Dipika, Doctrine of Atman and Anatman, and so on, *Annual Report*.

51 There were, for instance, eight regular students in Vidya Bhavan (Research Institute) of which two were from Gujarat, one from the central provinces, and five from Bengal. *Viswa Bharati Annual Report*, 1928.

52 Tagore, *Centre*, p. 486.

53 See Pradip Kumar Datta, *The Globality of Viswabharati: Sriniketan and Co-Operatives*, NMML Occasional Paper: Perspectives in Indian Development, New Perspectives, New Series, 1, 2013 for a detailed description of Sriniketan.

54 Tagore unequivocally said that we cannot only recognise the Hindu heart in India for there had been fusion of Islam in key elements of culture. 'Viswabharati' No. 4, *Rabindra Rachanabali*, Vol. 11, Kolkata: Paschimbanga Sarkar, 1368 [1961], p. 756.

4

FROM ERODE TO VOLGA

Periyar EVR's Soviet and European tour, 1932*

A. R. Venkatachalapathy

I

On 13 December 1931, E.V. Ramasamy Naicker (1879–1973), better known as 'Periyar,' set sail on the French ship *Amboise* from Madras port on what was to be a year-long tour of Europe. Barely a month earlier his wife, Nagammal, had issued a statement in the Self-Respect movement's organ, the weekly *Kudi Arasu*, that Periyar was ailing: he could barely speak for more than a minute, and if he tried to speak even for a few minutes he was out of breath; the statement requested readers and friends not to trouble him with demands to attend meetings and give talks.[1] The editorial duties of *Kudi Arasu* were now to be the responsibility of Sami Chidambaranar, his future biographer. This notice was followed by a statement that all future mails be addressed to Nagammal rather than to Periyar.[2] As the Special Branch of the Criminal Investigation Department (CID) observed, 'Their visit to Russia was not bona fide, and the lieutenants of Ramaswami Nayakkar have been asked to keep this fact as secret as possible.'[3] Another CID report recorded that 'It is said that the main objective of their visit was to study atheism.'[4] A general introductory letter addressed to fellow communists by that Shapurji Saklatvala gave to Periyar stated that he was 'on a hasty trip to Europe where they want to learn many sociological, political and working-class problems in a short time.'[5] What impelled Periyar to undertake this trip remains unclear to this day, and the tour definitely had a cloak-and-dagger flavour to it.

A *Kudi Arasu* editorial, 'Our Editor's European Tour,' provided some detail about Periyar's tour.[6] Taking a dig at Gandhi's earlier statement on his return from the Round Table Conference that it had ended in failure, the editorial said that there was no question of success or failure of Periyar's tour, for the objective of the tour was to further the development of 'our movement,' understand the culture and mores of the West, attain economic equality and promote the welfare of the working class. For 'Our social liberation will be attained only through our own social unity and not by reliance on others and tours to faraway lands.'[7]

Even though the *Kudi Arasu* editorial mentioned that the tour would take up to 3–4 months, Periyar ended up spending nearly a year abroad. What was often and repeatedly referred to as the European tour actually took him to the Soviet Union via Ceylon, the Suez, Cairo, Athens, and Constantinople. After his travels in the Soviet Union he journeyed through Germany, France, Spain, Portugal, and Ceylon,[8] spending considerable stretches of time in these countries. The bulk of his tour, over three months, was spent in the Soviet Union, meeting party officials, atheist organisations, state officials, and Indian émigré revolutionaries. Periyar then headed to Berlin, interacted with the League Against Imperialism, and spent a considerable time among Nudist activists. In Britain he participated in a number of Communist party events, meeting leading members of the Communist Party of Great Britain. During these hectic months he encountered some of the most active minds of the day who had led translocational lives – Abani Mukherji, Clemens Palme Dutt, Shapurji Saklatvala – linkages that caused ruptures not only in his life but also in his socio-political movement.

Though the *Kudi Arasu* editorial promised that 'the events of the tour and movement-related activities' would be periodically reported in its pages, the record is sparse. Apart from a few letters – from Cairo, Egypt – and the report of a speech that Periyar delivered at Locke Park in Barnsley, Mexborough, South Yorkshire, and in various parts of Ceylon on his way back, only some reports on events welcoming him on his return survive. The pages of *Kudi Arasu* are largely silent about his visit to the Soviet Union. A day after his return, in a statement in *Kudi Arasu*, Periyar's promise to write soon the details of his tour, and the ideas that he had imbibed and 'how far they can be adopted' did not materialise.[9]

Periyar had apparently maintained a diary and taken many photographs. Some of the pictures were mailed back home in the midst of his travels and a few of them were reproduced soon after his return in the pages of *Kudi Arasu*.[10] Thirty years later, his newspaper, the *Viduthalai*, carried excerpts from this diary in a souvenir to commemorate his 85th birthday – but few, his biographers not excepted – noticed it.[11] In 1997, V. Anaimuthu, editor of Periyar's collected writings, partially unearthed

103

Periyar's dairy of the tour and published a facsimile edition.[12] The note-book consisted of 151 pages. Evidently there had been at least two other notebooks, now untraceable. Incomplete as it is – beginning from Periyar's 66th day in the Soviet Union on 19 April 1932 and ending with his flight from London to arrive in Paris, it covers only 78 days of his 331 day-tour; only 30 days of his Soviet tour are covered by this diary – its value is beyond doubt, especially as there is no other record of his tour.[13] This chapter is largely based on this diary. And it has been supplemented by the perfunctory reports in *Kudi Arasu*, and two pieces by S. Ramanathan who travelled with him.[14]

Further, little has so far turned up in the British colonial archive while the Soviet and German archives await their scouring for this purpose. There are a few files in the Tamil Nadu archives which provide tantalizing glimpses of the tour. The British Government's Indian Political Intelligence Files (IPI) have been recently discovered; though they provide a wealth of information on a number of activists that Periyar met in Europe, they are surprisingly and inexplicably silent about him.

II

The tour came at a hectic period of Periyar's career. Periyar was a late entrant to politics. Born in 1879, in Erode, in a rich merchant family, Periyar, after a somewhat profligate life settled down to a successful career as a merchant and businessman. By the time of the First World War he was dabbling in local politics, rising to be the chairman of the Erode municipality. This brought him in touch with C. Rajagopal-achari, or Rajaji, famously described as Gandhi's conscience-keeper, his counterpart in the adjacent Salem municipality. Periyar was soon sucked into the vortex of the Indian nationalist movement in the wake of non-cooperation, 1920–1922. As a skilled agitator and organiser with remarkable leadership qualities, Periyar soon rose to become the secretary and president of the Tamil Nadu Congress. This was the time when the Brahmin – Non-Brahmin question occupied centre-stage in Tamil Nadu politics with the emergence of the Justice Party to champion non-Brahmin interests.

Even by 1920 Periyar was arguing for communal representation (or caste-based reservation) in representative institutions despite being in the Congress. His experience of leading the Vaikom Satyagraha (1924) for the entry of the low-caste Ezhavas into the temple streets of the famed Vaikom temple in the state of Travancore, and active participation in the Cheranmadevi Gurukulam controversy (1923–1925), where he agitated against the discriminatory dining arrangements made on the basis of caste, gradually led him to a position that non-Brahmin interests could not be guaranteed, whether in the Congress or in an India free of British rule. Following this, Periyar launched a strident campaign for social justice through communal representation, and a vehement attack on Brahminism, which, in his view, stalled its attainment. By mid-1927 there was a gradual shift in the content of Periyar's campaign – the attack on Brahminism and the championing of reservations quickly grew into a radical critique of caste and religion. He read religious texts critically, and condemned them, even calling for the public burning of all religious texts, and the abolition of all religion. By this time, he was also articulating radical feminist views, unprecedented in India. Raising the question 'Why women are enslaved,'[15] he traced its roots to lack of property rights, and the shackles of marriage and motherhood; he advocated contractual marriage, rather than one sanctioned by religion, and supported contraception. In a pioneering move he also looked at how language with its vocabulary of chastity and masculinity constructed and legitimised the enslavement of women. Communism in India was still nascent in the region, with neither leaders nor organisational structure. Periyar, however, opened the pages of his journal to the independent communist M. Singaravelu Chettiar, sometimes described as the first communist of South India.

Heralding his Soviet tour, Periyar, along with his long-time associate S. Ramanathan, began to publish in instalments, arguably the earliest translation in any Indian language, and certainly the first in Tamil, of *The Communist Manifesto*.[16] The translation was serialised in *Kudi Arasu* over five numbers from 4 October to 1 November 1931. The translation concluded with 'What the bourgeoisie, therefore, produces, above all, is its own grave-diggers. Its fall and the victory of the proletariat are equally inevitable.'[17] The promised translation of the second part never materialised, symbolic perhaps of Periyar's abortive attempt to embrace Communism.

In was in this context that Periyar set out on a year-long journey to many countries in the West, along with his co-translator S. Ramanathan,[18] and his namesake and young relative, Erode Rangaswami Ramasamy – his father was a cousin of Periyar's – called Ramu. This was indeed a team of Rams!

At the time of setting out on the tour, Ramu, aged about 24, after completing the second form in school, was studying motor mechanics and driving in an industrial training school in Chennai.[19] Ramaswamy holds that the purpose of the tour was to visit the Soviet Union, and fearing that passports may not be issued if the true destination was revealed, they excluded the Soviet Union from the list of countries to be visited. In any case, Periyar's passport (no. 9116) was issued on 9 April 1931 at Fort St George, signed by the Secretary in the Law Department of the Government of Madras. In those days, passports were not meant 'to allow the bearer to pass freely without let or hindrance' as now, but were endorsed for visits to specific countries. It is not clear for which countries his passport was endorsed. But it was definitely not endorsed for the Soviet Union as that required the express permission of the Government of India.[20]

III

Ever the penny pincher, Periyar had taken a fourth class ticket on the deck of *Amboise*. For the first four or five days, the passengers suffered in the sun and rain and had to keep shifting their seats whenever the cargo was moved. The ship docked at Colombo harbour on 16 December in the afternoon. The next morning the *Amboise* left Colombo and reached the French port of Djibouti on 24 December where the ship was anchored for a day. *Amboise* left Suez harbour on 29 December and dropped anchor at Port Said that night.

After a week at Port Said, on 5 January 1932 they took a train to Cairo, 150 miles away. Periyar and company then boarded the ship on the 16th at Alexandria and arrived at Athens on the 19th.[21] They had to wait for two weeks for Soviet permission and spent the time looking around the remains of the great civilisation and even toyed with the idea of a trip to Turkey. It is not clear how contacts were established with the Soviets but the pass eventually arrived on 2 February. Ramu claims that a typist at the local Communist Party office helped and they embarked clandestinely, shivering in the winter cold. However, they were seen off by the Soviet consul himself as they boarded the S.S. *Tchitcherine*, which passed through Smyrna on the 8th to arrive at Constantinople on the 10th.[22]

Periyar experienced a seasick crossing of the Black Sea and arrived at Odessa on 12 February. The sea was frozen and it took a while for the icebreakers to do the job before they could disembark. Ramanathan had managed to pick up twenty Russian words in preparation for his Soviet visit, and *tovarishch* (comrade) was one of them. Luckily they were received by an official, who claimed to be from the tourist department, who spoke fluent English – evidently their visit was expected.[23] However they were in for a shock when they were charged the equivalent of 250 rupees by the porters to carry their luggage, and began to contemplate going to Berlin right away. At this rate, Periyar feared, that they were already in the red as far as finances were concerned.

They took a train at Kiev and arrived in Moscow on the 14th. They checked in at a luxury hotel, Nova Moskva, an imposing building on the banks of the Moscow river, ahead of the bridge leading to the Red Square. After they found that a meal there cost 10 rupees they never set foot in the restaurant again. Instead they bought some bread and cheese, and heated water to drink. Luckily, members of what Periyar referred to as the atheists' society came to meet them and took charge of their day-to-day expenses.

Periyar and his companions promptly reported to the VOKS, the All Union Society for Cultural Relations with Foreign Countries, whose duty, according to British intelligence, was 'to keep in touch with foreigners, entertain distinguished visitors and organise reciprocal hospitality. . . . In reality it was an immense espionage and propaganda department working for the Communist Party and the third international of Comintern.'[24] It was through VOKS that J. M. Keynes, H. G. Wells, and Bernard Shaw had earlier been invited. VOKS offered free travel from the Soviet border to Moscow and return, accommodation, and guides, the last, needless to add, a key to ensure control. In late 1928, according to the same report, a section of VOKS was being planned for India.[25]

Soon after his arrival, Periyar made the mandatory visit to the Lenin Mausoleum in the Red Square. Despite 18 February being a holiday officials made special arrangements for his visit.

As indicated earlier, there is a gap in the record until the 64th day, and we are able to piece together their programme from fragmentary information, especially the uncertain reminiscences of Ramu, who remembers visiting the Dnieper Dam, the Baku oilfields in Azerbaijan, Sukhumi in Abkhazia, and Tbilisi in Georgia. A picture taken at The Primate Research Centre of the Institute of Experimental Medicine, Sukhumi, Abkhazia, also survives. There is evidence too that they went to Leningrad as a group photograph taken at the Leningrad League of the Militant Godless survives. They also visited Dneprostroi and Zaporozhia.[26] At Dneprostroi they are sure to have visited the Dnieper hydroelectric station, the world's largest, and a symbol of Soviet power. Zaporozhia was the site of another hydroelectric dam and as such a pilgrimage centre for Soviet industrial achievement.

The record is weak or non-existent until this point, but from 19 April 1932 we have Periyar's day-to-day record of his subsequent 30 days in the Soviet Union.

IV

On the evening of 18 April 1932, his 65th day in the Soviet Union, Periyar started on his return journey to Moscow – we do not know from where.[27] After 18 hours on the train they arrived the next day at Rostov. They dined in the dining car on the train and reached Kharkov station at 1 a.m. A party man brought an enlarged photograph of Periyar and a few other pictures to the train as souvenirs. In return they gifted him some French pictures and a thermometer – the purpose of these curious presents is not clear.[28]

Periyar observed the landscape and the settlements on the way. He noticed houses with sloping roofs all the way, much like those in India. Creepers climbed up the walls smeared with mud. He saw horse-drawn carts and tractors ploughing the fields. Noticing the sledges, he called them 'wheel-less carts'! He also observed that agriculture was practised 'as though in a factory.'

The team returned to Moscow at 6 p.m. on 20 April where they were received by what Periyar referred to as secretary of the Atheist society, one Feldman, who once again took them to Hotel Nova Moskva. From there they were taken to Hotel Nikitskaya, where they lodged for the reminder of their tour. In fact, what Periyar refers to as the Atheist society was the League of the Militant Godless.

The League had been established in 1925 by the Communist Party of Soviet Union (CPSU), at the height of the New Economic Policy of the new Soviet state, in the aftermath of the Revolution and the reaction to it, as a nominally independent organisation. At the time of Periyar's visit, the League was at its peak, claiming a membership of 5.5 million (a figure even higher than that of the CPSU) despite occasional outright hostility from Komsomol (The Communist Union of Youth). The League also published the atheist journal, *Bezbozhnik*. The League was well organised and connected by a wide network of local organisations across the Soviet Union.[29]

Periyar had arrived at an inopportune moment in the history of the world communist movement – what E. H. Carr termed 'the twilight of the Comintern.'[30] By this time Moscow had adopted a milder attitude towards Western powers and no longer held the hope that wars between imperialist powers was an opportunity for a workers' revolution. In any case communist parties, over which the CPSU had absolute control, were in place, especially in India, and there was little need for it to ally with an unknown entity of independent thinking such as Periyar.

Some literature was shared between Periyar and the League, including a letter from the German International Freethinkers' Association and the current bulletin of the Association. Two women interpreters, Havala and Kina, kept them company and took them around.

The trip was full of conducted tours to various organisations and institutions that bespoke the achievements of the October Revolution. One of the earliest organisations they were taken to was the Society of Old Bolsheviks, composed of all those who could claim to having been active in the revolutionary movement since before the Revolution of 1905. They were introduced to the dignitaries there, and 'an important person, the vice president,' whose name is not mentioned, delivered one of the many tedious lectures that were to be a feature of their tour. They were also permitted to watch the proceedings of their executive committee meeting.

Earlier, at Kharkov, Ukraine, the secretary of the town soviet had given an elaborate description of the working of the Soviet or Council system, including the eligibility criteria for voters, divisions, election of deputies, etc. The Town Committee President, who had been a driver during tsarist times, also gave a long speech. The descriptions bored them so much that Periyar was compelled to record, in an otherwise factual log, 'We were reduced to tears,' and underline it!

Periyar and his associates received excellent treatment wherever they went, which they contrasted with the privations of the Depression in other parts of the western world, information about which they had acquired from newspaper reports. 'Though France, Germany, Greece and United Kingdom,' he noted, 'were all democratic nations, unemployment is rampant. It is in Russia alone that there is no unemployment. There are a few beggars. But they are all old or infirm, and the state supports them.'[31]

They met an old man who had shot the tsar's brother, apart also from an old anti-religionist preacher, Logenov. They were impressed by the claim that 75,000 priests were out of business because of him, and of his having vanquished 300 well-known missionaries in debate. Periyar noted with agreement that 'Communist members are not required to be atheists, but should strive to be atheists' and quoted

Lenin's comment that 'Communism and atheism are related. Atheism is a programme of communism.'

The next day, on 23 April, they attended a children's event organised by the Society of Old Bolsheviks where they were asked to speak. Periyar spoke in Tamil, and was asked to take his seat on the podium as well. When the three spoke the children applauded and raised a din. Periyar was impressed that the children were all between 10 and 14, and that they had their own organisation and executive committee and that half the organisation was female. At the dinner they met many old Bolshevik members. And as could be expected, the entertainment that followed was full of revolutionary and war slogans. Periyar made note of their addresses in his notebook. Their itinerary was packed, and occasionally they had to turn down invitations, for instance, one from the Trades Union Congress.

Wherever they went, the visitors were bombarded with the commemoration of the Revolution. They were taken to the Red Army Club and visited its museum where the pictures of the ships and the leaders of the 1905 revolution were exhibited. Among the portraits was one of Rasputin who had, it was said, cuckolded the tsar. Long lectures on the counter-revolutionary resistance and international support for them were inflicted. Gruesome evidence of state torture of revolutionaries was on display, including a fingernail with its skin. The sights in an adjacent club room where women, the wives, and children of the Red Army's soldiers and officers, socialised, were impressive. They were dressed in vests and shorts playing football, practising on the bar with men, and working out in the gymnasium, providing a stark contrast to the poverty of tsarist Russia depicted in the museum. Periyar noted the many drama and cinema halls, hospitals, dining halls, etc., inside the club.

They were then taken to a crematorium. Periyar observed that it was a beautiful building. Noting that corpses are brought here, put in a cavern, and then burnt with electricity, Periyar's mind must have wandered to his repeated criticisms of the ways Indians handled their funeral rites. And the man who always talked of laughing at death noted a woman was weeping.

One of the detailed descriptions that Periyar provides of Soviet administration is that of Moskva Sarkozy Sakiz District People's Court. The counselling, the gender equity, and pro-labour stance of the courts left him impressed, though Periyar's recording, as his is wont, is very matter-of-fact. He noted that now anyone could become a judge and that the purpose of judicial proceedings was not to punish but to reform. There were also women lawyers and women judges. He made special notes on divorce cases, how they were not biased against women, and how adultery was not a crime. The speedy nature of justice delivery was also noted. He did not forget to record that death penalty could be awarded for political crimes; and also that the primary punishments for political offences were factory work, mental hospital, or solitary confinement. After noting the theoretical principles on which the courts were grounded, evidently supplied by a party official, they watched the court proceedings.

On the day of their visit, a male judge presided with a two-women jury, and a court secretary who was also a woman. An interesting case was in progress. A plaintiff had filed a suit that a newspaper salesman had not remitted the sales proceeds of 50 roubles. The defendant pleaded guilty but said he had no money. Laughing, the judge said, 'My duty is to determine whether you owe money. Whether you have money or not is a different matter,' and ordered him to pay 50 roubles. The salesman went away smiling. In another case, this time of assault, the interrogation by the female jury of the defendant went as follows.

'Do you do any social work apart from your factory job?'
'No.'
'Why?'
'I am unable to get such social work. The Komsomol.'
'Aren't you ashamed to say such a thing in the Soviet country? I think you are lazy.'
The defendant hung his head in shame.
'You say you are a member of the Komsomol. Can you then drink?'
'No. I drink only once a year.'

Then the lawyers argued both sides of the case. It was a police case of assault. Both plaintiff and defendant had been charged.

The visit to the court was followed by a visit to the Lefortovo prison, the notorious Soviet prison associated with the KGB and the Stalinist purges. Its director, one Moulin, a blacksmith before the revolution, and a party man for over 29 years, showed them around. With May Day fast approaching, the jail was being decorated. Periyar noted that prisoners were not distinguished by their clothing and that the jail was but a number of factories. They saw the manufacture of hosiery. The prison cells themselves, Periyar observed, were provided with cots, table and chair, commode, water tap, basin, heating, bookshelf, radio, etc. A veteran of prisons, Periyar's mind must have mentally compared these with the British jails that he had experienced. Built before the Revolution, he noted that new jails were even better constructed. The chapel inside was now a hospital. And prisoners were locked up only at night and had to work for only eight hours a day.

Periyar wondered to the director: 'Prisoners seem to be let free. Won't they run away?,' who replied that 'Once three prisoners ran away. But later returned on their own. Sometimes 100 or 200 inmates are sent out to watch the circus. They go out without escorts and return by themselves. The reason is their good conduct and the fact that without tickets they cannot easily buy provisions and lodging rooms.' Periyar would refer to the reformative nature of Soviet prisons in his later propaganda.

On 4 May Periyar went to the AMO (*Avtomobil'noe Moskovskoe Obshchestvo*, the Moscow Automotive Enterprise). The kitchen and the massive dining area at the AMO Factory left him impressed. The quality and cost impressed him even more. The efficiency of the assembly line production left him dazed. Once again he did not fail to note that men and women worked together in all sections, with women predominating in the sizing department and in the shock brigades, and that women even wielded the sledgehammer in the smithy. One day, on the way to AMO, they also saw the watch factory and the dynamo factory.

On 9 May they were taken to the International Agrarian Institute. Its director invited them to correspond with him, write about Indian agriculture, and offered to send them magazines related to agriculture, especially *The Agrarian Problem*, published in German, with branches all over Europe, India, Japan, China, and other colonial countries. Its scientific investigations were oriented to mechanising agriculture, 'the only path to emancipating peasants.' In the library Periyar noted that all magazines from the Indian agricultural department were being acquired.

It was a coincidence that the trio were in Moscow at the time of May Day, and they were witness to the joyous celebrations. At the League of the Militant Godless, red cloth was tied on their wrists for May Day. One woman even came to their rooms to tie the red cloth, and ended up playing chess with them. On May Day eve they were taken to the May Day celebrations at the Society of Old Bolsheviks. National songs and dances of various nations of the world were performed, and all of them pertained to atheism. As they stood on the road by the hotel a woman came forward to give alms, and a few women bystanders laughed at their mistake. It was unlikely that any of them had seen dark-skinned persons in their lives and therefore wherever they went women gathered around them. Periyar who was dressed in his dhoti but in a long overcoat, Turkish cap and shoes – as photographed in Aden – but had changed to trousers now, wore a turban. His walking stick was ever present. Ramanathan and Ramu were more sleekly dressed in half trousers in the early part of the tour, and in suit and tie in the Soviet Union.[32]

On May Day they saw lakhs of people going about in crowds with flags, and singing. People crowded together 'like bhajanai troupes,' and danced and sang. From every office and every factory people marched past in columns singing and dancing holding aloft the insignia and flags of their respective organisations and unions. Dressed in uniform and rifles and staffs some were mounted on horses, and thousands of men and women were milling around as they sang national songs. From Vladivostok a women's group had come, dressed fancifully with a music band accompanying them. From various provinces, both men and women of various nationalities too had come with their distinctive musical instruments, costumes, song, and dance. A big balloon, about 30–40 feet wide, with a basket of 10 feet circumference, was pulled down by many as it was flying up, and brought down to the square. Military vehicles and armoured cars, tanks and cannons, went on parade. Aircraft made an aerial display. Dioramas depicting various scenes such as those of the haves and have-nots – which reminded Periyar of the Mariamman temple festivals – were being paraded. Army units marched past the Lenin Mausoleum where Stalin, Mikhail Kalinin, Yemelyan Yaroslavsky, and other important leaders stood, waving to the crowds. The Turkish Prime Minister İsmet İnönü too had arrived in Moscow, for the May Day celebrations, to an ostentatious welcome. The town was festooned and decorated with colourful electric lights. As they walked with the League of the Militant Godless through the streets people of various organisations welcomed them as 'Indian Delegates.' On occasion Periyar and Ramanathan responded. They were photographed, and even filmed on a moving camera, and Periyar noted that at least 60 photographs were snapped on that day alone.

After a meal they were taken to watch a play enacting the 1905 Revolution. Bourgeois life, strikes, and the dropping of bombs were dramatised realistically. After the play was over, at midnight, they were driven round in motor cars to see the city with all its decorations and lights. Huge arches were decorated with lights. Fireworks lit up the sky. The most important festival of the entire Russian nation, it was also a celebration of the Revolution. 'Like the Aryans celebrate the killing of the rebel Narakasura as Deepavali, the people celebrate this festival with happiness and pride,' observed Periyar.

Some days later a welcome reception for all foreign delegates who had come for May Day was organised by the Society of Old Bolsheviks at the Great Kremlin Palace. Periyar represented India. The welcome address talked about the situation in the Soviet Union and in the rest of the world, and about the Five Year Plans. Mikhail Kalinin, whom Periyar referred to as Prime Minister, the titular head of the Soviet State, arrived and spoke. When the representatives of various countries were asked to speak, Ramanathan, as Secretary of the Self-Respect Movement, spoke on behalf of India. At the dinner, Yemelyan Yaroslavsky, the founder-editor of *Bezbozhnik*, sat beside Periyar and said that he was greatly pleased to meet the Indian delegates. Kalinin too sat next to him, shook his hands, and left with the words 'I'm personally very happy to have met you.' Periyar said to Yaroslavsky and Kalinin: 'In the very palace where the tsar had lived and enjoyed himself, that workers who had killed him should rejoice by dancing constitutes the greatest revolution in the world, and that's the most significant thing for the world.' He added that, 'The honour of putting in practice a theory that someone wrote in a bygone age belongs to Russia alone. If we told the Russians this they'd be hard put to believe this.'

This was followed by some dancing. A group of five women held Periyar by the hand and asked him to dance. One of them was Violet Lansbury, the 12th and last daughter of the English labour leader and leader of the opposition, the socialist and Christian pacifist, George Lansbury.[33] Violet – at that time married to a Russian professor of agriculture, Igor Reussner – was present at the May Day celebrations to act as interpreter to the British delegation of workers.[34] She apologised to Periyar for her father's behaviour as an imperialist politician, and said she would strive twice as hard to expiate. Ashamed of how the English behaved in relation to India, she asked for forgiveness. Periyar replied, 'There's no need for forgiveness. Indians are yet to regain their self-respect; the moment Gandhism is wiped out, Communism would come to India on its own; nobody's generosity is required for this and there can be no hurdle in that path.' Many took Periyar's address and got his autograph.

The next day they were invited to the Pioneer Day celebrations of the League of the Militant Godless. After an early dinner at 4 p.m. they went to watch a play on the Manchurian revolution called *The Armed Train*.

Émigrés of various hues were present in Moscow and Periyar met some of them during this trip. Periyar and Ramanathan met the early Indian revolutionary and a founding member of the Communist party of India, Abani Mukherji, at his home more than once. His execution during the purges was still some years away, and he was leading a quiet life, contributing, as he said, two articles a month. He lent them a few books and gave an article of his. Abani Mukherji made fond enquiries of Singaravelu, whom he had met in Chennai towards the end of 1922.[35] He offered to send them any communist literature that they may require. He desired to come to India, and work in a textile mill as in his youth, definitely a sign of alienation, but did not have a passport.

There were a number of émigrés in the USSR at that time but no design is evident from those whom Periyar met. By this time M.N. Roy had run afoul of Stalin, escaped to India and was serving a prison term in Bombay at the time of Periyar's visit. Virendranath Chatto-padhyaya was indeed in Moscow but Periyar did not visit him. In any case, Periyar was not in Moscow as a Communist or as a member of the Comintern, and was perhaps not therefore accorded privileges due to a member of the communist party.

Periyar was also taken to the Profintern (Red International of Labour Unions) office. This was probably more serious business, con-sidering that the passage of worker radicals to Moscow was discussed. The head of the Eastern Section, one Fidei, stated that if the workers knew English well, three or four of them could come for one to three years. If they could reach Germany or France, then their trade unions would send them here. Even if they were not elected, an executive committee resolution would do. One could come via Greece as well, or through the Philippine Trade Union where Russian representatives were present. One could go to the Philippines from Singapore and then reach Vladivostok. Workers could come in April or May. There was no objection to a guide accompanying them. Periyar wrote out 23 addresses and gave them to him. He was asked for a few more. The cir-cuitous route that was planned might indicate that it was clandestine.

In any case, they were treated as Indian representatives, coming from the Self-Respect League. Importantly, they did not meet any member of the CPSU except at the May Day reception where pleasantries were exchanged with Kalinin and Yaroslavsky.

Meetings with émigré communists appear to have been more courtesy calls than a serious discussion of the programme. Abani Mukherji was a recluse by that time, working as an Indologist in the Soviet Academy of Sciences. Ramanathan submitted a bizarre application when he wrote an application to Abani Mukherji, asking to be included in the Indian cabinet in exile, and requesting assistance to study Marxism-Leninism and economics in Leningrad, while he would teach English and Tamil.

Periyar tried to get Ramu to some training in engineering or place him in a factory in USSR. Periyar took him to the Industrial Director who agreed to give the young man a job in the AMO factory and provide him with lodgings and food. In the event, this did not work out as the Soviets dismissed him as a playful boy who could not be taken seriously.

By the end of April 1932, for reasons that are not entirely clear, there was discussion about concluding the trip. Considering that the objectives of the trip itself are not known, this is not surprising. There is confusing information on what Periyar and his two associates were doing or attempting to do in Moscow. Even though Periyar was in touch with CPSU officials, the logistics of the tour was being managed by the League of the Militant Godless. It is also evident that he was guided around to visit only the achievements that showcased the Soviet state. The jotting, 'Went to a coffee hotel by ourselves,' perhaps indicates that this was exceptional. Despite this, Periyar did not fail to enquire after general matters and record them: the cost of eggs (2 to a rouble); milk (2 glasses a rouble, and for children it's 4 glasses). For workers 10 eggs cost 90 kopecks in the cooperative store. 'A person requires 300 roubles to live here. 100 roubles would suffice for a worker.'

But wherever they went they were shown the theatre and the museum. The lifestyle of Russian nobles, their ostentatious life and rule, were the usual themes of enacted plays. Watching one of the plays Periyar noted, 'We should produce a play. Of workers bemoaning their fate; and their children espousing communism.' Never one for the arts, Periyar saw a huge oil painting of a Bolshevik committee meeting in progress. Its realism struck him as it 'looked as though the meeting was going on now.' Wherever they went photographs were taken, and Periyar seems to have promptly mailed back copies home.

There was also confusion about the dates of their return journey. While Periyar wanted to go to Germany en route to India the others wanted to stay back in the Soviet Union, and if that was not possible, wanted to return home via Turkey. Considering that the tour was to ultimately continue for another six months, talk of their return to India was either premature or ill-planned or both. The help of the

Vice-President of the League of the Militant Godless was sought when they reported to him about the tour and thanked him. While he promised to get tickets and make other arrangements for Periyar to go to Germany, he said he could do little to help S. Ramanathan and Ramu. He directed them instead to VOKS. Following this advice, the threesome went to VOKS and talked to its secretary where Ramanathan and Ramu wrote out an application to stay back. At first Ramu was given permission to stay back while Ramanathan was urged to return with Periyar via Germany and not Turkey as he had wanted. Later this too fell through, as, according to Periyar, Ramanathan had spoken indiscreetly during a meeting with Abani Mukherji. The official version communicated to them was that 'Ramanathan didn't know much, that he could not even write in the papers on what communism was, and that Ramu was a playful boy, and therefore permission was not accorded for their stay.'

Based on interviews with Periyar shortly before his death, Anaimuthu states that a meeting with Stalin had been arranged for 28 May 1932; that Ramanathan's contacts with Trotskyites had infuriated the apparatchiks and they were therefore asked to leave immediately. Not only is this not borne out by the tone or the content of Periyar's dairy, it also sounds somewhat implausible. Considering how closely the visitors' programme were monitored, it would have been impossible to have made any such contacts.

At this time Periyar was already in touch with the German Freethinkers Association, either on his own or through the League of the Militant Godless. The League was then closely involved in the International Proletarian Freethinkers, based in Germany, an organisation founded to counter the bourgeois Union of Freethinkers.[36] More contacts were promised by the Soviets. There was a setback to their plans as the papers reported that the German government had on 4 May outlawed the German International Freethinkers Association.

As the day for their departure from Moscow neared, Ramanathan fell ill on 11 May and a doctor had to be summoned. The next day Ali, Beelioff, Kina, the interpreter, and the doctor stayed back until the fever subsided. Kina, who had now become secretary of VOKS, brought the news that passports had arrived. Ramanathan, still hoping to stay back, asked 'Even for me and Ramu as well?'

By 14 May, Kina said that the departure of the three for Berlin was confirmed. But it kept being postponed every day. By that time Periyar had stayed long enough for the Soviet periodicals to carry reports and pictures of their visit. The *Bezbozhnik International Magazine* carried pictures of the three. Meanwhile the dailies were reporting that the first minister of Germany had been shot. The papers, moving through VOKS, finally arrived on 17 May. The secretary of the German International Atheists came to the restaurant with his family to see them off. Ali, Kina, Feldman, and Beelioff had a final meal together and saw them off at the railway station. The three travelled international first class on the train that departed from Moscow at 7:30. Ticket no. 4871, berth no. 9.

V

In Berlin

On 18 May 1932 the train crossed the Russian border into Lithuania at 11 in the morning. To acquire a passport, they borrowed 3.75 dollars from an American. They had to get another passport at Latvia, and borrowed 3 dollars from a German for this purpose. Travelling at 50 mph they reached the German border at 9:30 p.m. The people and the villages appeared very cultured to Periyar's eyes. On the first border town in Germany, a customs officer saluted Periyar with the words, 'You look like St Peter,' and did not check his bags.

On their arrival at Berlin, on the morning of 19 May, their first destination was the office of the League Against Imperialism (and for National Independence). The League had been floated by the Comintern in the heyday of the United Front strategy of the Soviet Union to effect cooperation of the communist parties with non-communist left and democratic parties. Its founding Congress had been held in 1927, in Brussels, providing a platform for nationalist protest against colonial and imperial rule, and proposed a fighting alliance between the national bourgeoisie of colonised countries and the international working classes. Jawaharlal Nehru, heavily influenced by this idealistic position, had played a leading part in the League's early stages. By this time, however, Stalin had put world revolution in cold storage and reconciled himself to 'socialism in one country.' By the time of Periyar's visit, the League Against Imperialism had, in Marxist speak, fulfilled its historical role, that is, it had become redundant. The League was formally liquidated a few years later in 1935.

This would not have been known to the bourgeois states. The League office had been raided by the German police some months previously in late December 1931, many of its staff arrested and correspondence seized. The League office had closed subsequently but had reopened by the time Periyar arrived.[37] Evidently, under Soviet direction, Periyar and his friend first met Clemens Palme Dutt (1893–1975)[38] – Clemens was the older brother (by three years) of Rajani Palme Dutt, and a founding member of the Communist Party of Great Britain (CPGB) like his brother. From 1931 he was International Secretary of the League Against Imperialism; he was also the Chairman of the Indian section of the Communist Party of Great Britain, and the Comintern's Indian section representative in Britain and the chief link with Indian communists.

They then called on A.C.N. Nambiar and visited the home of White Russian émigrés.

During his sojourn in Berlin Periyar made repeated visits to the League Against Imperialism office where they were given some propagandist literature. He also met Clemens Dutt and Nambiar frequently. Being diehard communists pursuing a sectarian line and with the Comintern in retreat, it is not surprising that they did not take Periyar seriously. But on 27 May a small meeting was held in the League rooms. Periyar's Self-Respect movement was discussed with an Indian called Mohan, Clemens Dutt, and another outsider. It was that suggested that Periyar join the Congress and win mass support. After listening to Periyar's counterarguments, his position on not joining the Congress was accepted.

Clemens Dutt gave Periyar two letters of introduction to London, one to Shapurji Saklatvala[39] and the other to H.P. Rathbone, a member of the Communist Party of Great Britain.[40] Nambiar too gave two letters: one for the YMCA Secretary Ayman, and another for Pulin Behari Seal. The YMCA letter would have been for lodging; Seal had arrived from Bengal to study in Cambridge and had earlier been close to both C.R. Das and the Congress. But after his return to England in 1925 he became a radical political activist and journalist founding the Oriental Press Service. He was closely associated with the CPGB, and especially close to Saklatvala.[41]

Probably through contacts provided by the League of the Militant Godless, Periyar was also in touch with the Freethinkers whose secretary visited their rooms. Given that Freethinkers were against religion – anti-Christian in the context of Europe – and insisted on logic and reason as the touchstone of thought rather than the authority of dogma and power, a natural affinity with Periyar's thinking can easily be discerned. Before the time of Periyar's visit the German Freethinkers had in fact splintered on class lines – the sectarian intervention of Communists cannot be discounted – with the emergence of a separate Proletarian Freethinkers Association.

Periyar mentions that he attended Marxist lectures in Berlin, while Ramanathan went to the library. They also visited the press where communist papers and books were printed. The press looked like a huge factory and Periyar was impressed by the many facilities provided for the workers.

Unlike in the Soviet Union Periyar met some persons in the communist party office. They visited the Kaiser's palace, various museums, galleries and memorials, and the Reichstag. An official of the Nudist Association accompanied them on these visits.

Periyar went to Hindustan House where Indian students lodged and boarded, to discuss politics. Ram Manohar Lohia was at that time a doctoral student at Friedrich Wilhelm University, now known as the Humboldt University, and might have been among the crowd. Periyar also did not meet the former Indian revolutionaries who lived in Berlin at that time – Champakaraman Pillai and M. P. T. Acharya – which is understandable given that Periyar was interested in social transformation and not a jingoistic anti-imperialism. One day, at a tea party hosted for Brij Lal Nehru, Jawaharlal's cousin, and his wife, Periyar and Ramanathan were also invited. At this gathering Nambiar and a few Indian students were present. Party differences were discussed at length.

The high point of the Berlin visit was Periyar's introduction to the Nudist Association. The Nudist movement was prominent at this time, with its origins in Germany earlier in the century. Apart from having many health fads in its ranks, the movement entertained utopian ideas, and was politicised by radical socialists who argued that it would lead to the destruction of class divisions. It was at its peak at this time, and the Berlin group had also hosted the first international conference of nudity only a few years earlier.

Periyar saw about 20 to 30 persons basking the sun, bathing in cold water, and exercising. Not to be left behind, Ramanathan too joined this group in the nude, though in the one surviving photograph while Periyar is evidently at ease, Ramanathan is attempting to hide himself. There were over 400 members, the men constituting three-fourths. Periyar paid the monthly subscription of 40 pfennigs, and watched a nudist film, *Sonne, Luft, und Freiköperkultur* (Sun, Air, and Nudism).

On 4 June Periyar went, by boat, to a restaurant on a nearby islet called Woltersdorfer Mühle. One hundred and fifty others were on the boat including many women. They disembarked on the islet and had their food. Lectures and dances were on, and Ramanathan joined the dance. It was all like a small carnival.

On 12 June they went to the garden of the Nudist Association, where he met someone who introduced his wife as 'my proposed wife.' This description would be etched in Periyar's memory, and he would quote this in his speeches many years later as an indication of the progressive nature of Western sexual morals. They went to a garden, 15 miles away, covering the distance by train, bus, and on foot. Over 200 people, both men and women, of various political hues – anarchists, fascists, social democrats, communists – were present. From 9 in the morning until 4:30 in the afternoon, all of them, in various groups, swam, exercised, sun-bathed, ran, played football, danced, and played musical instruments in the nude. Some 10 to 15 pictures of Periyar were clicked. Periyar gathered that often even 3,000 or 4,000 persons congregated in the nude while the total membership ran into lakhs, of whom 40,000 lived in Berlin alone. Some even lived in these gardens for months together. Then they went to the carnival of solidarity at 26 Victoria Park where 3,000 persons were present.

Periyar was extensively photographed on these occasions, including in the nude. In keeping with his iconoclastic and rebellious nature, he would include a description of his visits to the nudist colony in his authorised biography published in 1939; while there is evidence to show that he wanted to include his pictures in the nudist gathering in a new biography planned in the late 1940s, the revised edition of his authorised biography would carry it in 1962.

Meanwhile efforts to settle Ramu in Berlin continued – evidently he was considered too young to join Periyar and Ramanathan's adventures in Berlin. Apparently he wanted to join one Havro Trading Company. Periyar's meetings with engineers were perhaps to apprentice Ramu. In any case he was moved to a new room once arrangements for his training were made and their departure became imminent.[42]

By the end of May, the political situation in Berlin was fast changing. Ominously, on 30 May, there was a clash between fascists and communists, and some communists were shot.[43] On 1 June Periyar witnessed street demonstrations by the communists. The Nazi takeover was barely a year away. By this time, they had to register their passports with the police.

When he visited the League Against Imperialism on 11 June the interpreters asked Ramanathan to head back home, for reasons that are not clear. Nor is it clear why he was singled out. Meanwhile arrangements to meet Japanese communist youths had been made. At that meeting the youths introduced Periyar to an atheist association in Japan. During this time, they also visited the Bourgeois Nudist Association.

On 13 June Periyar went to the railway station and made enquiries. The next day they bought two tickets for London via Flushing. That night, Periyar and Ramanathan journeyed to London, probably from Charlottenburg station, after an eventful sojourn in Berlin of about four weeks.

VI

In Britain

Periyar and Ramanathan reached Hoek van Holland in the morning of 15 June and took the ferry to Harwich at 12:30 p.m. arriving there at 7:30 p.m. By the time they reached London Liverpool station it was 9:30 p.m. and they booked into the YMCA on Gower Street: 5 shillings for a night was exorbitant, thought Periyar.

The next day they did some sightseeing and saw the Thames, India House, the headquarters of the Secretary of State for India, and Hyde Park. Later they went looking for Shapurji Saklatvala at his Highgate home but were disappointed that he was not in town. (According to the *Daily Worker* reports he was touring in the western counties.) Similarly, they could not find H.P. Rathbone, who lived in Hampstead, some 3 kilometres away.

The following day they rented the front room of 28 Frederick Street, Gray's Inn Road, King's Cross. They went looking for Saklatvala and Rathbone, but once again without success. But the next day, on 18 June, they met Saklatvala at his home.

Shapurji Saklatvala (1874–1936), nephew of J.R.D. Tata, had rejected liberalism and joined the Independent Labour Party (ILP) in England; having failed to affiliate the ILP to the Comintern, he joined the Communist Party of Great Britain (CPGB) within a year of its founding in 1920. In the 1920s, as the sole Communist member of Parliament (though he was not an M.P. at the time of Periyar's visit), he was advocating India's freedom and was the most prominent M.P. to raise Indian issues. In the CPGB he toed Rajani Palme Dutt's line. His 1927 visit to India had brought him to Chennai as well, but evidently Periyar had not met him then.

According to a CID report Periyar was 'placed under the tutelage of Saklatvala' during his time in Britain.[44] Periyar kept in daily touch with Saklatvala until he left Britain a few weeks later.[45]

At this time Saklatvala was busy with organisational work among the coal miners of the Midlands and in Wales. Massive meetings were organised in places such as Crumlin, Pontywaun, Abertillery, Blaina, and Blaenau Gwent, and Saklatvala played a big role in them. The primary demand of the miners was for a seven-hour workday in place of the existing seven and a half hours. They were also opposed to wage cuts.[46]

On hearing from Saklatvala that he was going to Doncaster for a meeting, Periyar and Ramanathan decided to accompany him. Periyar bought return tickets, and armed with a letter of recommendation to one Dr Ramu, they set out. They reached Dr Ramu's home in Mexborough, South Yorkshire. The next day Dr Ramu drove them in his car to the meeting of the Conisbrough workers. Saklatvala too arrived and addressed the miners. It was a unity association of world workers. They lunched at a worker's home at Denaby Main near Rotherham. In the evening they attended a meeting at the Mexborough Royal Theatre where Saklatvala spoke for two hours. As Periyar did not fail to note, the meeting was presided over by a woman.

On 20 June, there was a rally of unemployed workers at Locke Park in Barnsley. According to a report in the *Daily Worker*, this was the Yorkshire Miners' Association's Gala Day, where George Lansbury and John Bromley were present. The communists held a rival meeting.[47] Over 70,000 workers had assembled. Walking in the vanguard of one group, Periyar noted that the crowd was as big as the one on May Day in the Soviet Union. The rally marched to music for 2–3 miles. Arrangements had been made for Periyar to address the rally but he could not as he was delayed. A rival platform was erected by the Communists, as noted by Periyar in his diary, as well.[48] Periyar spoke following Saklatvala's introduction.

The *Kudi Arasu* reported Periyar's talk, 'The Hypocrisy of the Labour Party,' a stinging attack on the Labour party.[49] Ridiculing Lansbury's Christian humanism as hollow – his meeting with Violet Lansbury at the Kremlin would have certainly crossed his mind at this time – Periyar pointed out that the Labour government had sentenced the Garhwal regiment which had refused to shoot unarmed people (during the Civil Disobedience movement) to 15 years of rigorous imprisonment. He also pointed out how miners in India had been imprisoned for unionising. The burden of his talk was that the Labour government's showing was worse than that of the Tory Baldwin's government in its handling of workers and in its war-mongering. Periyar was perhaps echoing Saklatvala's views that the Labour party was the worst of all reactionary English parties. They left Yorkshire late in the night and reached London in the small hours.

Periyar met Saklatvala again and the Secretary of the British section of the League Against Imperialism, Reginald Francis Orlando Bridgeman. At this time the British section of the League Against Imperialism was no longer housed in Great Ormond Street as the landlord had ended their lease, and was therefore temporarily housed in the office of the International Labour Defence office on Theobald's Road, and would shortly move to Gray's Inn Road.[50]

Periyar and Ramanathan went to the Rationalist Publishing Association (R.P.A.) and its Watts & Co., and also met the secretaries of *Labour Monthly* and the Clerks' Union. The Rationalist Publishing Association, founded in 1899 by Freethinkers, published anti-religious books including those by Charles Bradlaugh, H.G. Wells, Julian Huxley, and Ernst Haeckel; many of its books were published through its Watts & Co. A forerunner to Victor Gollancz, the Left Book Club, and Penguin, at the time of Periyar's visit, it was managed by Frederick Watt, the son of its founder Charles Watt.[51]

Saklatvala also accompanied them to the office of *Searchlight* and Workers International Relief (W.I.R.) – the organisation started as an adjunct of the Comintern in 1921 to provide relief to famine-stricken Soviet Union and was to counteract the USA's American Relief Association. At W.I.R. they attended a meeting of the Clerks' Union where Saklatvala spoke. The World Congress of W.I.R. had been held in late 1931, and there had been discussions about opening its work in India as well.[52] A resolution was passed in the meeting to completely abolish arms and the military.

Late that night they attended a meeting at the Radical Club where Saklatvala spoke on India. When they entered the hall many applauded and cheered Periyar mistaking him for Saklatvala.

The next day they went with Saklatvala to the *Daily Worker*, the organ of the CPGB, and their bookshop. The following day there was a meeting at a park at 8:30 p.m., where many, including Saklatvala, spoke on communism. There was a minor incident when at the meeting venue some gathered together and sang from the Bible. Saklatvala rebuked them and launched a blistering attack on religion. The Christian group returned the abuse. Both parties sang songs in rivalry. As Periyar recollected in his obituary of Saklatvala some years later, 'his hair would stand on end at the sight of Christian priests.'[53]

On 27 June Periyar again went to the League Against Imperialism and met one Mazumdar, probably Niharendu Datta Mazumdar. He then visited the Labour Research Department, the independent trade union based research organisation which provided support to unionist

124

activity and campaigns, and collected some bulletins. The visit was repeated the next day with Saklatvala. They went to a meeting conducted in a chapel. He also met Ranchhodas Bhavan Lotwala, the proprietor of the *Sunday Advocate*, Bombay, a rich Parsi merchant and, according to the Intelligence Bureau of India, an 'intimate friend' of Saklatvala. A leading patron of the communists in Bombay, Lotwala had assisted both S.A. Dange and M.N. Roy financially, and was the first to print the *Communist Manifesto* in India in 1922.[54] Lotwala spent practically every summer in London, and engaged in communist propaganda.[55] This meeting took place either at his home at Beaufort Gardens or at Parton Street. Periyar was witness to a heated argument between Lotwala and Saklatvala. At this time Lotwala was taking a decidedly anti-Stalin stance and leaning towards a Trotskyite position which led to his arguments with Saklatvala. Here Periyar also met and talked to Indulal Yagnik, the Gujarati politician who was active in the Gandhian movement and in the peasant movement, who was working for Lotwala. Curiously Yagnik's multi-volume autobiography, which devotes a long chapter to his sojourn in London, makes no mention of his meeting with Periyar.[56]

On 28 June Periyar was taken to a meeting of 'Negroes,' as the *Daily Worker* described them, held at Club & Institute Hall, Clerkenwell, to condemn the death penalty to nine African-American boys in Scottsboro, Alabama, in 1931, for the alleged rape of two white girls.[57] The Scottsboro Boys was a cause célèbre – Harper Lee's *To Kill a Mocking Bird* is said to have been inspired by this case – a classic case of racism in the south, including every ingredient such as false charges, attempted lynching, and an all-White jury. The boys were defended by the American Communist Party: despite its best efforts, and many appeals, they could only win reprieves for the innocent boys. The meeting was conducted in the presence of Ida Wright, the mother of two of the accused boys – Andy and Roy, the latter only twelve.

According to the *Daily Worker*,[58] at the meeting presided over Hedley, 'a London Negro seaman,' 'inspiring scenes were witnessed' as Ada Wright opened her campaign in Britain. As she walked to the platform, she was escorted by 'Negro and Indian comrades' and 'the audience broke into rounds of cheers and spontaneously rose and sang the International.' 'The toil-worn woman,' 'the Negro mother told her story as only a mother can. Just a simple story of life at home, the departure of the boys in search of work, and then – prison, the menace of the electric chair.' Periyar was in the audience which 'strained to catch every word,' though we do not know what Periyar made of

Ada Wright's words as she 'spoke quietly in the soft, pleasant drawl of the South.' She moved the audience with the fervent words, 'I appeal to you all here tonight to free my two boys and the other seven boys. When you are fighting for the Scottsboro boys you are fighting for the class war prisoners all over the world.'

Many of those present in the meeting were blacks. Saklatvala, who played a leading role in the defence campaign in Britain, spoke. Money was collected and in the auction Periyar bought a German silver chain for half a pound. The presence of Periyar and Ramanathan was appreciated by the meeting. Isobel Brown, Secretary of the Workers International Relief, spoke at the meeting, and impressed by her fiery speech, Periyar met her again the next day and had a discussion.[59]

Periyar returned to the Rationalist Press Association (RPA) and to the Workers International Relief, where he ordered 1,000 copies of R.P. Paranjpye's book, *The Crux of the Indian Problem*, published by Watts & Co. a year earlier. R.P. Paranjpye, a Cambridge Wrangler, and later vice-chancellor successively of Bombay and Lucknow universities, was an early member of the RPA, and the burden of his book was that given the 'rigid hold of religion' there was no hope for India without following rational thinking.[60] In London Periyar also bought and read Lenin's *On Religion*. Tamil translation of these works was undertaken by Ramanathan immediately and would be published soon after they reached India. While Lenin was serialised in *Kudi Arasu*, Paranjapye's would be published as a separate book.

There was an occasional indulgence when they ate at Veeraswamy's, the only south Indian restaurant, and the earliest Indian restaurant, of London in those days. The London trip was not all work. They met some friends and acquaintances from India. They met G.D. Naidu of Coimbatore, who would become a leading, if eccentric, industrialist and philanthropist, and Periyar's lifelong admirer and friend. They also met many Indian students. Hearing that R.K. Shanmugam Chetty, at this time a member and Deputy-President of the Indian Central Legislative Assembly, was in London, they caught up with him at India House.

On 1 July Periyar and Ramanathan joined Saklatvala to catch the 1 p.m. train to Cardiff, South Wales. The CID followed Saklatvala. As soon as they alighted at Pontnewydd, a meeting was held where Saklatvala spoke on India and Indian labour, and argued against Indians enlisting in the army. They slept at a worker's home that night. There was another meeting that night at Pontnewydd. Periyar would remember in his obituary of Saklatvala that his voice could be heard even among a crowd of 20,000 workers, and that even if he spoke at three meetings a day, his voice would be none the worse for it.[61]

The next day a meeting was conducted beside a canal that reminded him of Pondicherry. At 7:30 p.m. there was another meeting at Brynmawr with 1,000 people present. A Salvation Army meeting was also in progress at that time. With song and instrumental music there was a clash causing disturbance. At 11 p.m. there was another meeting at Nantyglo.

On 3 July, after breakfast, they went to see the coal mines, some of which had been closed down. In the afternoon they went to Blaina, 3 miles away where a meeting was attended by 500 workers. Later they went to a worker's home, drank tea and then went by bus to Crosskeys, 15 miles away. Saklatvala and Periyar spoke for 2 hours. Again they ate and slept at a worker's home.

On 4 July they attended a meeting at a theatre hall at Crumlin, 6 miles away. After the meeting a policeman accosted Periyar and Ramanathan and made a note of their passports. That night they once again slept at a worker's home in a nearby village.

The next day too, a policeman accosted them, asking for their passports and making a note of the various places stamped on it. Considering that Periyar was noticed by police on many occasions, and that practically every one of whom he met or tried to meet had an intelligence dossier – Clemens Dutt, Lotwala, Abani Mukherji, Saklatvala, P.B. Seal, Niherendu Mazumdar – it is not a little curious that there is no trace of Periyar's visit in the Indian Political Intelligence files.

Thereafter Saklatvala asked them to leave Britain for India immediately. Periyar and Ramanathan took his advice and went to Newport station and boarded a train to London. On the 55th mile to London they saw the aeroplane factory, and a little ahead of London the gramophone factory of His Master's Voice. On 6 July, they bought tickets, took leave of Saklatvala and others, and departed for Paris at 2 p.m. and reached the French city in the night.

Details of the later part of Periyar's tour are not available. There is a gap of over three months in the record. Anaimuthu mentions that he travelled to Madrid and Lisbon. Ramanathan went to Geneva after seeing off Periyar at Marseilles.

Periyar arrived to rousing welcome receptions in Colombo on 17 October 1932. He spent nearly three weeks in Sri Lanka, travelling to Kandy, Matale, Ukuwela, Nawalapitiya, Hutton, Kodikamam, Point Pedro, Vaddukoddai, and Jaffna. Periyar left Colombo on

7 November, reached Tuticorin the next morning and arrived at his Erode home via Madurai and Tiruchirappalli on 11 November 1932.

Conclusion

What was the import of Periyar's European tour, and what impact did it have on his subsequent political career, considering that he was alive and active for another four decades and more?

The short statement he released immediately on his arrival at Erode was ominous. The third and last paragraph of the statement exhorted members of his Self-Respect movement to forthwith desist from using the honorifics Maha-ganam, Sri, Thiru, Thirumathi, Srijut, etc., as prefixes and urged them instead to employ 'Thozhar,' or Comrade. Periyar also stated that his *Kudi Arasu* would implement this policy from the very next issue. It was Periyar and his movement that popularised this usage, and the Communists adopted it later.

It is a custom in Tamil Nadu to ask elder and venerated people to name children. Such was his fascination for the Soviet Union that Periyar named the daughter of a leading Dravidian intellectual 'Russia' and another child 'Moscow.' When queried, he replied – referring to the Tamil habit of giving place names of pilgrim centres to children – if one could name children Madurai, Palani, and Chidambaram why not Russian place names. Following Periyar it was not uncommon for people influenced by him to name their children after Russian, European, and American Enlightenment figures. The 'L' in the initials of the distinguished translator of Tamil classics, M.L. Thangappa, born soon after Periyar's return from Russia, stands for Lenin. Names such as Rousseau and Ingersoll are quite common in Tamil Nadu to this day. M. Karunanidhi's son, born in the year of Stalin's death, was named after him.

According to a secret police report, Periyar 'lost no time in starting the spread of Communist doctrine,' and within three months of his return had addressed no less than 44 meetings. He 'expressed unbound admiration of the Russian regime' and stated 'his intention to end the present administration and establish a Socialist form of government.'[62] Hectic parleys and discussions with party leaders followed in the wake of Periyar's return. In a matter of a month and a half Periyar had announced the formation of the Samadharma (Periyar's neologism for Communism/Socialism) Party of South India, a political party, 'from the body of Self Respecters,' the draft programme of which he released in early January 1933. Endorsing the progress that the Self-Respect Movement had made in 'rousing the masses to the enormity of their superstitious habits, customs and practices of their religion and caste and of their degraded economic conditions' as the aims and ideals listed the attainment of complete independence from the British and other forms of capitalist governments, the cancellation of national debts, public ownership of railways, banks and transport, cancellation of all private debts of workers and peasants, changing of all the native states into one common Indian federation, minimum wages, etc.

The year or so that followed were 'days of bliss' quivering with idealism. There was a veritable churning in the Self-Respect Movement with a band of young men such as P. Jeevanandam and A. Raghavan pushing for an even more radical programme. The hard core of the Self-Respect Movement was especially uncomfortable with the socialist turn and wanted to keep to the original agenda of social emancipation. This was the only moment in the history of modern Tamil Nadu that the political (anti-colonial and national), economic (socialist), and social (anti-caste and secular) came together, and the scenario was pregnant with possibilities. The Madras CID at this time found that it was the Self-Respect Movement which was championing socialism in the Tamil country rather than the Communist Party of India. The pages of *Kudi Arasu* are full of strident writings espousing socialism. In the wake of the global depression and its attendant restiveness among the people, the government was far from happy. The heat was turned on the movement. A *Kudi Arasu* editorial (29 October 1933), 'Why the Present Government Must Be Destroyed' was considered to have exceeded the limit. And it was repeatedly called on to furnish securities. *Kudi Arasu*'s premises were searched and its de jure publisher, Periyar's sister S.R. Kannammal, and Periyar himself, were arrested. When *Kudi Arasu* folded, Periyar launched two other journals, *Puratchi* (Revolution) and *Pakutharivu* (Reason), to keep his propaganda going. By this time Periyar had also published a Tamil translation of Bhagat Singh's *Why I Am an Atheist*.[63] The Madras government proscribed it, and arrested its translator Jeevanandam and publisher E.V. Krishnaswami, Periyar's brother. Periyar was forced to take a call on the party's programme and its immediate future. He asked the translator and publisher to tender an apology, while openly taking unqualified responsibility for the backtracking. In March 1935, in a public statement, he openly declared that he was withdrawing his socialist programme in the larger interest of the movement and the present strength of his movement.

Thus ended a definitive moment in Periyar's life and by extension in the history of Tamil Nadu. The hectic three years discussed here constitutes a rupture in Periyar's long life and political career.

Periyar remained impressed by the achievements of the Soviet Union all through his life. The complete control of society and economy by the state made a deep impact on him. As he observed in an interview with the correspondent of *Ceylon Daily News* on his return to India via Colombo, 'It is a new world. Such a transformation has never ever taken place in any country.'[64] Only a state such as that of the Soviet state could rid India of its poverty. Periyar either did not follow what happened in the Soviet Union subsequently or did not care for the reality of lived Soviet socialism, and preferred to believe in an idealised version of a socialist society. This was quite in keeping with his politics, as it had less to do with the travails and vicissitudes of international socialist reconstruction than with building a just society in India. His engagement with socialism, intense during 1932–1935, never really surfaced in the next 40 years of an eventful political life. The socialist fringe of his movement left him and joined the still, and forever, nascent Communist Party. Periyar made frequent comments on his Soviet tour and favourable statements about the Soviet Union, he also supported the Communist Party in the 1952 general elections, contributing significantly to its successes. While he was the most vociferous champion of the human rights of Communist prisoners, and mourned the death of Stalin as a calamity, he maintained no truck with the Communist Party itself. Periyar remained critical of Indian Communists, stating that they were mostly Brahmins, did not have an anti-caste orientation, and took orders from Moscow.

Notes

* This chapter has gained immensely from Madhavan K. Palat's close reading of the draft and his deep scholarship in European and Russian history.
1 *Kudi Arasu*, 15 November 1931.
2 *Kudi Arasu*, 6 December 1932.
3 Under Secretary Safe (USS) file No. 839 dated 28 September 1933; CID report dated 13 September 1932.
4 USS file No. 839 dated 28 September 1933; CID report dated 12 August 1932.
5 Letter by Shapurji Saklatvala, 5 July 1932. (I am grateful to K. Veeramani, President, Dravidar Kazhagam for giving me access to this document).
6 *Kudi Arasu*, 13 December 1931.
7 *Kudi Arasu*, 13 December 1931.

8 A police report also mentions Ireland. USS file No. 839 dated 28 September 1933. CID report dated 13 September 1932.

9 *Kudi Arasu*, 13 November 1932.

10 *Kudi Arasu*, 30 April 1934.

11 'Periyarin Melainattu Suttruppayana Anubhavangal,' and 'Periyar Kanda Pothu Undichalai,' *Viduthalai Thanthai Periyar 85vathu Piranthanal Malar*, 1963: 137–140.

12 In 1988, with help from the son of Periyar's faithful older brother, E.V. Krishnaswamy, E.V.K. Selvaraj, Anaimuthu located the manuscript in the safe of the trust named after Periyar's father, Erode Venkata Naicker.

13 Apart from these notebooks, Periyar seems to have maintained another calendar dairy and a notebook, probably of addresses. None of these have survived. Periyar's hand was notoriously difficult to read, and the Tamil transliteration (complicated by the Tamil alphabet being more a syllabary and lacking in aspirates) of European names poses a further challenge. I have verified and corrected Anaimuthu's reading, or rather, decipherment, of Periyar's orthography.

14 While remaining indebted to Anaimuthu's vast and long experience of deciphering Periyar's hand, I have made emendations based on my reading of the facsimile. The diary notes are short and cryptic.

15 This was the title, in Tamil, of his book *Pen En Adimaiyanal*. Consisting of a series of essays in the late 1920s and early 1930s, it was first published in book form in 1942.

16 For a history of the translation of the Communist Manifesto in the various Indian languages, see Prakash Karat (ed), *A World to Win: Essays on the 'Communist Manifesto,'* New Delhi: LeftWord Books, 1999, especially. 'The *Manifesto* in India: A Publishing History,' pp. 131–140. For an interesting analysis of Periyar's translation, see Matthew H. Baxter, '*Bhutams* of Marx and the Movement of Self-Respecters,' *History of Political Thought*, Summer 2016, 37(2): 336–359.

17 *Kudi Arasu*, 1 November 1931.

18 S. Ramanathan (1896–1970) began his political career in the Congress, played a leading role in the Khadi movement, and was a close associate of Periyar before rejoining the Congress to become a minister in the first Congress ministry (1937–1939). Despite his shifting political positions, he was a lifelong rationalist and edited the *Indian Rationalist* for many years from 1954.

19 This is based on an interview conducted with R. Ramasamy in 1989 by V. Anaimuthu, *Chinthanaiyalan Periyar 111 avathu Pirantha Nal Vizha Malar*, 1989.

20 USS file No. 839 dated 28 September 1933.

21 The following is based on 'Periyarin Melainattu Suttruppayana Anubhavangal,' *Viduthalai Thanthai Periyar 85vathu Piranthanal Malar*, 1965: 137–140.

22 This and the subsequent two paragraphs are based on S. Ramanathan, 'Azhiyatha Russia,' *Kalki Deepavali Malar*, 1942: 102–106.

23 Ramanathan, 'Azhiyatha Russia,' pp. 102–106.

24 India Office Records (IOR): L/PJ/12/315. VOKS was the Vsesoiuznoe obshchestvo kult'turnoi sviazi s zagranitsei.

25 IOR: L/PJ/12/315.
26 Hiren Mukherjee, *Time-Tested Treasures: Recollections and Reflections on Indo-Soviet Friendship*, Bombay: Allied, 1975, p. 79.
27 He was probably returning from one of the Transcaucasian Republics. As we shall see below he definitely went to Azerbaijan.
28 This section is fully based on Periyar's travel diary unless specified otherwise.
29 For an excellent study of the organisation see Daniel Peris, *Storming the Heavens: The Soviet League of the Militant Godless*, Ithaca: Cornell University Press, 1998.
30 E. H. Carr, *The Twilight of Comintern, 1930–1935*, London: Macmillan, 1982.
31 *Kudi Arasu*, 30 October 1932. Evidently, they were not aware of the onset of the famine of 1932–1933.
32 For a contemporary report on the May Day celebrations in Moscow, see *Daily Worker*, 3 May 1932.
33 A year later Violet Lansbury would meet Clemens Palme Dutt, elder brother of Rajni Palme Dutt, in Moscow – whom Periyar would encounter a number of times in the tour subsequently – and marry him.
34 Violet Lansbury, *An English Woman in the USSR*, London: Putnam, 1942, p. 263.
35 IOR: L/PJ/12/212.
36 Peris, *Storming the Heavens*, p. 109.
37 IOR: L/PJ/12/272.
38 Anaimuthu misreads the references to Dutt in Periyar's tour record as Rajani Palme Dutt. RPD, as he was commonly referred to, was a leading figure in the CPGB and in the international Communist movement. A friend of Nehru and V. Krishna Menon, he also directed the Communist Party of India. His *India To-Day* (1940), a classic Marxist analysis of India, influenced generations of Indian left historians (translated into many Indian languages; twice in Tamil alone). RPD was married to an Estonian-born Communist Salme Anette Pekkala who had been sent by Lenin to help create CPGB. She did not have a British passport, and it was therefore difficult for RPD and his wife to travel to Britain. Consequently, they moved to Brussels where they took up more or less permanent residence until 1936 (John Callaghan, *Rajani Palme Dutt*, London: Lawrence and Wishart, 1993, p. 59). A reading of the Indian Political Intelligence (IPI) files makes it clear that it was Clemens Dutt who was shuttling back and forth between Berlin and London at the time of Periyar's European tour.
39 Corroborated by USS file No. 839, 28 September 1933, CID report dated 12 August 1932.
40 If it is the Hugh Rathbone that M. N. Roy mentions in his *Memoirs*, Delhi: Ajanta, 1984, p. 513.
41 www8.open.ac.uk/researchprojects/makingbritain/content/pulin-behari-seal (accessed on 9 July 2012).
42 In the event Ramu returned to India on 23 October 1932. At the Dhanushkodi port he was subjected to a thorough search which yielded nothing incriminating. USS file No. 839, CID report dated 27 October 1932.

43 This was the day that Chancellor Brüning's government fell. Periyar has a cryptic one-line entry in his diary, and it is not clear whether he witnessed a street fight or repeated a news item or even hearsay.

44 USS file No. 839, 28 September 1933, CID report dated 12 August 1932.

45 Despite the close contact that he maintained with him during these weeks, the *Kudi Arasu* (26 January 1936) sub-editorial when Saklatvala died in January 1936 lacks all personal touch but rather focusing instead on his indefatigable energies, oratorical skills, his sharp critique of Gandhi, and his anti-clericalism.

46 *Daily Worker*, 5 July 1932.

47 *Daily Worker*, 21 and 22 June 1932.

48 Periyar's attendance at this meeting was noted by the CID as well: USS file No. 839 dated 28 September 1933, CID report dated 12 August 1932.

49 *Kudi Arasu*, 18 December 1932.

50 IOR: L/PJ/12/272.

51 For more on the Rationalist Press Association see Bill Cooke, *Blasphemy Depot: A Hundred Years of the Rationalist Press Association*, London: Rationalist Press Association, 2003.

52 IOR: L/PJ/12/272.

53 *Kudi Arasu*, 26 January 1936.

54 IOR: L/PJ/12/167. Rajni Kothari, the pioneering political scientist and founder of the Centre for the Study of Developing Societies, Delhi, recollects in his autobiography that he was radicalised in the later 1940s by reading the left literature in the enormous library of 'one Mr Lotwala' at Deolali, Maharashtra. Rajni Kothari, *Memoirs*, Calcutta: Rupa & Co., 2002, pp. 23, 80, 98.

55 *The Autobiography of Indulal Yagnik*, Vol. 2, New Delhi: Manohar, 2011, p. 434.

56 *The Autobiography of Indulal Yagnik*, Vol. 2, pp. 463–486.

57 For more on this case see Susan D. Pennybacker's magnificently researched *From Scottsboro to Munich: Race and Political Culture in 1930s Britain*, Princeton: Princeton University Press, 2009.

58 *Daily Worker*, 30 June 1932.

59 For more on this see A. R. Venkatachalapathy, 'Periyar's Brush with the Mocking Bird,' *The Hindu*, 22 August 2015.

60 R. P. Paranjpye, *Eight-Four, Not Out*, Delhi: Publications Division, Government of India, 1961, p. 113.

61 *Kudi Arasu*.

62 USS file No. 839 CID Report dated 28 September 1933.

63 Bhagat Singh, *Naan Nathigan Ean?*, translated by P. Jeevanandam, Erode: Pakutharivu Noorpathippu Kazhagam, 1935.

64 *Kudi Arasu*, 30 October 1932.

5

THE INDIAN CIVIL SERVICE
AND INDIAN FOREIGN POLICY

Amit Das Gupta

Has 15 August 1947 been the zero hour in modern Indian history?
Though formally the Indian Union attained independence at midnight,
there are many continuities over this threshold. The most obvious argument against any zero hour is the appointment of the Interim Government under Vice-President Jawaharlal Nehru on 2 September 1946.
Apart from the British Viceroy, all portfolios came under Indian politicians, who took fundamental decisions regarding the future political
order in South Asia. There is even less of a zero hour in Indian foreign policy. The Asian Relations Conference from 23 March to 2 April
1947 is but one major event taking place before formal independence
that both saw India as an important international player and shaped
Indian foreign policy. Mahatma Gandhi, Nehru, or Subhas Chandra
Bose had since long established themselves as heavyweights in international affairs in the interwar period. They took part in international
conferences, lobbied the Indian case and – in the case of Bose – looked
for military allies to drive the British out of the subcontinent. In a
rather unfair generalisation, Gandhi and Nehru are considered pursuing foreign policy along moral principles and visions, whereas the
Netaji stands for pragmatism rather than morals.

The usual focus on the politicians has taken care that another group
of key actors in Indian foreign policy has been completely overlooked.
From the early 1920s, a group of Indian administrators of the Indian
Civil Service (ICS) had made (British) Indian foreign affairs their
day-to-day business, and they left an imprint on the foreign policy of
independent India that can hardly be overstated. They worked in the
department responsible for Indians overseas, which from 1923 ran
under the misleading name Department for Education, Health and

Lands (EHL). The key figure among them was Girja Shankar Bajpai, whom in late 1946 Nehru asked to establish the Indian Foreign Service and set up the Ministry of External Affairs. He functioned as India's de facto foreign minister until 1952. After his departure, his two main discoveries from the colonial period continued to influence Indian foreign policy, though in different directions. Subimal Dutt became India's longest-serving foreign secretary. Whereas by pursuing a realist and anti-communist line he proved to be Bajpai's true heir, K.P.S. Menon stands for India's opening towards the Soviet Union. After his term as Indian Agent in Ceylon, Menon had soon distanced himself from Bajpai and had become very much Nehru's man instead. He hardly left an imprint when working in Delhi, but shone when posted abroad.

Regarding the foreign policy of independent India, this chapter focuses rather on the relations with the Soviet Union and the United States. The author has covered those with other powers, in particular the People's Republic of China, in the political biography of Subimal Dutt[1] and an edited volume on the 1962 war[2] and will do so again in a monograph, due in 2018, on the impact of ICS officers on Indian foreign policy.

How the issues of Indians overseas became Indian foreign policy

The fate and the treatment of Indians overseas began to rouse emotions in India already before the outbreak of the First World War. Ironically, the large majority of them belonged to classes for whom nobody cared much while in India. With the abolition of slavery in two steps, 1833 and 1843, throughout the British Empire, the demand for unskilled labourers in various British controlled territories was satisfied from overpopulated parts of the world like China and in particular South Asia. As Amitabh Ghosh in his highly acclaimed novel *Sea of Poppies* has brought home to a global public, their fate was not much better than those of slaves.[3] It took the Gandhian campaigns in South Africa, however, to make Indians at home aware of the grievances of their countrymen abroad. The story of Kunti, a young Indian woman narrowly escaping an attempt of rape by overseers in Fiji, received wide publicity. The demand that the Government of India should look after the interests of Indians abroad grew even stronger with India's enormous contribution to the First World War. Against the background of this very self-confidence and the Gandhian campaigns, the British, however, tried to tighten their control over the subcontinent.

Among the few tokens of gratitude was that they gave in to the demands to protect Indians overseas. A new department was created in 1923 by merging those of Revenue and Agriculture on the one hand and Education and Health on the other. Like the Law and the Finance Departments, it came under an Indian member, in this case Sir Muhammad Shafi. With three Indian members in the Viceroy's Executive Council, nominal parity was established between Europeans and Indians. Nevertheless, the British kept the key portfolios – Defence, Home, and Foreign and Political.

The personnel of the last department were nearly exclusively European. For being something like a branch of the Foreign Office in London, its competences were rather limited. Responsible for the regions neighbouring British India and the Gulf, those in the top ranks played the last rounds of the Great Game with the Soviet Union. The EHL Department was initially meant to keep itself busy with the issue of Indian migration. Accordingly, the first officers sent to Ceylon and Malaya in 1923 were called Emigration Agents. There is good reason to believe that the strange name of the department was chosen in order to indicate there was no rivalry with the Foreign and Political Department. In fact, however, the two departments were competing from the first day. Already from May to October 1922, V.S. Srinivasa Sastri had undertaken a journey through the dominions and crown colonies to investigate the condition of Indians living there, which had had foreign policy repercussions. The South African Prime Minister Jan Smuts had refused to invite Sastri, arguing that the latter was prone to agitate public opinion in South Africa by demanding equal franchise for Indians. 'In other dominions he has made people alive to the issue – indeed he has largely created it.'[4]

In India, Sastri was considered a moderate. Among others, he had been nominated to the Madras Legislative Council and the Imperial Legislative Council. He had resigned from the Congress Party in protest against the non-cooperation movement in 1922. The Government of India obviously held him to be both loyal and credible in the eyes of his countrymen. It sent him on numerous delegations abroad, be it to the Imperial Conference in 1921 or the League of Nations. The key figure in that field, however, was to become the Officer on Special Duty accompanying him on his journey in 1922 – Girja Shankar Bajpai.

The rise of Girja Shankar Bajpai

Bajpai was born on 3 April 1891 in Allahabad. His father Pandit Seetla Prasad Bajpai had made his career as a judge, finally rising to the rank of Minister of Justice in Jaipur State. Educated at the Jubilee High School in Lucknow and Trinity College, Cambridge, he passed the ICS entrance examination in London in 1914. Standing first in the final examination at the end of the one-year probation,[5] he joined the ICS cadre of the United Provinces and in late 1915 was posted to Varanasi.[6]

No archival evidence regarding Bajpai's early years in the service in UP districts has been found. Many years later, however, one of his subordinates, N.B. Bonarjee, described Bajpai as belonging 'to the school of thought which looked on District Officers as a somewhat uncouth species, addicted to riding and shooting and generally lacking in spirit and polish.'[7] Bajpai's true passion was international affairs. How he initially established himself on that field is unknown, but he had made enough of a name by 1922 to be sent along with Sastri. A year later, a Calcutta publisher asked him to write a book on the issue of Indians overseas.[8] In August 1924, he was appointed Officer on Special Duty for that very task in the EHL Department.[9] Bajpai quickly made himself indispensable. His extraordinary command of English and a number of other languages, his photographic memory, and his capacities as writer and orator together with his ambition, his strong self-confidence, his liking for socialising, and the capacity to play along in Delhi and Simla networks were all ingredients for an outstanding career. His presence at the Round Table Conference in South Africa was crucial for the signing of the Cape Town Agreement in 1927. In Delhi, the publication of the final version of the half-yearly report of the Indian Agency in South Africa in 1928 was delayed for months until Bajpai had returned from Europe.[10] It appears that Muhammad Habibullah, the member of the department from 1924 to 1930, shared Bajpai's views in general and left most decisions to him.

Creating a cadre of foreign policy experts

The Cape Town Agreement provided for the establishment of an Indian Agent in South Africa. Due to the delicacy of the task, the Government of India decided to send an Indian politician. Srinivasa Sastri was appointed, but Bajpai insisted that his secretary had to be an experienced ICS officer.[11] The constellation in South Africa, nevertheless, remained an exception. The Government of India was well aware that trusting such a task to a politician included risks. Accordingly, Habibullah cabled to Viceroy Lord Irwin that he would convey to Sastri 'that, while we completely trust his discretion, he must appreciate desirability, during the tenure of appointment, of avoiding public pronouncements or making commitments on questions of policy without previous consultation with Govt. of India.'[12]

Already in 1923, two agencies had been opened in Ceylon and Malaya. As the Indian communities consisted mostly of plantation workers from South India, the EHL Department asked the Government of Madras for experienced Indian officers fluent in Tamil, preferably from the ICS cadre.[13] That is why India's first generation of de facto diplomats were South Indians throughout. Arunandalam Pillai from the Madras Civil Service was sent to Malaya, at the age of 53 commanding decade-long experience, whereas with S. Ranganathan a very junior ICS officer was appointed to the post in Ceylon. The island was seen as the more demanding task, but it seems that belonging to the ICS elite outweighed the handicap of a mere six years in service.

Many ambitious young ICS officers were keen to be sent on deputation from the provinces to the Central Government. The new postings came with an increase of prestige and higher salaries, and the officers after their return either hoped for a career jump or staying on in the capital. Until 1937, there was no formal procedure for applications. Whenever Delhi needed an officer, it asked the provincial governments to suggest suitable candidates. For the higher ranks in its departments, the Central Government asked for officers with an experience in service of around 16 years,[14] though this was ignored whenever there was a junior, but suitable candidate.

Bajpai in particular was proud to select only the very best for work in the EHL Department or with the agencies.[15] Whenever an officer or agent did not fulfil expectations, he was rather blunt in his comments. The annual report for Malaya in 1927, authored by R. Subayya Naidu from the Madras Civil Service, Bajpai found 'characteristically long, indiscreet in many parts, and full of controversial or impractical suggestions . . . We must, in due course, call the agent's attention to the impropriety of cramming into the report his pet theories and favourite schemes, regardless of their effect on public opinion in India. . . . The proper place for them . . . is a confidential memorandum or letter and not a proper report.'[16] Even harsher were the comments on K. V. Reddi, in 1931 Indian Agent in South Africa, who, according to Bajpai, did not have the necessary presence of mind in his talks with representatives of his host country.[17] He regularly raised issues without any practical importance[18] and his suggestions were considered 'unintelligible'[19] and 'really inconsistent with our instructions.'[20] Those whom Bajpai sorted out as substandard, of course, were not at all fond of him. Deputy Secretary N.C. Mehta, for example, imposed 'almost all vices on Bajpai,' who allegedly held Indian officers for unworthy and inefficient, but flattered the British and Habibullah.[21]

India's first top diplomat – K.P.S. Menon

Bajpai, however, was also hunting for outstanding officers. The first of his two main 'discoveries' was K.P.S. Menon, born on 18 October 1898 in South Indian Palakkad. Like many of his ICS colleagues, his father, too, made his living as a lawyer. Menon had all the skills for a distinguished academic career with an outstanding performance as student of history at Oxford. Although he chose to join the ICS, all his life he excelled as writer and orator, demonstrating a deep knowledge of Indian and Western humanities. To no surprise, he stood first in both the competitive and the final examination. Menon shone for many more reasons. He had an extraordinary capacity to make himself popular and to establish and maintain networks. To no small extent, his wife Saraswati, the daughter of Sir Sankaran Nair, President of the Congress Party in 1897, helped his career. Unlike the wives of many other Indian ICS officers, she fully participated in British Indian social life.

Belonging to the 1922 Madras batch, in 1925 Menon was only the second Indian officer to be selected for the prestigious Foreign and Political Service, his performance in the princely state of Hyderabad and later the North West Frontier Province (NWFP) winning him attention. Menon's many talents helped him overcome the prejudices both British and North Indians harboured against the short 'black' men from the south. It even did not hurt his career that his sympathies with the independence movement were well documented since his Oxford days. When the British government interrogated Menon before letting him sign the covenant, he held 'that India should in time have a place like that of the dominion in the federation of nations forming the British Empire.' Nevertheless, 'he agreed that to work for anything like disruption would be incompatible with . . . his covenant.'[22]

Being one of the very few Indians in the Political Service, however, seemed to limit his career options to postings in the NWFP or as dewan in a princely state. During the 1920s, only European officers were sent abroad. In 1929, his chance came when Bajpai urgently insisted on the return of the Indian Agent in Ceylon, M.S.A. Hydari, his best official, whom he needed for the Haj Committee.[23] As a substitute for Ceylon, he wanted 'an ICS officer possessing tact and resource' and suggested

Menon.[24] The latter was enthusiastic about a higher salary and to get a chance to prove himself.[25]

The Indian Agents' main duties were to keep contact with their countrymen abroad, inspect rubber and tea estates, and maintain close relations with the colonial administration. Their competences were 'little more than those of a welfare officer.'[26] At the end of the day, however, much depended on the personality and the diplomatic skills of individual agents. Menon, for example, throughout his four-year term acted as a proper ambassador, earning Bajpai's praise as 'the best Indian Agent who ever went there.'[27]

Menon faced enormous difficulties. Nine days after his arrival on 15 October 1929, with the Black Thursday at the New York Stock Exchange the world economic crisis reached its peak. As the prices for raw products dropped, many rubber estates became unprofitable. Some planters closed their estates and released the Indian labourers unemployed, others demanded either a substantial reduction of the minimum wages as fixed in the Delhi Agreement or a massive reduction of the general labour force by 50,000 to 60,000.[28] Menon emphasised that during the earlier rubber boom the planters had not cared to share their enormous profits with the labourers, but in the moment of crisis wanted them to carry the burden.[29] Typically, planters, along with colonial officials, considered him as a sort of enemy representing the interests of labourers, backed by a powerful government.[30] Menon made the best of a difficult situation. Given the further falling rubber price, in September 1930 he gave up 'the inflexible attitude recommended in my previous letters.' Ceylon did not want to violate the Delhi Agreement and suggested keeping the daily wage as stipulated in the agreement, but wanted the labourers to work fewer days per week – a solution the latter found agreeable.[31]

When the economic situation deteriorated further, the planters' associations with the backing of the Ceylon government suggested reducing both the minimum wages and the price of rice sold by them to plantation workers. Menon found the demand 'well-nigh irresistible.'[32] In his typical pragmatic approach, Bajpai agreed, arguing that 'a legal quibble cannot dispose of hard economic facts and quibbling is only likely to lose us the good-will both of the Ceylon Government and the employers of Indian labour.'[33] With Member Fazl-i-Husain, he held that the earlier position 'could hardly be sustained in a time of economic depression . . . when our own Retrenchment Committees are talking of reduction in salaries because of a fall in the cost of living.'[34]

Another task keeping Menon busy was the franchise of Indians abroad. A part of the agents' work was creating the sort of political awareness, which Indians in British India had developed but Indians overseas often lacked. Indian labourers could be registered in the voter's roll when either born in Ceylon or having been residents since five years. The second precondition was difficult to prove, and poor Indians could not afford counsel for a hearing. Menon foresaw it as the attack point for Sinhalese organisations,[35] who campaigned against South Indians as economic rivals.[36] To make things worse, there was 'total lack of organization and leadership among Indians in Ceylon.' The agency promoted registration and Menon and his staff toured the estates. They tried to counter Sinhalese propaganda that Indians with registration might lose Indian citizenship together with the privileges guaranteed by the Delhi Agreement. Menon, however, was sure that he did not convince many.[37]

Nevertheless, his superiors in Delhi found his performance outstanding. Whereas Foreign Secretary Aubrey Metcalfe wanted him to return to the Foreign and Political Department,[38] the EHL Department extended his term for another year.[39] Bajpai wanted him to continue in the proto-diplomatic service, and Menon was just as keen to do so. Menon fancied the post of Indian Agent in South Africa,[40] but Bajpai in August 1934 sent him on a two-month tour to Zanzibar, British East Africa, and Uganda to investigate allegations of discrimination against Indians. Thereafter, he promised him a Deputy Secretaryship in the EHL Department,[41] a promise redeemed in late June 1935.

Menon, however, soon discovered that he both disliked deskwork and working under Bajpai. He preferred to travel around, to negotiate, and to give speeches instead of the dry work with files. Moreover, the self-confident officer did not at all appreciate that the powerful secretary corrected his drafts.[42] 'Baji,' as he called him in his diaries in a derogatory manner, 'is a clever fellow, but an egoist. A little too much of a tactician, too. He may overreach himself.'[43] Whereas he admired Bajpai's knowledge and ability, he found him 'a little pompous.'[44] Though Menon hid his deep antipathy well, he soon returned to the Political Service.

The latent conflict between the two by the then-leading Indian foreign policy experts never surfaced, but it was much more than personal dislike from Menon's side, which Bajpai in return obviously did not feel at all. The former had no ambition to rise to the top of a department, but loved to explore the world, whereas the latter stayed on in the capital for two decades, as close as possible to the centre of power. Both appreciated good work, but whereas Bajpai focused on the content, Menon gave more weight to personality. For him, the message was less relevant than the messenger. In this regard, he stood in the tradition of the Political Service, where character and masculinity counted more than anything else.[45] Whilst these different approaches led to no controversy during the colonial period, after independence Bajpai and his heir Subimal Dutt stood for certain political and moral principles, whereas Menon became the very face of the opening towards the Soviet Union, less bothered by ideology and appalling reality but deeply impressed by leaders like Nikolai A. Bulganin or Nikita A. Khrushchev.

Subimal Dutt – a most unlikely discovery

In late 1937, Bajpai's efforts to win Menon for another diplomatic mission failed. Due to manpower shortage in the Foreign Department, Metcalfe rejected the proposal to release Menon to take over the post of Indian Agent to Burma.[46] The candidate himself, then Political Agent in the princely state of Zhob in Baluchistan on a sort of diplomatic mission at the outskirts of British India, turned down the offer, too.[47] At the same time when Bajpai and Menon lost touch, a complete outsider arrived at Delhi, to work with the EHL Department. Compared to Bajpai, Menon, and most other ICS officers, Subimal Dutt was of a very different kind. Born on 5 December 1903 in the village Kanungopara in Chittagong District, he grew up far from any wealth, privileges, or European influence. Like his ten brothers, he excelled in school and university. Due to his superior intellect, after an extremely short period of preparation, he managed the ICS entrance examination in London in 1927. Notwithstanding two years in Great Britain and ten years in the service, he had never transformed into one of those proverbial 'brown Englishmen,' but – with some pride – considered himself 'totally of the vernacular type.'[48] He felt that the powerful Bajpai initially looked down on him, the unpolished newcomer from Bengal.[49]

Again unlike Bajpai and Menon, Dutt had no genuine interest in politics, let alone foreign relations. His dearest ambition was to rise to the rank of secretary in whatever department. Being introverted, shy, and stiff, he hardly qualified for a diplomat's career. Apart from a tremendous work discipline, however, he had a knack for administrative issues. As soon as Bajpai had discovered this, he became Dutt's mentor. The latter rose to the rank of Deputy Secretary in the Overseas Branch of the department, keeping himself busy with Malaya. In late 1939, Bajpai offered him the post of dewan in the princely state of Cooch Behar,[50] but Dutt declined. Like his mentor, he was keen to remain as close as possible to the centre of power. Joining the Political Service with its enormous prestige and a higher salary seems not to have been attractive for one of the most Indian of ICS officers. Due to new rules, however, Dutt would have had to return to his home province after a maximum of three years of deputation to the centre. As the only alternative, Bajpai sent him as Indian Agent to Malaya.

Once again, Dutt was a rather unlikely candidate for such a posting, speaking no Tamil or Malayalam at all. He was not only the first agent from outside the Madras Presidency but the first ICS officer there. In comparison with Ceylon and South Africa, Malaya was considered the least difficult and least relevant agency. Notwithstanding the Rubber Slump, things had developed rather smoothly. Shortly before Dutt's arrival, however, the situation had become critical when Indian labourers had gone on strike. The colonial government, against the background of the urgent need for rubber in the Second World War, had sent troops, and to make things worse, Indian units. A number of strikers were shot dead and the Government of India demanded an investigation. On his first posting abroad, Dutt tried to investigate the backgrounds of the strike and – among others – found economic grievances, whereas the British Governor Sir Shelton Thomas held there were none. According to him, Congress agitators had caused the unrest,[51] and he incorrectly reported to London that the agent agreed to his point of view.[52] Dutt protested, which triggered an intense dispute between the Colonial Office and the governor on the one hand and the India Office, the Government of India and the agent on the other hand. The latter, though still a junior officer, stood his ground and was supported even by the Viceroy Linlithgow, at least over a couple of months.[53]

Dutt found the old-style colonialism in Malaya appalling, where Europeans and a few rich Indians did not care about the living conditions and even lives of foreign labourers as long as they secured their profits. His predecessor as a 'black' man as a matter of course had not been admitted to European clubs.[54] Dutt did not cope with the climate and the food as well. Suffering from acute health problems and horrified by the prospect of becoming a prisoner of war with the Japanese invasion looming, Dutt quit after little more than eight months. The Government of India could also hardly resist any longer the demands to replace him by a more experienced officer with the appropriate language skills.[55]

Self-confident anti-colonialism in the colonial period

Dutt and Menon were different, but the parallels were remarkable. The former painfully avoided offending superiors, but in Malaya with great self-confidence challenged a powerful British governor. He clearly understood himself as representing his countrymen in Malaya rather than British India. When exactly the earlier avowedly apolitical Dutt had turned into a staunch patriot is impossible to say, but it seems that his three years in the EHL Department, fighting for the emancipation of Indians overseas, had left a strong imprint. Dutt's anti-colonial attitude corresponded with that of K.P.S. Menon while in Oxford and later in Ceylon. Both displayed great self-confidence and did not want to accept the role of mere welfare agents. There could be no doubt about their patriotism and their sympathies with the independence movement. Whereas Dutt used the opportunity of a commemorative speech for the late Rabindranath Tagore,[56] Menon's regular public speeches to all sorts of topics occasionally raised eyebrows in Delhi.

Interestingly, this did not affect their careers. The shy and cautious Dutt at least at home did not indicate any political sympathies, but Menon knew and appreciated Jawaharlal Nehru at least since 1931.[57] At the same time, he was friends with die-hard British imperialists like Olaf Caroe, Aubrey Metcalfe, or Hugh Weightman. Other than his two temporary subordinates, Bajpai has not left any collection of private papers allowing insights into his thinking. He found one of Menon's speeches provocative but was restrained in his criticism, which might be explained by the fact that he was otherwise greatly pleased with the agent's performance.[58] Bajpai, however, must have been aware that the policy the EHL Department pursued had a strong anti-colonial touch by demanding equal rights for all citizens of the Empire. British rule over large parts of the world was de facto based on the idea of the inequality of races – the 'white man's burden.' Although many British, particularly those in the Foreign Department, disliked Bajpai's craving for power, they must have considered him a loyalist. At least the British officers working with and under him supported his policy. Whether they and Bajpai were aware that, thereby, they were undermining the foundations of the Empire, remains an open question.

From irrelevance back to power (1942–1947)

Bajpai was no friend of the Congress Party or Nehru, proven by his vitriolic propaganda during the war. By late 1941, the powerful official, having been appointed member of the EHL Department in March 1940, met his downfall. Linlithgow's declaring war on the Axis Powers without any consultation with Indian political leaders caused continuous unrest, culminating in the Quit India Movement in 1942. In order to mollify the Indian public, the Viceroy's Executive Council was expanded and the two Indian officials replaced by politicians.[59] Bajpai was appointed Agent-General for India in Washington, a posting attached to the British Embassy without any prestige and deliberately vaguely kept competences. To complete his humiliation, the Agent-General was instructed by Foreign Secretary Caroe that all correspondence had to go through the External Affairs Department.[60] Bajpai had finally come under his arch-rivals' thumb. This also meant that Dutt's career in the EHL Department came to an end. Without support from his mentor, he returned to Bengal and completely lost touch with foreign affairs.

Bajpai was complimented for his performance in Washington from all sides,[61] but actually spent a most miserable term there. Suffering from health problems, getting involved in petty fights over his powers and being widely ignored, he grew deeply depressed and concerned about his future.[62] Menon was better off, not having made enemies with the British. In September 1943, he was appointed Indian Agent to China, where he stayed on until early 1948. He went on giving patriotic speeches, but to little effect in the midst of the world war and the Chinese Civil War. For a short moment in autumn 1945, Viceroy Wavell considered him 'the Indian best fitted by ability and experience' for becoming Foreign Secretary. 'But Menon, though attractive and good with his pen, is rather a light weight and I doubt if he could cope with an Indian Member for External Affairs if one is appointed next year.'[63]

Bajpai's return to power began with the end of the Second World War, when numerous conferences regarding the post-war global order took place in North America. Given the critical situation in South Asia, the Government of India was happy to have a knowledgeable and experienced diplomat on the ground. It appears that the Agent-General was still considered a loyalist. His anti-Congress propaganda during the war gave that impression, and in conversations with Sir Frederick Puckle, Secretary in the Department of Information and Broadcasting, he had expressed by then moderate hopes that India might achieve full dominion status after the war.[64] Bajpai's participation in various conferences must have helped him overcome his frustration. In late 1945, he authored a unique paper. Formally a quarterly report, it actually was a full-fledged analysis of the foreign policy options for an independent India – the only such analysis known from a key-decision maker in Nehruvian foreign affairs. Given that many of those who joined the Indian Foreign Service (IFS) had gone through Bajpai's school, one can hold that the essay provided the direction for the thinking in the EHL Department.

The text is characterised by three key-features – realism, anti-communism, and scepticism regarding the United States. India was considered too weak to stand alone, hence alignment was the need of the hour. Pan-Asian dreams like those of an alliance with China seemed naïve to Bajpai – 'a combination of the weak does not add up to power.' The Soviet Union was not to be trusted, as any closer partnership would inevitably make Moscow attempt to overthrow the political system in the partner country along socialist lines and make India another satellite. The United States was the most powerful country in the world, but they were immature and unpredictable. What remained was an alliance with the Commonwealth, 'a partnership with security and honour, a partnership of mutual advantage in which, in return for her manpower, her growing industrial capacity and the immense value of her strategic position, India will have at her disposal the resources in science, in technical equipment, in modern armament and, last but not least, in political experience of the U.K. . . . No nation can shape a safe and progressive future by the lone light of memories of a wronged past.' His concluding sentence shows him in the tradition of realists, too: 'Sentiment must serve, not master the national interest.'[65]

To no surprise, Bajpai's conclusions were fully in harmony with those views dominant in Great Britain throughout the interwar period. The idea of an aligned India, however, ran contrary to Nehru's visions. The same is true regarding Asian solidarity and relations with the Soviet Union. Nevertheless, with independence approaching, Nehru as Vice-President of the Interim Government called Bajpai back from Washington in order to establish the Ministry of External Affairs and the IFS. The appointment must have surprised many. Nehru had earlier massively criticised the ICS as 'self-satisfied and self-sufficient, narrow, with fixed minds, static in a changing world and wholly unsuited to a progressive environment . . . No new order can be built up in India so long as the spirit of the ICS pervades our administration.'[66] In December 1946, however, Nehru found 'that in spite of his past, Bajpai is a man of considerable ability which should be used by us,'[67] who like most of his ICS colleagues was 'quite capable of adapting yourself to the new India' lacking trained administrators.[68]

Bajpai was appointed Secretary-General and lost no time to assemble his confidants around him. Already on the journey back from the United States, he asked Dutt to join the IFS.[69] The Secretariat Reorganization Committee, also termed the Bajpai Committee, in its report of 10 August 1947 recommended that 'the Indian Civil Service officer, both because of his education and the training in administration he receives in the formative stages of his career, must continue to remain an important source of recruitment for the higher administrative and Secretariat posts.' The MEA had the most pressing need for 33 such officers to fill the ranks of joint, deputy, and under secretaries, excluding headships of missions.[70] Ironically, the committee consisted of six ICS officers and two officers of the Audits and Accounts Service – not the sort of men to recommend anything else but man the top ranks with ICS officers, though admittedly there were hardly any reasonable short-term alternatives.

The ICS troika on the top of the MEA with Bajpai as Secretary-General and Dutt as Commonwealth Secretary was completed in April 1948, when K.P.S. Menon was appointed Foreign Secretary. The latter, however, actually did not fully fit into the picture. Trained rather in the spirit of the Political Service, unlike his two colleagues, he did not at all like deskwork. Moreover, he was horrified at the idea of working under Bajpai again.[71] It needed a personal message from the Prime Minister to make Menon change his mind.[72] Being Nehru's man, however, did not guarantee him any influence. As earlier in the EHL Department, Bajpai called the shots, and Menon and Dutt implemented his decisions.[73] India's first Foreign Secretary during his four-year term did not leave any lasting impression.

The ICS school in Indian foreign policy

The troika on top of the MEA had all acquired experience abroad. Most of the officers of the newly established IFS, however, were newcomers to international affairs. There were a few men and women of public life, and a few military officers. The majority, however, had grown up in the ICS or other British Indian services. There can be no doubt about their loyalty to independent India, in particular to Nehru, whom most of them admired from the bottoms of their hearts. Nevertheless, their thinking inevitably was coloured by patterns and views they had developed and used over many years.

One element was a deep-rooted anti-communism, which in a rather mild form Bajpai had expressed in late 1945. His anti-communism was based in part on his close-up view of the West's major difficulties with the Soviet Union leading up to the Cold War. The expectation that cooperation with Moscow entailed becoming a satellite was no fixed idea of Bajpai's. A world revolution had been among the top priorities of the communist movement and the Soviet Union right from the start. The British in South Asia considered communism an even more severe threat than the Congress-led independence movement. Whereas the latter, genuinely a civil-rights movement, played along certain lines, the former was considered capable of all evils. District officers of the ICS or the provincial services had had their share fighting political unrest, and whereas sympathies with the Congress had grown, hardly any of them indicated any support for Indian communists.

There was a certain scepticism regarding the United States, which had its roots rather in British attitudes than in practical experiences. Apart from Bajpai and those officers who had represented India at UN conferences, most prominently among them K.P.S. Menon, hardly any ICS officers had been in touch with Americans until the outbreak of the war. In the United Kingdom, which had dominated world affairs over more than a century, the rise of the United States to world power status with the First World War had caused resentment. Politicians in Washington were seen as commanding enormous means without the experience and reliability the British appreciated. Moreover, British politics and cultural life were considered much more sophisticated. The often strongly anglicised 'brown Englishmen' of the ICS took over such attitudes. The stationing of American forces in South Asia during the war apparently had played a role as well.

The third factor in the approach of ICS officers to foreign affairs was a deep-seated realism. District work meant mostly handling day-to-day affairs and hardly left time for visionary schemes. There was need for practical, manageable solutions, whereas long-term planning was left either to the departments in Delhi or those in London. Menon, who by regularly publishing on historical and political topics thought in wider dimensions, was a rare exception. That sentiment had to serve the national interest, therefore, was a commonplace among India's administrators, though not necessarily among the politicians.

Anti-communism

Beyond doubt, the point of view where former ICS officers clashed most with the prime minister or V.K. Krishna Menon, first high commissioner in London, then from 1955 to 1962 de facto foreign minister, was their attitude to communist countries. Whereas Nehru and Menon were known for open-mindedness if not sympathy, for most IFS officers this was anathema. In a conversation with the Australian High Commissioner Warwick Fielding Chipman, Bajpai confessed that he was 'not worried so much by the economics of communism but my whole soul revolts against its totalitarianism. I find it difficult to be more than polite to the Russian and Chinese ambassadors. I am not a hypocrite. How can I converse with [Soviet Ambassador Kirill Vasilyevich] Novikov?'[74] Such deep-seated anti-communism affected practical politics. This was true even of career changers like Nehru's sister Vijayalakshmi Pandit, who, as India's first ambassador, found the Soviet Union so appalling that she never asked for an interview with Stalin.[75] Whereas the lower ranks in the embassy found Moscow a sort of paradise where 'everyone was well-housed and had enough to eat' and there was no racial or caste-feeling, to no surprise, the higher ranks in the embassy, all ICS officers, shared Mrs. Pandit's point of view.[76] Another career changer, India's first ambassador to Burma, M.A. Rauf, a businessman by upbringing, reacted with outrage when blamed by Deputy Secretary Y.D. Gundevia for having ignored news about communist activities in the Indo-Burmese border region: 'What makes you think that we did not sufficiently appreciate the communist menace? . . . Let me assure you that this is not so. You know my views about communists. If there is any disturbing factor in India, which is likely to become dangerous, it is the CPI.'[77]

That the Communist Party of India was suspected to be under the control of Moscow was consensus in the Government of India including Nehru. There was no consensus, however, on cooperation with communist countries. The anti-communism of former ICS officers can best be seen around the first state visit of Soviet leaders to India in late 1955. In an inter-departmental meeting at secretary level, held in advance of the arrival of Bulganin and Khrushchev, with all participants being officials with an ICS background, it was decided in unison that Soviet offers for cooperation schemes were 'motivated by political considerations' and, therefore, to be avoided if possible.[78] Not only Foreign Secretary Dutt found the partly stage-managed welcome and the enormous expenses for it a shame for democratic India. Nevertheless, some IFS officers, though known for their anti-communist attitudes, found it appropriate to demonstrate even-handedness in public.[79] In the aftermath of the visit, the anti-communist attitude resurfaced, when the offer of Ilyushin-28 bombers was discussed. Those would have been the first weapons system procured from Moscow, and Nehru was enthusiastic to get the chance to overcome the hitherto exclusive dependence on Western sources. Secretary-General N.R. Pillai, Dutt, and Defence Secretary M.K. Vellodi, ICS, strongly opposed it, the latter holding that 'if we buy a few bombers from USSR our supplies from western sources will dry up.'[80] It took a visit of former Viceroy Mountbatten, however, to talk Nehru out of the deal.[81]

The next clash regarding the Soviet Union took place but a year later in the context of the Red Army's intervention in Hungary. As the bloodbath coincided with the Suez War, Nehru and above all V.K. Krishna Menon read the news from Budapest as a red herring produced by the Western press, though the Chargé d'Affaires Mohammed Ataur Rahman telegraphed home most accurate reports. Krishna Menon, generally distrusting everyone holding different views and in particular civil servants,[82] held that Rahman was taken in by Western propaganda. On 9 November 1956, at the UN, Krishna Menon without authorisation voted against a resolution demanding the withdrawal of Soviet forces and free elections, thereby completely isolating India.[83]

Surprisingly, K.P.S. Menon, ambassador to both the Soviet Union and Hungary though spending most his time in Moscow, held the same view.[84] Four years in the Soviet Union had not only made him most popular with Soviet officials and politicians, but, typically for diplomats stationed in a host country for too long, had coloured his perception. In the typical manner of a former officer of the Political Service, he counted more on personality than anything else. When Bulganin, who impressed the ambassador in general, wrongly assured him that Western news were largely exaggerated and there were no deportations of Hungarian dissidents into the Soviet Union, Menon accepted those words at face value.[85] Only when Nehru sent him to Budapest to investigate the state of affairs did he immediately change his mind.[86]

In the meantime, Nehru had gone through weeks of changing his mind on a daily base. Blindly trusting both Menons, one his confidant, the other regularly sending marvellously written reports directly to the prime minister, he faced strong resistance from Pillai and Dutt. They not only trusted Rahman but held the Soviet Union capable of committing atrocities. Dutt, the foreign secretary, even considered quitting his job,[87] but Pillai, the Secretary-General, convinced him that if they left the MEA, those succeeding on the top ranks would be less prone to put a foot on the ground and challenge Nehru's wrong perceptions.[88] Finally, with the mission of K.P.S. Menon and the Ambassador in Prague J.N. Khosla, the anti-communists won the battle. Though, to their deepest embarrassment, Nehru still defended Krishna Menon's unauthorised vote, from then on the prime minister, mostly via Dutt, behind closed doors exerted enormous pressure on the new Hungarian government to release political prisoners.[89]

K.P.S. Menon played a rather doubtful role in the early stages of the Hungarian crisis. Nevertheless, he definitely contributed to the warming of relations with the Soviet Union, which were to become a crucial element of Indian foreign policy. The US–Pakistan alliance, the Sino–Soviet split and the Sino–Indian border dispute, all helped to bring Moscow and Delhi together. Menon's part mostly was the human factor. On the one hand, he was immensely popular with Soviet politicians and officials, the first Indian ambassador not feeling any contempt for the country. The former officer of the Political Service typically did not much care for ideologies but was often impressed by the personalities of those he interacted with.[90] After the end of his term in 1961, he spent every summer vacation in the Soviet Union.[91] On the other hand, because of his elegant style and the friendship with Nehru, the latter even when extremely occupied always enjoyed reading his reports. When the prime minister had come in personal contact with the Soviet leadership in 1955, he had not been impressed at all, the guests giving anti-western propaganda speeches on Indian soil and Khrushchev drinking heavily.[92] Menon's rather sympathetic reports created more understanding. He must be understood as a sort of interpreter between the two countries, helping to close a deep gap.

Realism

It is more difficult to trace the typical realist approach of ICS officers in Indian foreign policy, even more as only a few ever discussed fundamental questions of foreign affairs. In 1952, Bajpai published an article 'India and the balance of power,' which gave evidence of his thoroughly realist approach once again.[93] The few others who authored essays were once in a while driven rather by ambition. Badr-ud-din Tyabji, a somewhat hyperactive officer who felt that he was bound for the highest ranks, pestered the MEA with grand schemes about a new policy in the Gulf or Southeast Asia when he was posted in Tehran and later Jakarta.[94]

Perhaps the advice of Khub Chand, the head of the Indian Military Mission in Berlin, revealed more of the general approach of former ICS officers. He was discussing whether India should recognise West

Germany in 1949. This ambitious officer belonged to the 1935 batch of the ICS cadre of the United Provinces. Owing to urgent need in the capital during the Second World War, he had been sent as a very junior officer to the Department of Defence. When he was transferred to Berlin in February 1948, he commanded neither any knowledge of international affairs nor had he ever been in touch with Bajpai. He rather got the chance because there was nobody else available or interested.

Khub Chand's worldview had much in common with Nehru's. He deeply distrusted the Americans who he believed were waiting for an excuse to re-arm Western Europe for a war against the Soviet Union. He regarded the West Germans as not having learned their lesson and as waiting for their chance to regain control of Europe.[95] On the other hand, the Soviet Union, though most unhelpful whenever the Indian Military Mission asked for assistance, was considered blameless. Distrusting the West and giving the Soviet Union the benefit of the doubt went down well with Nehru or Krishna Menon, but not at all with Bajpai or Dutt. When, however, after the foundation of the Federal Republic of Germany in May 1949, the question arose whether India should follow the invitation of the Western Powers to open an office in Bonn, where the Federal Government had taken its seat, Khub Chand found a Solomonic, deeply realist solution. If India were acting according to its commercial interest, which lay with West Germany, it had to open an office in Bonn; but it had to keep the mission in Berlin for possible contacts with the East German authorities. Otherwise, it would be 'dubbed stooges of American imperialism.'[96]

This suggestion, approved by Bajpai,[97] actually was not consistent with non-alignment, as de facto it made India support the Western case against the Soviet Union, which naturally did not see the Federal Government as the only legitimate representation of all Germans. A recognition of the German Democratic Republic (GDR), carved out from the Soviet Occupation Zone, would have ensured return to a neutral position, and, therefore, was favoured for example by Foreign Secretary K.P.S. Menon.[98] Khub Chand, however, successfully pleaded for a wait-and-see strategy. He argued that national interest should be 'our paramount consideration. All the logic and all the loyalty to principles in the world will defeat their own ends if the country goes under. We are deeply interested in financial and technical assistance from the United States; otherwise, we run the risk in 10 or 15 years of an internal revolution fed on hunger and distress. We must not therefore turn Congress and private American businessmen from the task of Indian reconstruction by premature and ill-considered political moves in Europe.'[99] Notwithstanding Khub Chand's well-documented dislike for the United States, realism had won the day. As neither the East German authorities nor Moscow approached India for recognition of the second German state, the window of opportunity when Delhi could have afforded a step most unpopular with its Western trade partners closed. The wait-and-see strategy resulted in the non-recognition of the GDR until October 1972.

Scepticism vis-à-vis the United States

Among the basic attitudes of the ICS and IFS, the most difficult to trace is a certain scepticism regarding the United States. The reason is obvious: with the Americaphobic Krishna Menon and the nearly as critical Nehru, their subordinates' differing viewpoints tended not to surface at critical moments. Indo–US relations, apart from short episodes, were in a rather bad shape during the Nehru years. The dogmatic position of Secretary of State John Foster Dulles that other countries were either friend or foe was intensely disliked in non-aligned countries and vice versa. The exception was during the months of late 1962 and early 1963, when spontaneous American helpfulness at the moment of India's defeat in the border war with China created enormous goodwill in India. Moreover, the visit of President Dwight D. Eisenhower in 1959 for a moment seemed to end the ice age caused by the US – Pakistani military alliance from 1954.[100]

Khub Chand's views as expressed in Berlin could be said to represent in general the attitudes of ICS trained officers. Rather better documented are the views of Foreign Secretary Dutt, who once in a while asked himself whether it was a wise policy to criticise everything that came from Washington whereas Moscow was given the benefit of the doubt. He agreed with Vice-President Radhakrishnan that the continuous criticism of the US had contributed to Washington's close links with Pakistan.[101] As he said: 'I distrust the communists; I distrust their friendly approaches . . . I do not share the view held by quite a few high up in the country, if not the highest, that the US are trying subversive tactics in our country.'[102] As Nehru warmed up to Eisenhower once personal contact was established, Dutt appreciated US ambassadors for their personal integrity and the seriousness with which they tried to improve bilateral relations. He, however, also noticed that given the political environment, they had little hope of success.[103] Beyond doubt, given the fundamental differences between the two countries, Dutt had never suggested a closer cooperation with

Washington as Home Minister Vallabhbhai Patel and obviously Bajpai had in 1950.[104] This was both an outcome of realpolitik and the general Indian dislike for the American approach to international affairs.

Conclusion

It is most difficult to measure the influence of the ICS mind-set on Indian foreign policy for later years. Jagat S. Mehta belonged to the first generation of the IFS, recruited in 1947. Whereas his ideas regarding foreign policy certainly were shaped by Bajpai, whom he served as private secretary,[105] he otherwise did not undergo the typical training of ICS officers. Mehta retired from the IFS in 1980, but one might rather take Kewal Singh from the 1939 batch as the last former ICS officer of influence, holding the rank of foreign secretary between 1972 and 1976. His diplomatic career ended in 1977.

By then, the political environment had changed completely. With Nehru, an era of global visions and ambitions had come to an end. After Dutt's departure from Delhi in spring 1961, it had appeared that with the now unchallenged Krishna Menon ever more strongly influencing foreign affairs, the typical ICS realism had become history. The defeat in the border war with China in late 1962, however, ended both Menon's career together with visions and illusions. The terms of Nehru's successors Lal Bahadur Shastri and, even more, Indira Gandhi are characterised by a deep pragmatism. In a manner of speaking, ICS realism continued to play a key role.

Thereafter, with both the Sino–Soviet split and the declining American interest in South Asia, Moscow became Delhi's preferred partner, as India's negative obsession with the United States grew further. Dutt certainly had been the most profiled anti-communist in the leading ranks of the IFS during the late Nehru years. When he was called back from retirement in early 1972 to represent India as High Commissioner in Bangladesh, there was nothing left of the seemingly extremely deep-rooted attitude. Dutt not only cooperated closely with the Soviet embassy, but he even organised fraternisation, with the staff of both missions visiting each other at an exclusively social level.[106] Among the parties in Bangladesh, the high commissioner considered the communists as the only ones standing for Nehruvian secularism, in his eyes the best option for the hopelessly divided host country.[107]

Dutt was perhaps among the last proselytes. Some of his generation had changed their mind much earlier. In some cases, this had been due to immediate contact. K.P.S. Menon fell in love with the Soviet

Union during his term in Moscow, and the same can be seen with T.N. Kaul after serving in Beijing in the early 1950s. Others found leftist leanings useful. Due to his immense influence on the affairs of the MEA, Krishna Menon made or ended diplomatic careers, and his favourites, apart from never criticising their master, had to demonstrate anti-American and pro-Soviet leanings. Dutt wondered whether 'we [are] approaching a time when to be dubbed pro-American is to ruin a man's career. McCarthyism in reverse?'[108] Loathing Krishna Menon, Dutt counted Arthur S. Lall or M.J. Desai among those. In a neutral assessment, one might say that civil servants over the long run usually adapt to changes, be it career options or a modified political environment. Although the selection of candidates for the Indian Administrative Service until today shows some parallels with the ICS, and officials – not only in India – tend to be pragmatic rather than visionary, the ICS anti-communism had disappeared. The next generation in the IFS formed its worldview in a totally Indian environment.

Notes

1 Amit Das Gupta, *Serving India: A Political Biography of Subimal Dutt*, New Delhi: Manohar, 2017.

2 Amit R. Das Gupta and Lorenz M. Lüthi, *The Sino-Indian War of 1962: New Perspectives*, New Delhi: Routledge, 2017.

3 Amitav Ghosh, *Sea of Poppies*, London: John Murray, 2008.

4 Statement of Prime Minister Smuts at the Imperial Conference of 1923, 18 October 1923, Department for Education, Health and Lands (EHL), March 1924, B-Proceedings no. 4–3 Appendix. National Archives of India (NAI).

5 Application, 45/1915, India Office, Public no. 217, 17 December 1915. Uttar Pradesh State Archives (UPSA).

6 Application, 45/1915, Note, 25 November 1915. UPSA.

7 Neil Bruniat Bonarjee, *Under Two Masters*, London: Oxford University Press, 1970, pp. 140–141.

8 Bajpai to Deputy Secretary E. B. Ewbanks, 10 May 1923, EHL, B-Proceedings no. 35, May 1923. NAI.

9 Note, 24 August 1925, Bajpai, EHL, B-Proceedings no. 68–74, August 1925. NAI.

10 Note, 22 August 1929, A. B. Reid, EHL, February 1930, B-Proceedings no. 94–95. NAI.

11 Note, 12 May 1927, Bajpai, EHL, July 1928, B-Proceedings no. 263–340. NAI.

12 Private telegram from Habibullah to Viceroy Irwin, 7 April 1924, EHL, July 1928, B-Proceedings no. 263–340. NAI.

13 Letter D.O. no. 173-Emi from Deputy Secretary R.B. Ewbank to the Government of Madras, Moore, 20 February 1923, EHL, January 1924, B-Proceedings no. 36–82. NAI.

14 Appointment, 389/1937. Circular no. F.128/37-Ests to all Chief Secretaries of the Provinces, 12 August 1937, Secretary Home Dept. F.H. Puckle. UPSA.

15 Bonarjee, *Under Two Masters*, p. 141.

16 Note, 11 September 1928, Bajpai, EHL, January 1929, B-Proceedings no. 122–127. NAI.

17 Note, 24 March 1931, Bajpai, EHL, August 1931, B-Proceedings no. 2–26. NAI.

18 Note for Member Fazl-i-Husain, 14 March 1931, Bajpai, EHL, August 1931, B-Proceedings no. 2–26. NAI.

19 Note, 25 February 1931, Bajpai, EHL, August 1931, B-Proceedings no. 2–26. NAI.

20 Note for Member Fazl-i-Husain, 7 March 1931, Bajpai, EHL, August 1931, B-Proceedings no. 2–26. NAI.

21 Subimal Dutt Diary 4a, 28 April 1938. Original in Bangla.

22 Secret letter J&P(S) 6487 from J.E. Ferard. Judicial and Public Department, India Office, to S.P. O'Donell, Secretary to the Government of India, Home Department, 22 November 1922. British Library (BL), India Office Records (IOR), L/PJ/12/115.

23 Bajpai to Sir Denys Bray, 13 March 1929, Foreign and Political Department (FP), Establishment, 60(2)-E. NAI.

24 Confidential letter from Bajpai to Sir Denys Bray, 4 March 1929, FP, Establishment, 60(2)-E. NAI.

25 K.P.S. Menon Files. Diary 1929, 5 March 1929. Nehru Memorial Museum Library (NMML).

26 Telegram to the GoI no. Pol. 3947/41, 13 August 1941, W.C. Wallis, India Office. BL, IOR, L/PJ/8/264.

27 K.P.S. Menon Files. Diary 1934, 13 March 1934. NMML.

28 Demi-official letter from Menon to officiating Joint Secretary Ram Chandra, 7 August 1930, EHL, Overseas, 1931, B-Proceedings no. 1–49. NAI.

29 Demi-official letter from Menon to officiating Joint Secretary Ram Chandra, 18 August 1930, EHL, Overseas, 1931, B-Proceedings no. 1–49. NAI.

30 Confidential letter from Menon to Joint Secretary Bajpai, 5 March 1930, EHL, Overseas, March 1930, B-Proceedings no. 19. NAI.

31 Demi-official letter from Menon to officiating Joint Secretary Ram Chandra, 15 September 1930, EHL, Overseas, 1931, B-Proceedings no. 1–49. NAI.

32 Demi-official letter from Menon to Joint Secretary Bajpai, 22 April 1931, EHL, Overseas, 1931, B-Proceedings no. 1–49. NAI.

33 Note, Bajpai, 5 May 1931, EHL, Overseas, 1931, B-Proceedings no. 1–49. NAI.

34 Bajpai for Member Fazl-i-Husain, 15 July 1931, EHL, Overseas, 1931, B-Proceedings no. 1–49. NAI.

35 Demi-official letter from Menon to officiating Joint Secretary Ram Chandra, 9 September 1930, EHL, Overseas, 1931, 29–49. NAI.

36 Half-yearly report for Ceylon for the months from July to December 1930, Menon, 7 January 1931, EHL, Overseas, 1931, 49–52. NAI.

37 Half-yearly report for Ceylon for the months from July to December 1930, Menon, 7 January 1931, EHL, Overseas, 1931, 49–52. NAI.

38 Foreign Secretary Metcalfe to Political Secretary B.J. Glancy, 6 June 1932, Foreign and Political Department, 99-E. NAI.
39 Joint Secretary Ram Chandra to Member Fazl-i-Husain, 22 April 1932, EHL, Overseas, 1932, 256. NAI.
40 K.P.S. Menon Files. Diary 1934, 18 March 1934. NMML.
41 K.P.S. Menon Files. Diary 1934, 25 October 1934. NMML.
42 K.P.S. Menon Files. Diary 1935, 28 August 1935. NMML.
43 K.P.S. Menon Files. Diary 1935, 15 July 1935. NMML.
44 K.P.S. Menon Files. Diary 1935, 13 August 1935. NMML.
45 Note, 7 June 1932, Political Secretary B.J. Glancy, FP, 99-E. NAI.
46 Confidential letter from Foreign Secretary Metcalfe to Bajpai, 16 December 1937, External Affairs Department, 4(74)-E/37.Confdl 1937. NAI.
47 K.P.S. Menon Files. Diary 1938, 9 January 1938. NMML.
48 *Subimal Dutt Diary*, 4a, 8 May 1938. Original in Bangla.
49 Amit Das Gupta, *Serving India: A Political Biography of Subimal Dutt*, New Delhi: Manohar, 2016, p. 45.
50 Letter to Deputy Secretary Dutt, 6 November 1939, Bajpai, *Private Papers Subimal Dutt*.
51 Confidential telegram no. 42 from Thomas to Secretary of State Moyne, 10 May 1941. BL, IOR, L/PJ/8/264.
52 Confidential telegram no. 43 from Thomas to Secretary of State Moyne, 12 May 1941. BL, IOR, L/PJ/8/264.
53 For Dutt's term in Malaya see Das Gupta, *Serving India*, pp. 50–65.
54 Copy of letter no. 1331/41 to the GoI, 20 August 1941, Dutt. BL, IOR, L/PJ/8/264.
55 Important, personal telegram no. 27556 from Linlithgow to Secretary of State for India Amery, 2 November 1941. BL, IOR, L/PJ/8/264.
56 *Subimal Dutt Diary*, 4, 14 August 1941.
57 Diary 1931, 11 May 1931, K.P.S. Menon Papers. NMML.
58 Diary 1932, 22 November 1932, K.P.S. Menon Papers. NMML.
59 Draft letter from Secretary of State for India Amery to A. Hardinge, Secretary to the King, 11 July 1941. BL, IOR, L/PO/196.
60 Letter D.O. no. D.1411–1(c)/41, Foreign Secretary Olaf Caroe to Agent-General Bajpai, 7 October 1941. BL, IOR, L/PS/12/2636.
61 Mission to the U.S.A. of Sir Frederick Puckle, Secretary, Department of Information and Broadcasting, Government of India, and Mr A. H. Joyce, Adviser on Publicity to the Secretary of State for India, p. 8. Centre of South Asian Studies Cambridge (CSAS), Frederick Puckle Papers.
62 Diary 1945, 9 July 1945, K.P.S. Menon Papers. NMML.
63 Private and confidential letter from Viceroy Wavell to Secretary of State for India Frederick Pethick-Lawrence, 5 November 1945. BL, IOR, L/PO/10/22. No. 75.
64 Mission to the U.S.A., p. 6, Frederick Puckle Papers. CSAS.
65 Quarterly report for the months from October to December 1945, Bajpai. BL, IOR, L/P&S/12/4627.
66 Jawaharlal Nehru, *Autobiography*, London: Bodley Head, 1938, pp. 442–445.
67 Nehru to Vijayalakshmi Pandit, 5 December 1946. *Selected Works of Jawaharlal Nehru (SWJN)*, series 2, Vol. 1, p. 135.

68 Letter from Nehru to Chargé d'Affairs of the Indian Embassy Washington G.S. Bajpai, 5 December 1946. *SWJN*, series 2, Vol. 1, p. 549.
69 Dutt, *Autobiography* (unpublished), pp. 86–87.
70 Secret Report of the Secretariat Reorganization Committee, 10 August 1947, MEA, 319-AD/47. NAI.
71 Private letter from Menon to Prime Minister Nehru, 23 September 1947. M.O. Mathai Papers, Correspondence with K.P.S. Menon. NMML.
72 Diary 1947, 4 November 1947, K.P.S. Menon Papers. NMML.
73 Badr-ud-din Tyabji, *Memoirs of an Egoist: Vol. I, 1907 to 1956*, New Delhi: Roli Books, 1988, p. 257.
74 Despatch no. 1198, 30 November 1951, Chipman. Document forwarded by Lorenz Lüthi. Library and Archives Canada, RG25, Vol. 3262.
75 Confidential letter no. 690 to MP Earnest Bevin, 12 September 1947, Chargé d'Affairs Frank K. Roberts. FO 371/66320. National Archives of the United Kingdom (NAUK).
76 Confidential report from the British Embassy in Moscow, No. 690 (213/15/47), 12 September 1947, Chargé d'Affairs Frank K. Roberts.FO, Vol. 371/66320, NAUK.
77 Secret letter to Deputy Secretary Gundevia, 25 October 1948, Rauf. MEAA, 104-SB/48.
78 *Subimal Dutt Diary*, 9, 16 November 1955.
79 Das Gupta, *Serving India*, pp. 172–173.
80 *Subimal Dutt Diary*, 9, 15 October 1955.
81 Sarvepalli Gopal, *Nehru: A Biography*, Vol. 2, Delhi: Oxford University Press, 1979, p. 274. See also Paul M. McGarr, *The Cold War in South Asia: Britain the United States and the Indian Subcontinent, 1945–1965*, Cambridge: Cambridge University Press, 2013, p. 217.
82 Das Gupta, *Serving India*, p. 93.
83 *Subimal Dutt Diary*, 10, 10 November 1956.
84 *Subimal Dutt Diary*, 10, 22 November 1956.
85 Telegram no. 21 to Foreign Secretary Dutt, 3 January 1957, K.P.S. Menon. MEAA, 9/13/56.
86 Secret telegram to Joint Secretary M.A. Husain, 5 December 1956, Rahman. MEAA, 9/13/56.
87 *Subimal Dutt Diary*, 10, 16 November 1956.
88 *Subimal Dutt Diary*, 10, 17 November 1956.
89 Das Gupta, *Serving India*, pp. 195–197.
90 Das Gupta, *Serving India*, pp. 296–297.
91 Dutt, *Autobiography* (unpublished), p. 185.
92 Das Gupta, *Serving India*, pp. 174–175.
93 G. S. Bajpai, 'India and the Balance of Power,' in *Indian Year Book of International Affairs*, Madras: Indian Study Group of International Affairs, 1952, pp. 1–8.
94 Note for Prime Minister Nehru, 18 September 1957, Dutt, SDP, SF 29. NMML.
95 Military Mission Berlin, fortnightly report no. 36, 1 November 1948, Khub Chand. MEA, 9(15)-EUR/47. NAI.
96 Telegram no. IMM/DIP/283 from Khub Chand sent via the High Commission London, 3 August 1949, MEA, 5(42)-EURII/49. NAI.

97 Note, 25 July 1949, Bajpai. MEA, 5(42)-EURII/49. NAI.
98 Note, 12 November 1949, K.P.S. Menon, MEA, 5(115)EUR.II/49. NAI.
99 Secret letter no. IMM/DIP/300 from Khub Chand to Foreign Secretary K.P.S. Menon, 19 October 1949. MEA, 5(115)EUR.II/49. NAI.
100 Denis Kux, *Estranged Democracies: India and the United States, 1941–1991*, New Delhi: Sage, 1993, pp. 164–168.
101 *Subimal Dutt Diary*, 9, 20 February 1957.
102 *Subimal Dutt Diary*, 11, 18 May 1957.
103 Das Gupta, *Serving India*, p. 184.
104 Das Gupta, 'Nehru, Patel and China.'
105 Jagat S. Mehta, *The Tryst Betrayed: Reflections on Diplomacy and Development*, New Delhi: Penguin Books, 2010, p. 32.
106 Bangladesh Diary II, 29 October 1973, Subimal Dutt Papers, NMML.
107 Das Gupta, *Serving India*, pp. 356–357.
108 *Subimal Dutt Diary*, 11, 23 April 1957.

6

INDIA–USSR, 1946–1949

A false start?

Rakesh Ankit*

History-writing on the early years of India-Soviet Union (USSR) relationship remains incomplete, inadequate, and unbalanced seventy
years on. There are two main reasons for this: first, the restricting
prism of the Cold War and second, a limited availability of primary
sources. Until very recently, this meant either participant reminiscences
or celebratory writings or Cold War accounts.[1] Since 2008, important
articles have emerged drawing upon archival research in Russia, India,
and Eastern Europe. However, these ground-breaking contributions
begin from the 'years of late Stalinism' when, according to Andreas
Hilger, 'the Soviet interest in South Asia manifest[ed] itself in its relations with the Communist Party of India (CPI),'[2] instead of the Government of India. Following him, Vojtech Mastny started his account
of the Soviet Union's partnership with India 'from the elusive period
after Stalin's death.'[3] This approach leaves the inter-governmental
exchanges between India and the USSR in the period 1946–1049
largely untouched in the twin beliefs that first, nothing much happened
then, and second, there is not much material to describe and analyse
whatever little happened.[4] This understanding is in striking contrast
to the vast literature on India's relations with America, Britain, and
India's participation at the United Nations (UN) in the same period.[5]
The aim of this chapter, therefore, is to provide the 'pure particular' of
the first years of India–Soviet Union relationship.[6] It does so by examining the Indian and the Russian archives, for both official and private
papers, and supplementing them by relevant British sources. In doing
so, it recovers and reconsiders the first years of the India–Soviet Union
relationship when it was dominated by the internal threat of communism in India, the upcoming institution of the new Commonwealth

and the security imperatives of the Cold War. Taken together, these represent bilateral diplomatic and economic dimensions, issues of international relations propaganda, and, above all, ideological perceptions and predispositions.

Prelude to Moscow: September 1946–August 1947

The question of India, while still a British dominion and when other older dominions like Canada had only recently done so, establishing diplomatic relations with the USSR arose because of Jawaharlal Nehru's 'desire' to do so upon becoming vice-president and member, external affairs, of the interim government on 2 September 1946. This was as much a product of his much-remarked fascination with the Soviet economic system[7] as of India's urgent need for wheat at the time. He also had 'a very suitable person to explore informally possibilities' in this regard: his confidante V. K. Krishna Menon.[8] Educated at the London School of Economics, Menon had worked tirelessly for the India League in Britain since the 1930s, served as Nehru's unofficial spokesman there and revelled in his communist sympathies and friendships.[9] Unsurprisingly, Archibald Wavell, the viceroy, considered Nehru's proposal to have Menon make enquiries from Soviet Foreign Minister Vyacheslav Molotov about getting wheat from Russia an 'embarrassing, ill-advised and ill-timed adventure.'[10] Lord Pethick-Lawrence at the India Office in London wondered, 'how to deal frankly or consistently with [Nehru when] all references to Russia have to be bowdlerised.'[11] Above all, at the foreign office, Ernest Bevin was 'anxious to delay' any such initiative.[12]

Krishna Menon's meeting with Molotov in Paris in September 1946 did not yield any grain owing to the less-than-expected harvest in the USSR, but Menon got Molotov's agreement to his visit to Moscow to discuss opening diplomatic relations. Notwithstanding Nehru's caution otherwise, born out of his awareness of the less-than-total-enthusiasm for Russia in his Congress party,[13] Menon indicated to Molotov 'India's desire to line up in the international field with Russia.' Molotov, in turn, replied that 'Russia will support India in the UN.'[14] Indeed, elements in the Soviet foreign ministry had been emphasising the 'essential' nature of establishing relations with India since July 1945.[15] By the end of October 1946, having reckoned with Nehru's determination to establish direct relations with Moscow, as well as Bevin's displeasure, especially at Nehru's choice of Krishna Menon as the unofficial envoy,[16] British officials at the external affairs department (EAD) in Delhi decided that the next-best thing would be 'to make an official approach to Russia leaving Krishna Menon to go to some other European countries.' Foreign Secretary H. Weightman advised Wavell to send K.P.S. Menon (Indian Civil Service-ICS, 1920) as the official special representative to Moscow, while the 'potentially embarrassing' Krishna Menon could go to Europe though even there, he was to keep clear of Yugoslavia and Poland.[17] Nehru conceded on this point to Wavell,[18] though this decision to send the 'British government servant antagonistic to the Soviets' to Moscow 'depressed' Krishna Menon and left Nehru's sister Vijayalakshmi Pandit 'unhappy.'[19]

The India office was relieved that mandarin Menon was going to Moscow as opposed to mercurial Menon. The foreign office too shared in its view of K.P.S. Menon's 'sound and healthy views,' lack of 'strong political affiliations' and support of 'retaining the British connection' and asked the British embassy in Moscow to help him.[20] Nehru responded by making it clear to K.P.S. Menon that he was not to enter into any policy discussions and was to only fix up technical details about the exchange of diplomatic representatives. Fully aware that there was 'not much love lost' between Moscow and London, Nehru made it clear to Menon that he was not going to be a party to 'British Foreign Policy or the old methods of the British Foreign Office.'[21] As it turned out, K.P.S. Menon did not need to go to Moscow. In early-December 1946, at the UN, Molotov informed Pandit, leading the Indian delegation in New York, that his earlier talk with Krishna Menon had 'covered a wide field' and all that was left was a swift exchange of missions.[22] Nehru now instructed K.P.S. Menon to obtain all the relevant information from Leolyn Dana Wilgress, the Canadian ambassador in Moscow.[23] 'Anxious' for diplomatic relations, Nehru was himself 'eager' to visit Moscow, 'as early as possible – if things go well . . . about the middle of next year [1947] or earlier.'[24]

The official wheels started turning upon the return of the principals to Delhi in the new year of 1947: Wavell and Nehru from London and Vijayalakshmi Pandit and K.P.S. Menon from New York. On 17 February 1947, the external affairs department sought London's approval for an exchange of diplomatic relations with the USSR. K.P.S. Menon, by now consul-general in China, was to pursue the formalities with Soviet Ambassador Petrov there.[25] On 25 February, Petrov signified his government's agreement.[26] In mid-April, relevant press communiqués were issued,[27] and on 22 May, the external affairs department sent Vijayalakshmi Pandit's name to London for approval as India's first ambassador to Moscow. Subsequently, on 5 June, K.P.S. Menon approached Petrov to seek the Kremlin's agreement.[28] It came two weeks later, and on 25 June 1947, King George VI approved Pandit's appointment. It had neither been easy nor straightforward, in fact indirect and rather random, for the Muslim League members in the interim government had made it clear that they did not wish to see an ambassador appointed to Moscow, let alone Nehru's sister.[29] However, earlier neither they nor Wavell and not even key Congressmen like Vallabhbhai Patel and C. Rajagopalachari had liked Nehru's choice of the Muslim lawyer Asaf Ali as India's first ambassador to Washington, principally because of his card-carrying communist wife, Aruna, and now, they were above all equally keen to prevent Krishna Menon from going to Moscow.[30] The Muslim League was also unwilling to accept Nehru's nomination of Akbar Hydari (ICS), another non-Leaguer Muslim like Asaf Ali, as Indian high-commissioner in London though Hydari had Wavell's support.[31] Pandit's name offered a way out. She would go to Moscow and Krishna Menon to London.

Simultaneously, appointments were made to the embassy staff. A.V. Pai (ICS, 1924) was appointed minister-counsellor and T.N. Kaul (ICS, 1937), first secretary.[32] Terence Shone, the UK high commissioner in New Delhi, perceptively remarked that Pandit was 'emotional, sensitive and impatient with delay and regimentation – [qualities] which may not serve her well in Moscow.'[33] Shone's deputy, A.C.B. Symon, assessed Pandit's deputy Pai as 'very well-disposed to us.' T.N. Kaul was an 'unknown quantity' but Symon could not help notice that all three were Brahmins.[34] They were going to be accompanied by a skeletal staff of less than twenty, which would remain so till February 1950.[35] Among the many letters of congratulations on her appointment, Pandit received one from a friend that was especially encouraging. Pearl S. Buck sent her wishes and rather high hopes from America. Calling Moscow 'the most strategic post in the world,' Buck wrote: 'You are the one person who can fill the post . . . Help them to understand us and us to understand them . . . Peace lies in your hands, more than in any others just now.'[36] This was too optimistic for Lord Listowel at the India office, for whom this entire exercise was a 'folly at [a] critical juncture.'[37]

Anyhow, the Indian ambassador's first task in Moscow was going to be the food department's continuing request for wheat. In view of his 'very cordial relations' with Petrov at Nanking, K.P.S. Menon had been dealing with this since early May 1947. He had stressed 'the gravity of the food situation in India' to the Soviet ambassador, while reminding him of India's failed approach in September 1946.[38] Petrov had 'expressed deep concern' and explained that in 1946, the USSR had been affected by 'the worst drought in half century.' The food situation there was still unsatisfactory and Petrov could do no more than 'make enquiries.'[39] In mid-June 1947, Delhi had asked Menon to approach again,[40] and Petrov regretted 'that he had not yet heard from his government [and] it was too soon for Moscow to estimate prospects of next crop and possibilities for export.'[41]

August 1947–January 1948: 'inferiority complex'

Pandit's entourage left New Delhi on 3 August 1947 and reached Moscow three days later via Karachi, Sharjah, Basra, Baghdad, Tehran, and Baku.[42] In its first days, the Indian embassy was run out of six rooms at the hotel Metropole and four at the Grand.[43] On 8 August, Pandit had her first meeting with the Deputy Foreign Minister Andrei Vyshinsky. The cordial conversation centred on the South African government's treatment of Indians there, an emotive issue in India and the theme of Pandit's finest hour at the UN in 1946,[44] and an informal query by Vyshinsky if Nehru could visit Moscow in the near future.[45] This brief and limited first talk shows how, notwithstanding Nehru's desire and Menon's efforts, India–USSR relations at this time were sporadic and symbolic. An instance is the failed request by the food department to secure groundnut seeds from the USSR in April 1947. This particular file had taken a circuitous route illustrative of the-then 'interim' governance in India. From the food department in Delhi, where incidentally Kaul worked then, the note went to the external affairs department and the chancery, which sent it to its counterpart in London. From there it was forwarded to the foreign office, who finally sent it to the British embassy in Moscow, where the matter gathered dust between June and September 1947, when Kaul picked up the thread again![46]

While Pandit waited to present her credentials, her good reception produced 'considerable conjecture,'[47] not least at the British embassy, which noted that Pandit had been allowed to come in her own aircraft, an honour that had previously been accorded only to the American and the British ambassadors, and offered a habitable house immediately while some other delegations, like the Belgians, the Argentines, and the Brazilians, who had arrived before her were still staying in hotels. She surprised the British by expressing a wish to have a joint party on 15 August in her first meeting with Frank Roberts, chargé d'affaires. However, they demurred given the Soviet understanding of Indian independence as 'disguised subordination' and, instead, Roberts invited Pandit and her staff for lunch.[48]

Pandit presented her credentials to Marshal Shevernik and Vyshinsky three days before the transfer of power in India. In her first report to her brother and to Girja Shankar Bajpai, the secretary-general of the external affairs department, she exclaimed 'an inferiority complex' at the 'deep knowledge' that Shevernik and Vyshinsky seemed to possess of India, like when Vyshinsky knew the names and portfolios of the new ministers in India but Pandit did not,[49] and confessed at being 'just a little frightened' in the diplomatic game.[50] Nehru, for whom the USSR remained 'unique', was excited to read his sister's personal impressions while Bajpai had 'never expected otherwise.'[51] As regards wheat, Pandit was given to understand by Vyshinsky that Russia might send some wheat pending their assessment of the year's harvest. Mikhailov in the foreign ministry impressed her with his 'wide and accurate knowledge' of India,[52] but also left her under no illusions that, in international matters, the Kremlin did not make much of the implications of the transfer of power in India.[53] This shadow of the international situation on the bilateral relations was to plague Pandit's tenure throughout: from the partition of British India in 1947, the continuing British involvement in India and Pakistan and the ensuing Kashmir conflict, developments in China in 1948 and Indonesia in 1949, and, finally, the question of India's membership in the new Commonwealth.

Pandit left Moscow on 10 September 1947 to lead the Indian delegation at the UN. To Frank Roberts, it seemed an appropriate time for a 'stock taking' of the Indians. Confirming the 'happy relations' with them, Roberts noted that the Indians had been 'uniformly friendly . . . grateful for assistance but not unduly dependent.' Roberts had been a bit surprised that 'the Soviet authorities had gone out of their way to be helpful to Mrs Pandit' but politically, thus far, 'nothing very important' had happened though Pandit had told Roberts that she wanted to show the Soviets that the 'Indian Embassy was not just a member of the Commonwealth bloc.' The Soviet foreign ministry itself did not seem to regard India as a normal member of the Commonwealth and India was being dealt with by its south-east Asia department. The Soviet Press's treatment of India had been puzzling. While the transfer of power on 14–15 August had passed unnoticed, the trip of the Indian communists S.A. Dange and K.J. Shah, about which the Indian embassy knew nothing, had received much publicity. *Trud* had published an interview of Dange alongside an article, which re-asserted that with 'reactionary governments in Karachi and Delhi, India and Pakistan were yet to achieve real independence.' Dange had

met Andrei Zhdanov (the chief organiser of the Communist information bureau) and Mikhail Suslov (head of the foreign policy department of the Communist party's central committee) on 6 September
and had wide-ranging discussions on the re-organisation of the CPI
post-partition, agitation for land and labour reforms, efforts to eradi-
cate the caste system, and frequent visits of trade union delegations to
the USSR. However, anticipating the displeasure of the independent
Indian government, Zhdanov referred to 'difficulties in having direct
[CPI-CPSU] ties' and advised, 'for the time being, to limit ourselves to
certain "occasions."'[54] Thus, Roberts felt able to conclude optimisti-
cally that 'there is no threat to Anglo-Indian relations.'[55]

In the ambassador's absence, Pai took charge, pursued the supply
of wheat and found that India was at the back of the queue. He had
a talk with Mikhailov and, on 23 September, got a letter from Jacob
Malik, deputy foreign minister, informing him that Moscow would
not be in a position to give any reply until the end of the year. Pai felt
it to be 'an attempt to temporise' as the Soviet government wished to
use their wheat surplus for 'their East European neighbours.' He met
Malik on 29 September but he refused to add anything, leaving Pai
'without hope that we shall get any grain from Russia this year.'[56] Sym-
bolically, on the other hand, there seemed a lot of interest in India. Dr
Hiranmay Ghosal, the cultural relations officer at the Indian embassy,
was enthusiastically approached by Soviet writers on the theme of
Russia–China–India as eastern allies.[57] Moscow also seemed to give
little notice to the burgeoning dispute in Kashmir bar noting the presence of British army officers in both dominions' armies. By November,
it seemed to give little notice to India altogether as trade delegations
from France, Czechoslovakia, Bulgaria, Finland, Poland, and other
neighbouring states were camped there.[58] The presence of the French,
in particular, was for Pai, 'another pointer that the Soviet Government
would like to use [wheat] as a lever for political purpose. This will
make it more difficult for us to get wheat from Russia.'[59] It seemed to
him that the Soviet government wanted to export wheat for either 'US
dollars or Communist goodwill' and as India could not offer either,
there was 'nothing more to be done until the middle of December.'[60]

In early-December, a UK trade delegation arrived and swiftly signed
an exchange agreement on the supply of machinery from UK and export
of wheat from the Soviet Union. Soon, Czechoslovakia got 250,000 tons
of wheat at the rate of $122 per ton alongside a promise of another
additional 200,000 tons before the elections there in May 1948, leaving Pai further 'disappointed.'[61] By now, enquiries were also beginning

to be made about Pandit's return and, more ominously, criticism was starting to emerge on Nehru government's attitude to the repression of the CPI as well as the creation of the new Commonwealth.[62] This was accompanied by the Soviet foreign ministry's posture of 'delay and denial' on grant of entry of visas to Indian nationals, except members of the CPI.[63]

After shouldering her UN duties, Pandit had returned not to Moscow but to Delhi in December 1947. There she told Shone that she had no love for the Soviets after their unhelpful role in India's recent failed bid for a non-permanent seat at the UN Security Council. She was not looking forward to going back to Moscow as neither had she seen Stalin nor had she found it easy to make contacts with Russians. She was 'exasperated' with Soviet bureaucracy, 'disillusioned' with the Soviet state, and wished for close relations with the British embassy in Moscow, but was wary of getting close to the Americans.[64] Upon her return, one of Pandit's first meetings was with the British Ambassador Maurice Peterson. She told him that while Home Minister Vallabhbhai Patel and Governor of West Bengal C. Rajagopalachari were getting uneasy about the CPI, Nehru wanted to neutralise the communists by cultivating the Kremlin, but faced with the ambiguous Soviets and apprehensive of the Americans, her brother was not feeling assured as 1948 began.[65]

January 1948–June 1948: 'disturbing trends'

It was in the second-half of January 1948 that the Indian ambassador sent the first of her doubtful letters to Delhi about the near future of India-Soviet Union relations. Noting the 'recent disturbing indictment against the "reactionary Congress Party,"' she warned Nehru to not bank on Soviet professions of friendship and understanding at the UN because while there may have been 'sympathy to India on Kashmir [the conflict reached the UN in January 1948], [there was] no open condemnation of Pakistan.'[66] In his reply, Nehru acknowledged that India was placed in a difficult situation because it refused 'to line up with any group' but asserted that there was 'no possibility of adopting any other policy.' He asked her to speak frankly to the Russians that it was quite absurd for them to think that India was tied to England. Moreover, India had no wish to be caught up in America's foreign or economic policy but it did not desire to quarrel with the West either. Nehru wanted Moscow to know that he wished to be 'especially friendly' with Russia because it 'represents, in many ways, the future pattern.' But this old admiration was also accompanied by the new annoyance that he felt vis-à-vis the CPI. Nehru would not have cared much for it but he knew that many people in Russia formed their opinions from reports of the Indian communists.[67]

Pandit's replies in end-January and early-February 1948 summed up her woes and wishes alike. The USSR had signed a grain-for-manganese agreement with Sweden, while Pandit was reading from Delhi that India was short of 200,000–300,000 tons in its grain imports for 1948 and anything she could do was welcome.[68] In its exchanges with the Slav bloc, the Indian Embassy was feeling that 'impartiality does not seem to be acceptable any longer.'[69] Her exchanges with the Kremlin were totally 'one-sided' but what was worse was the 'suspicious atmosphere.'[70] She reflected on the warm welcome she had received as the 'UNO heroine': 'I was made to feel I was to be one of them.' But she also noted the Soviet dislike of the ICS men serving in the Indian Embassy, as 'reactionary servants.' She was sad that the Kremlin was 'not convinced of our impartiality' due to the continuing Commonwealth connection but what bothered her, above all, was the sense that there was 'very little one can do here' given that 'contacts [both official and personal] were very difficult.' Exactly six months to the day she had presented her credentials, she wished to be shifted out to Washington, given her 'personal success [and] large number of American friends and admirers.'[71]

What she wrote next also throws an unflattering light on foreign policy making in early independent India and the specific conditions of Indian diplomacy after partition. She claimed that when she went to Moscow she was given 'no instructions at all' as to what she was supposed to do, had 'functioned according to [her] own understanding of Government's foreign policy' and hoped that she 'shall not be brought to task for having said or done something which did not fit in.'[72] She was hurt when she came to know that Stalin had met with the Polish and Romanian trade delegations while she was still waiting.[73] Her disillusionment near complete, she wrote to Nehru's personal assistant M.O. Mathai: 'You cannot imagine what a difficult place Moscow is for anyone but a Slav or an American.'[74] Ironically, Asaf Ali, Nehru's envoy in Washington, was also unhappy at this time and suggested to the Prime Minister to shift him to London, from where Menon could go to Moscow and Pandit could then come to Washington. But Nehru did not want to remove Menon from London, where he was deeply involved in the Commonwealth discussions, and encouraged Pandit to stay on in Moscow, 'our most difficult assignment.'[75]

In March 1948, Pandit reported the 'Soviet desire to make the isolation of the foreign colony in Moscow complete.' Diplomatic privileges were on the decline, outside contacts were reduced, and surveillance was tightened.[76] In a silver lining of sorts, the Soviet press was talking about British attempts to form a 'Muslim League' against the Soviet Union containing Iran, Iraq, Afghanistan, Turkey, and Pakistan – but not India – and Soviet officials came to see the 'Kashmir Story,' India's propaganda production on the conflict, while not a single member of either the UK or the US embassy in Moscow turned up. On internal issues though, first mentions of the 'leftist Nehru under the influence of reactionary Patel' had also appeared.[77] However, it was the Communist victory in Czechoslovakia and the death of Jan Masaryk that 'shocked' Pandit into 'resentment' against the Soviet bloc's 'indifference.' Earlier, no Soviet official had come to express condolence on Gandhi's death, while, Dr Foo, ambassador of China, regularly asked to 'keep in closest contact' and warned against the CPI's activities. Pandit's other illusions against the Soviet Union were breaking too. She was aghast at the 'acute shortage of bread, butter and sugar' and the illicit trade therein.[78] These experiences of hers can be embedded in the general situation of foreign representatives in Moscow at this time, with an almost hostile Soviet policy towards all non-socialist countries, which made engaging with the Soviet diplomacy especially challenging.

At this time, the Indian embassy produced a comprehensive report on its five months of 1947 in Moscow and it makes for pitiable reading. The embassy had no consular or trade section and while it had issued visas to 56 Soviet citizens by now (35 in 1947), the Soviet Foreign Ministry had issued a grand total of one visa to Indians – to R.M. Nanavati, who had experience of trade in Russia from before the Second World War and acquaintance with the Soviet trade commissioner in Calcutta. Pai and Kaul had concluded that with little political communication, no commercial agreements, and no opportunities for 'systematic public relations,' the only way to establish inter-governmental relations were by developing cultural exchanges.[79] Meanwhile, on the key pending issue of wheat, while Belgium, Luxemburg, Poland, Romania, and Switzerland had signed various agreements with Moscow, the Indian embassy was offered ancillary agricultural equipment and protested to about 'repression' of the CPI.[80] On 4 March 1948, Kaul had sought instructions for making a definite offer to the Soviet government as 'mere feelers are not treated seriously' and suggested that the whole question could be explained to Rajeshwar Dayal (ICS,

1933), the new counsellor in succession to Pai, as he was coming to Moscow.[81] In early March 1948, an Egypt-Russian wheat deal took place,[82] and, while Pandit and Pai were trying to contact Mikhailov and Vyshinsky about it 'without success,'[83] the Indian embassy in Cairo furnished the details. Egypt was to supply 38,000 metric tons of cotton in exchange for 216,000 tons of wheat and 19,000 tons of maize.[84] When Pandit finally saw Vyshinsky on 23 March 1948, he had a surprise for her. As she wrote in her personal telegram to Nehru:

> Vishinski tells me that Bhabha [Commerce Minister] personally met Soviet Commercial Counsellor last September when it was agreed that 35000 tons of Russian wheat could be given for same amount of cotton. Since then, no further steps taken by our government.[85]

Nehru immediately asked the commerce department to clarify.[86] It was soon revealed that the food department was as ignorant as the external affairs department,[87] that the Russian trade commissioner had indeed approached the commerce ministry multiple times for a wheat-for-cotton deal in mid-December 1947 and mid-January 1948.[88] Vishnu Sahay, the food secretary, now called for a meeting with the commerce and external affairs departments on whether the threads be picked up in Delhi or be pursued in Moscow.[89] Meanwhile, on 30 March 1948, Pandit was called in for a 'hurried, brief and sudden' interview with Molotov, where she was informed of the 'Soviet willingness to sell immediately to India 50,000 tons of wheat in exchange for tea or shellac or hard currency.'[90] Pandit was surprised at this attitude of 'take it or leave it.'[91] Sending a vivid description of the meeting to her brother, she wrote: 'Talking with Molotov is like a fencing match . . . It is a most difficult and irritating business . . . I always feel as weak as water when I enter the Kremlin.'[92] She was relieved of the fencing match on wheat when, on 2 April, the 'official mind' in Delhi decided to take the next steps with the Soviet embassy there.[93]

By the end of March 1948, the Indian embassy in Moscow had started an *India News* and granted Indian visas to 39 Soviet citizens in the first three months of 1948 for nothing in return.[94] Moreover, like Dange and Shah in August 1947, Suhasini and R.M. Jambhekar – a communist couple from Bombay – were visiting the Soviet Union and again Pandit's embassy 'knew nothing about' them. One silver lining was that Czechoslovakia was keen to sell textile and other machinery for skins and hides. Another was that Molotov acknowledged to Pandit that India 'would have prior claim' for a non-permanent seat at the UN Security Council as the 'proper representative of South-east Asia.' She advised Nehru to have a south-east Asian conference before the UN meet in September and also to think about a trip to Moscow, as Kaul was told that 'visit by PM would [take relations] forward.'[95] The advice was not outrageous for by mid-April, with the arrests of communists in many parts of India and the ban on the CPI in West Bengal, the Soviet attitude was 'stiffening.'[96] This was reflected in the slow response of the Soviet embassy in Delhi to the external affairs department's initiative for the wheat/ tea barter agreement.[97] At least, this time, Pandit was kept informed of the developments, as they took place.[98]

On 30 April 1948, first formal discussions were held in Delhi between Indian and Soviet officials. The latter wanted to buy tea, shellac, and castor oil apart from some groundnut oil and raw jute. In return, they offered 50,000 tons of wheat at a price of $186 per ton. When the Indian officials replied that this price was high, the Soviets said that Russia had sold wheat to Egypt at the same price and the terms offered to India were more advantageous as in return Egypt had sold cotton at a price 25% below its market rate. Indian officials were also wary about this transaction from the political point of view and were concerned 'whether our relations with USSR would be adversely affected, should the deal not materialise by our insistence on a price unacceptable to Moscow [as] generally political motives underlie Russia's trade policy.'[99]

Away from all this, Pandit was attending her first and only May Day parade at the Red Square in 1948. She reported 'tremendous, genuine, spontaneous and personal love for Stalin and enthusiasm for USSR.' She was also able to visit a school, permission for which had come after four months of 'very annoying interminable delay' but when she finally went, she was 'greatly impressed' with the 'free education.'[100] However, she was still waiting for permission to travel in Soviet Central Asian republics, 'while every facility was given to Jambekars [apart from a] long interview with Stalin,' and thus feeling 'properly snubbed.'[101] By now, feted in Moscow, the communists appeared 'definitely hostile and violent' in India and the Nehru government was intensifying its moves against them.[102] This prompted a protest by Mikhailov (now heading the far-east division) and Molochkov (head of protocol), who complained to Pandit against the 'repressive policy against progressive elements in India.'[103] Similarly, the retention of British General Sir Roy Bucher as independent Indian army's commander-in-chief did not go unremarked.[104] This continuing British influence (military, politico-official, economic, and cultural) in independent India remained an issue with the Soviets as late as February 1951, when none other than Stalin himself raised it with the visiting CPI leaders.[105] Earlier, in January 1950 too, he had bluntly asked Pandit's successor, Sarvepalli Radhakrishnan, 'if India was entitled to have her own army without any restriction and if there was a navy.'[106]

Meanwhile, May 1948 saw some serious bargaining in Delhi for the elusive wheat. The original Russian offer of 50,000 tons at $5 per bushel came down first to $3.3 per bushel and eventually to $2.7. At that time, the American price was $2.6 per bushel plus 3–5 cents. But, firstly, American wheat was not available to India and secondly, it would have cost precious dollars. Moreover, India had paid Australia at the same rate in 1947. India's demand for wheat for the period August 1948–August 1949 was around a million tons or 37 million bushels. Australia was giving 20 million bushels, with a possibility of another 5 million. Delhi was thus short by 12 million. Under the international wheat agreement, India was entitled to get 27.5 million at $2 per bushel but 'dollar difficulty' made it imperative to get considerable quantities from elsewhere. To the Food Secretary Vishnu Sahay, it was unlikely that wheat sold outside the international wheat agreement would have been available to India any cheaper. Moreover, as a barter deal, the Soviet offer had no repercussions on other negotiations. It was also desirable because the tea that was being given to the Russians was not subject to any export quotas and they were free to buy it, anyway. Finally, Sahay also considered the fact that this offer had come 'after many approaches by our Embassy in Moscow and our High Commissioner in London also recently approached the Russian Ambassador there on the subject.'[107]

June 1948–August 1948: 'moral defeat'

While all this was going on, Nehru agreed in end-May 1948 to transfer Pandit to Washington acknowledging her feeling that the present situation between the Soviet government and the West made any understanding of Indian aims by the Kremlin impossible and reduced the Indian embassy to an 'observation post.'[108] Bajpai congratulated Pandit on the shift to America, 'a freer field [to the] sphinx-like USSR' but it was not going to be an immediate shift so as to 'avoid offence to Moscow.'[109] By mid-June 1948, the wheat deal, for which Pandit had worked hard, too was on the verge of being inked,[110] and, on

12 July 1948, a tea-wheat barter agreement was signed. Pandit was kept informed throughout to make sure that she was not 'behind' in her talks with Molotov and Vyshinsky.[111] Simultaneously, a battle began among Indians to take credit. Pandit complained to the external affairs department about a report in *India News* (London) claiming that Krishna Menon had negotiated the wheat agreement with the Soviet embassy there. She slammed 'the impression given by Menon that negotiation [between India and the USSR] cannot take place without help' from him.[112] Bajpai concurred that Menon's trouble was his 'expansiveness.'[113] Pandit also protested to Menon directly,[114] who waved the news off as an unofficial expression.[115] Away from this jockeying for credit between them, a spanner in the works was thrown in Delhi by H.L. Khanna (regional food commissioner), which shows the presence of an attitude of suspicion within the Indian bureaucracy towards Moscow. Khanna had returned from a visit to Egypt and called the Egypt–Russian deal as heavily advantageous to Russia as it also included a 'most favoured nation' status clause and warned that 'the Russians will demand from us as well [this] status [and] not only in trade [with] likely long-term repercussions.'[116]

Notwithstanding the breakthrough in wheat, June 1948 was a watershed in India–USSR relations. On 21 June 1948, a day after the Mountbattens left Delhi; Nehru sent a long letter to Pandit setting the Indian case against Moscow. He wanted Pandit to meet Molotov and tell him that while India was 'anxious to develop friendly relations' with the USSR, it would not align in international affairs with the Soviets, 'in the nature of things even apart from our general policy.' But India was 'certainly not lining up with British or Americans.' The cooperation in defence and industry between India and England was due to India's colonial past but, in political and international matters, 'India was completely free to decide what it wanted.' Secondly, Moscow would have to understand that India's internal policy towards the CPI had nothing to do with its foreign relations. The CPI behaved as a 'hostile force' and yet, he had refrained from inflicting a country-wide ban on them. Nehru was disappointed and almost bitter that India's attempts to increase interactions with the USSR had been ignored with scant courtesy. Pandit had not met Stalin while Indian communists Suhasini and R.M. Jambhekar had a long interview. 'What did all this signify? Was it that the USSR wanted to squeeze the Indian Embassy out?' If the Kremlin thought that the CPI was going to capture power in India or even come anywhere near it, 'it was very much mistaken and exceedingly foolish.' Nehru could not understand why Moscow was being so 'gauche' in dealing with a country which intended to remain 'neutral subject to developments.'[117]

Bajpai summoned the Soviet Ambassador K.V. Novikov four days later and repeated that there was not even the 'remotest possibility' of India being influenced by Britain. Special relations with the UK in defence due to old associations did not mean either alliance or subservience. Reminding Novikov of Nehru's desire even as interim prime minister in 1946 for diplomatic relations, Bajpai pointed out that Pandit's appointment was the proof of importance Nehru attached to Moscow. The Kremlin's 'cooling off' was an 'inexplicable contrast' to this. Similar was the Soviet Press' treatment of India as a 'camp follower' when India was supporting Russia on Greece. Internally, except in West Bengal, the communists were not banned anywhere else. In any case, Indian economic policy of state ownership of basic industries was in common with Russian economic plans. In reply, Novikov claimed that no specific request was made by Pandit for an interview with Stalin, pointed out that Indian newspapers were more hostile to the USSR but, crucially, mentioned the possibility of a permanent trade treaty.[118]

Sending a report of the Bajpai–Novikov meeting to Krishna Menon, Nehru wrote to him that the 'time had come to clear the progressive deterioration in Indo-Soviet relations' as people were being antagonised by the condemning Soviet attitude and the rebellious CPI. Nehru was annoyed that 'completely isolated, my sister finds nothing useful to do there . . . She was frustrated and had the sensation of a moral defeat.' He might not 'see eye to eye' with the Soviets on many matters but had a 'great fund of friendship' towards them, which was gradually disappearing because of their attitude 'that no essential change had taken place in India.' This was 'complete nonsense' and he 'resented [it].'[119] This issue of non-meeting with Stalin was becoming a curious episode. When Bajpai asked Pandit whether she 'had ever *specifically* asked to see Stalin,' she replied that she had 'not ever *applied* for an interview' but had mentioned it on a couple of occasions. She was told that 'unless she had something specific to speak about, it was no use asking.'[120] Bajpai's 'inclination' was to treat this 'as equivalent to a polite request.'[121] Robert Andrews in his *A Lamp for India*, a book whose manuscript was read by Pandit, writes that she 'asked repeatedly for a meeting with Stalin.'[122]

Anyhow, as the Indian embassy in Moscow approached its first anniversary, it felt the critical gaze of the 'eastward turned Soviet eye' on the treatment of communists in Bombay, West Bengal, Madras provinces, and Hyderabad state (Telangana).[123] The Soviet foreign ministry continued its policy of 'deliberate delay and denial' in granting visas to Indians, and the only activity of note the Indian Embassy could manage was an 'Indian evening' organised by VOKS (institute of cultural relations with foreign countries).[124] The British embassy prepared its own appraisal of the Indians, which began by noting that the Indian ambassador was 'not sympathetic to Communism at all.' Her second-in-command, Dayal was also considered very friendly to the West. Kaul continued to be another matter though. He was considered 'hostile' but the British Embassy could not ascertain whether this hostility was due to 'national or ideological' reasons. Dr Hiranmay Ghosal, Pandit's interpreter, and his Polish wife were termed 'openly, frankly Communist.'[125] In August 1948, the British high commission in Delhi sent the first intimations to London that there was a likelihood of Pandit's transfer to Washington by year-end.[126] However, as 1948 wound down, rumours began that Pandit was due to change places with Krishna Menon as her leadership of the Indian delegation to the UN had not been regarded favourably by Governor-General Rajagopalachari. These rumours became so persistent that Delhi had to issue a denial.[127]

In the meantime, Pandit had a surprising and significant encounter in Moscow. She was invited to meet the remarkable Alexandra Kollontai on 3 August 1948. Kollontai, twenty-eight years senior to Pandit, was a trail-blazer in the Russian left movement since 1899 and was the first woman ambassador of modern times when she represented the USSR in Norway (1923), Mexico (1926–1927), and Sweden (1930–1945). She had met Pandit on many occasions informally but this meeting was officially arranged and Pandit rightly concluded that Kollontai was 'conveying a message,' perhaps as one woman diplomat to another. Kollontai told Pandit that 'as a friend' she was deeply disappointed to find Nehru at the head of the present 'reactionary' government in India, which was suppressing the communists. She added that when Molotov had returned from San Francisco in 1945, he had spoken admiringly of Pandit's 'courageous fight,' only to be disappointed. Pandit, 'stunned' at this assertion of primary loyalty to ideology as opposed to country, in her turn, reiterated India's non-alignment, termed the CPI a threat to law and order and told Kollontai that 'friendship was a matter of reciprocity [and not] pin-pricks.'[128]

This disappointment was also reflected in her meetings with other diplomats. Frank Roberts, a good friend and observer of Pandit's early enthusiasm, found the Indian Ambassador a 'sadder' woman in

August 1948 than a year before. Sharing with him her conversation with Kollontai, Pandit also expressed unhappiness about her failure to make any headway in trade relations after the promising start of the wheat-for-tea agreement and blamed Krishna Menon for it.[129] Nehru found Kollontai's interview 'most surprising – culmination of many things,'[130] and agreed with his sister that better relations were not 'a one-sided matter.' Writing to Krishna Menon about the 'very short-sighted, impossible, discouraging, bitterly critical and bullying' Soviet attitude, towards which he found it 'impossible to feel friendly,'[131] he hinted at downsizing the seventeen-member Indian embassy. However, on 15 August 1948, despite the consistently 'hostile' attention on persecution of communists, Soviet officials turned up in strength for the Independence Day celebrations. One vice-foreign minister, the head of the south-east Asia division, the deputy chief of protocol, three Red army generals, and the head of VOKS came bearing Stalin's greetings.[132]

August 1948–January 1949: 'great strain'

Pandit left Moscow on 30 August 1948 for Delhi from where, a fortnight later, she left for the UN session in Paris. She would not return until January 1949 – a gap of almost five months.[133] In Paris, she had a long talk with Bajpai. In light of the confidence-building talks that Nehru had with the Americans and the Soviets there, she felt that it would be 'a grave political error' for her to leave Moscow immediately. She wanted to avoid 'a direct change from Moscow to Washington' lest 'it be construed as an unfriendly act.'[134] She made it quite clear though that she could not stay in Moscow beyond March 1949 and wanted to go once a decision was taken on India remaining in the Commonwealth, reasoning that then 'there will be no special antagonism.' Nehru agreed that 'it would be a bad thing for you to leave Moscow at present. I know that this will mean a great strain on you.' Expressing surprise at receiving a personal telegram of greetings from Stalin on his birthday, Nehru felt that it indicated 'friendliness' and was keen that India 'should take advantage of this.'[135]

In her absence, Dayal had taken charge and felt, from early-September, the Soviet anxiety 'to prevent India from going over to West'; notwithstanding their continuing 'concern about failure of CPI to gain mass support.' Moreover, in reports welcomed in India, Dayal wrote that while the annexation of Hyderabad was 'increasingly being understood as a domestic quarrel,' and on Kashmir, the Soviet 'wait and watch policy' was beginning to 'tilt towards India given the presence of British officers in Pakistan army as well as rumours of a British Arab League.'[136] To Dayal, trade relations were the big 'hope' as the USSR was interested in not just tea but jute too, and he recommended that in view of the proposed trade treaty with America, he should be allowed to revive similar talks in Moscow.[137] By early-October, Dayal detected 'a slow loosening up of the Soviet attitude.' India's interventions on disarmament at the UN were getting 'prominent and favourable notice.'[138] Probably the frank talks with Novikov were finally beginning to produce an effect or perhaps the Soviets wanted to go slow on India while the question of its relations with the Commonwealth was 'on the tapis.' Maybe they had begun to realise the futility of alienating possible friends. Whatever the reasons, it seemed to Dayal that things were beginning to look 'somewhat easier.'[139]

In the last week of October it was reported that Uday Shankar, the Indian classical dancer, was being invited for the fiftieth anniversary of the Moscow Art Theatre, Mulk Raj Anand would be hosted by the Writers' Union,[140] and the VOKS was showing interest in articles by Indian progressive writers.[141] Mikhailov told Dayal that Nehru's speech at the UN as well as his meetings with Vyshinsky on the sidelines had covered 'everything' and impressed the Soviets that it was possible to work with him;[142] so much so that there was no adverse comment on Nehru's participation in the Commonwealth prime ministers' conference.[143] Over November–December 1948, Dayal continued to affirm 'a slight softening of the Soviet attitude.'[144] Uday Shankar was given an enthusiastic reception at the VOKS on 3 November, Mulk Raj Anand's trip stretched to three successful weeks,[145] and the Soviet press appeared sympathetic to India on Kashmir. In December 1948, India continued to escape 'any embarrassing attention.'[146]

The only remaining fly in the ointment seemed India's relationship with the Commonwealth, and Mikhailov did not mince any words in expressing the 'clear and unequivocal Russian attitude that anything short of an independent republic with a single nationality will detract from India's sovereign and independent status' and would be considered 'unnatural.'[147] The Commonwealth conundrum would continue to complicate the differences between Indian and Soviet interpretations of non-alignment/neutrality and impact their bilateral relations. In January 1950, when Radhakrishnan asserted to Stalin that 'India's policy of neutrality was real and positive, and in Colombo [in spring 1949], Nehru had reaffirmed India's anxiety to avoid cold war tactics and anti-communist pacts,' Stalin replied that 'he did not hear about it'![148]

January 1949–April 1949: 'carrot and stick'

In January 1949, however, India's leading role in rallying Asia against the Dutch action in Indonesia brought adverse reactions in Moscow. Although agreeing with the Indian position, the Kremlin was not prepared to play 'second fiddle' to an Asian organisation emerging from the Delhi conference on Indonesia.[149] Dayal wrote, 'Living in a state of prolonged encirclement-psychosis, the Soviets have promptly read an ulterior motive into India's Asian Conference.'[150] Despite this overt critical focus on Indonesia, Dayal also discerned a growing and supportive if covert interest in Kashmir, where the fifteen months–long India-Pakistan war ended at this time, which the Soviets were increasingly referring to as a 'meeting point of five frontiers.'[151] Twice in 1948 they had voiced criticism of the composition of the UN commission on Kashmir; and in 1949 they would condemn the selection of the UN representative on it.[152] On 13 January 1949, he sent a long note on the Soviet policy towards India, in which, notwithstanding their differences on the CPI and the Commonwealth, Dayal remembered that in September 1947 Moscow had listed India, alongside Egypt and Syria, as sympathetic to the USSR. Arguing that there would be no support from the Anglo-Americans for India's 'middle of the road policy,' Dayal recommended a policy of 'positive neutrality' towards Soviet Russia.[153]

When Pandit returned to her desk in February, she too felt a 'carrot and stick' policy towards India with the Kremlin being alternatively 'impressed at India's growing influence in Asia' and 'chagrined that India [was] keeping the Soviets at arm's length'[154] internationally and 'repressing the Communists'[155] internally. She had got a taste of this in her last substantial meeting with Molotov on 10 February 1949. The Soviet foreign minister had opened the meeting with caustic remarks on the Delhi conference on Indonesia claiming that 'we were not invited; nor, unfortunately, have we received any information about it.' Pandit expressed surprise, pointed that the Soviet press had a good deal of news on it and averred that there was no question of bypassing USSR at what was essentially a 'regional conference.' Molotov then criticised Nehru for inviting the Philippine delegate Carlos Romulo – 'for whom the Soviet does not have the slightest respect.' Then, he reasserted the Soviet Union's anti-colonial credentials by reminding Pandit that 'even at San Francisco [1945], I had the privilege of speaking for India, which had not then attained her freedom.' Pandit replied that India had always appreciated the Soviet stand on this question and had openly expressed gratitude more than once for his San Francisco speech. Molotov ended the meeting by revealing the Kremlin's growing interest in India, albeit with qualifications:

> India and the USSR can and must come closer together even [without] a common ideology. We have adopted a positive policy toward India and I would like you to [reciprocate]. All that is required is respect for each other as sovereign states, non-interference in each other's national policies and a consistent international policy.[156]

This increased governmental attention was matched by a prominence in the Soviet press and, by early-March, Dayal felt that 'the wind blowing against India has dropped.'[157] Meanwhile, on 19 February 1949, Pandit had read from her brother that she was to go to America in late-April.[158] India was 'turning a big corner,' and he wished 'to build up our publicity in America.'[159] It was another month before agreement came from Washington to her appointment and she was allowed to formally inform the Soviet foreign ministry.[160] Pandit's last days in Moscow were rather quiet. They coincided with the creation of the NATO, which brought 'a gradual paling of the brown-out on India . . . a respite in Soviet cavilling at India.'[161]

Coda

The first Indian ambassador to the Soviet Union left Moscow for the last time on 1 April 1949 without seeing any senior member of the Soviet government.[162] Kaul also left with her and Dayal was left in Moscow without an Ambassador as well as a first secretary for five months. Radhakrishnan's name as Pandit's successor was announced in July, and Dayal advised him as well as Foreign Secretary K.P.S. Menon that Radhakrishnan should come to Moscow before the UNESCO meeting, present his credentials, and then go to Paris else it would create a bad first impression.[163] Radhakrishnan wanted to go to Paris first but was prevailed upon and eventually reached Moscow on 2 September 1949. He met Vyshinsky on the 7th, presented his credentials two days later and left for Paris on 12 September. In their meeting, Radhakrishnan assured Vyshinsky that India and the USSR had 'identical foundations' in their external politics. Vyshinsky agreed but argued that for the USSR, internal and external politics were identical, whereas India saw no contradiction in siding with the communists internationally and suppressing them

179

internally. Radhakrishnan responded to this by emphasising another shared goal between the two countries, namely creating equal economic opportunity for everyone. Finally, Radhakrishnan made a request for a 'visit to Stalin,'[164] which was granted in January 1950. Three months later, meeting Vyshinsky again on 20 December, Radhakrishnan was re-emphasising non-alignment by pointing out that there could be no better evidence of this than Nehru's US visit during which he 'was not lured' to do any pact. An unconvinced Vyshinsky asked, if so, then why did India not find it possible to come closer to the USSR? Why did it put itself under the 'constraints' of the Commonwealth? Radhakrishnan argued that in continuing to hold this impression, Vyshinsky was ignoring the continuing British departure from India.[165]

Soviet interest in India continued to grow, reflecting a wider change in the Kremlin's endeavours with regard to worldwide anti-colonial peace movements, economic relations, and cultural contacts from this time. Events in China in October, Nehru's trip to America in November, and India's mediatory conduct during the Korean War especially rejuvenated the Soviet interest in India. Stalin would approvingly tell the visiting CPI leaders in February 1951 that 'in its deeds the Nehru government plays off England and America.'[166] On Kashmir, by now, it was clear to Dayal that contrary to appearances, the Soviets were 'greatly interested.' He summed up their position in a prescient formula: 'they would dislike most Kashmir's accession to Pakistan . . . they would like best an independent Kashmir.'[167]

How right he was can be seen from a note prepared by Mikhailov on the 'present position in Kashmir' on 23 May 1949. In it, Mikhailov analysed the Anglo-American strategy on Kashmir through war (British presence in Pakistani army and civil service) and diplomacy (appointment of an American plebiscite administrator) and weighed on the idea of an independent state of Kashmir. He also noted that this strategy suited Pakistan's 'dissatisfaction' with India on Kashmir, Hyderabad, and other post-partition matters.[168] The report pointedly noted that unlike Indian Kashmir, Azad Kashmir was looked after by the British governor of Pakistan's North-West Frontier Province, mentioned the visit of Loy Henderson, the American ambassador in India, whom Mikhailov called the 'well-known master of intrigue,' to Kashmir on 11 May, and argued that the division of Kashmir between India and Pakistan was an important part of the British strategy on this regional border of the USSR. Secondly, the United States had already 'penetrated' in Kashmir through the UN commission and its military observers. The report claimed that this was an Anglo-American plot that looked at the Kashmir conflict through a 'big lens' and a division of Kashmir guaranteed their interests by securing Gilgit, in the north of Kashmir, where military units could be based. The report ended by emphasising that the UK–US interest in Kashmir had deepened after the communist success in China and the political activities of the socialist bloc in south-east Asia. The scene was set for the subsequent Soviet support to India on Kashmir.

On the Commonwealth, which it considered 'old empire in new guise,' the Kremlin certainly 'pre-judged' the issue. In 1950, Stalin bluntly asked Radhakrishnan, 'if [India] was more or less independent than, say, Canada.'[169] Delhi would have to work hard to regain its 'formerly somewhat distinctive status' and it did so by its conduct during the Korean War. Thus, in 1951, Stalin was telling the visiting CPI leaders that he 'cannot consider the government of Nehru as a puppet.'[170] The other inexorable delinquency on the part of India was to 'organise labour according to production' instead of vice-versa.[171] Dayal was told of a Russian proverb that summed up Kremlin's view of India in May 1949: 'when the devil is ill, he becomes a monk.'[172] Developments here would take longer and need Nehru's and Khrushchev's trips to each other's countries in 1955.

Notes

* I am grateful to Professor Madhavan Palat for his encouragement, support, and this opportunity. Professor Ian Talbot read the first draft, supervised the subsequent ones, and has been a pillar of strength. Many thanks to him, as ever. My special thanks to Professor Vijay Singh for the many conversations, comments, and suggestions.

1 For examples, see K.P.S. Menon, *The Flying Troika*, London: Oxford University Press, 1963; T. N. Kaul, *Stalin to Gorbachev and Beyond*, Delhi: Lancer, 1990; S. R. Sharma, *India-USSR Relations, 1947–1971*, Delhi: Discovery, 1999; J. Bakshi, *Russia and India: From Ideology to Geopolitics, 1947–1998*, Delhi: Dev, 1999; R. C. Horn, *Soviet-Indian Relations: Issues and Influence*, New York: Praeger, 1982; P.J.S. Duncan, *The Soviet Union and India*, London: Routledge, 1989; R. E. Kanet, *The Soviet Union, Eastern Europe and the Third World*, Cambridge: Cambridge University Press, 1987; E. A. Kolodziej and R. E. Kanet (eds), *The Limits of Soviet Power in the Developing World*, London: Macmillan, 1989; R. Thakur, 'India and the Soviet Union: Conjunctions and Disjunctions of Interests,' *Asian Survey*, 1991, 31(9): 826–846; R. Thakur and C. A. Thayer, *Soviet Relations with India and Vietnam, 1945–1992*, New York: St. Martin's Press, 1992.

2 Hilger, Andreas, 'The Soviet Union and India: The Years of Late Stalinism,' *Parallel History Project on Cooperative Security (PHP)*, September 2008, www.php.isn.ethz.ch (accessed on 8 December 2016), pp. 1–2.

3 Vojtech Mastny, 'The Soviet Union's Partnership with India,' *Journal of Cold War Studies*, 2010, 12(3): 50–90, p. 52.

4 An exception being Surendra Gupta, 'Stalin and India: 1946–47: From Cooperation to Hostility,' *Australian Journal of Politics and History*, 1987, 33(1): 78–92; also see Surendra Gupta, *Stalin's Policy towards India, 1946–1953*, New Delhi: South Asian Publishers, 1988.

5 For examples, see Manu Bhagavan, *The Peacemakers*, New Delhi: HarperCollins, 2012; Paul McGarr, *The Cold War in South Asia*, Cambridge: Cambridge University Press, 2013; Rudra Chaudhuri, *Forged in Crisis*, London: Hurst, 2013.

6 Paul Schroeder, 'History and International Relations Theory: Not Use or Abuse, but Fit or Misfit,' *International Security*, 1997, 22(1): 65.

7 Ramachandra Guha, *India after Gandhi*, London: Macmillan, 2007, pp. 161–162; Michael Brecher, *Nehru: A Political Biography*, Oxford: Oxford University Press, 1959, pp. 586–587; Judith Brown, *Nehru: A Political Life*, New Haven: Yale University Press, pp. 259–260.

8 21 November 1946, Nehru to Wavell, Correspondence File, M. O. Mathai Papers, Nehru Memorial Museum and Library (NMML), New Delhi.

9 Paul McGarr, 'A Serious Menace to Security: British Intelligence, VK Krishna Menon and the Indian High-Commission in London, 1947–52,' *The Journal of Imperial and Commonwealth History*, 2010, 38(3): 441–469.

10 Wavell-Pethick Lawrence exchange, Item Nos. 357 and 500, Nicolas Mansergh and Penderel Moon (eds), *The Transfer of Power 1942–7*, Vol. 8, London: HMSO, 1970–82, *TOP*.

11 14 October 1946, Anderson to Turnbull, Item No. 446, Volume VIII, *TOP*.

12 28 September 1946, Bevin to Roberts, Item No. 378, Volume VIII, *TOP*.

13 5 May 1946, Nehru to Menon, Correspondence File, Mathai Papers, NMML.

14 11 October 1946, Pethick-Lawrence to Wavell, Item No. 431, Volume VIII, *TOP*.

15 28 July 1945, Dimitrov to Molotov, Fond 82, Opis 2, No. 1196, V. M. Molotov Papers, the Russian State Archive of Socio-Political History (RGASPI), Moscow.

16 Paul McGarr, '"India's Rasputin"?: VK Krishna Menon and Anglo-American Misperceptions of Indian Foreign Policymaking, 1947–1964,' *Diplomacy & Statecraft*, 2011, 22(2): 239–260.

17 30 October 1946, File No. 1-EUR/47 (MEA & CR), National Archives of India (NAI), New Delhi.

18 21 November 1946, Nehru to Wavell, Correspondence File, Mathai Papers, NMML, 28 November 1946, Item No. 109, Volume IX, *TOP*.

19 29 November 1946, Pandit to Nehru, Subject File Serial No. 47, Vijayalakshmi Pandit Papers (I Installment), NMML.

20 5 December 1946, FO to Moscow, T. No. 3940, L/P&S/12/4639A, India Office Records (IOR), the British Library, London.

21 5 December 1946, Nehru to KPS Menon, Correspondences File, Mathai Papers, NMML.

22 6 December 1946, Pandit to Nehru, GA-57, L/P&S/12/4639A, IOR.

23 8 December 1946, Menon to Nehru and 11 December 1946, GOI to New York, L/P&S/12/4639A, IOR.

24 5 December 1946, Nehru to Pandit, Correspondence File, Mathai Papers, NMML.

25 17 February 1947, GOI to India Office, L/P&S/12/4639A, IOR.

26 10 April 1947, GOI to India Office, L/P&S/12/4639A, IOR.

27 15 April 1947, Moscow to FO, T. No. 935, 26 April 1947, Cabinet Office to New Delhi and 25 April 1947, Shone to CRO, T. No. 35, L/P&S/12/4639A, IOR.

28 4 June 1947, Nanking to FO, T. No. 570, L/P&S/12/4639A, IOR.

29 Philip Ziegler, *Mountbatten: The Official Biography*, London: Collins, 1985, p. 395; Penderel Moon (ed) *Wavell: Viceroy's Journal*, Oxford: Oxford University Press, 1973; Vijayalakshmi Pandit, *The Scope of Happiness: A Memoir*, New York: Crown, 1979, p. 227.

30 14 February 1948, Patel to Mountbatten MB1/D50 (Folder 2), Louis Mountbatten Papers, Special Collections, Hartley Library, University of Southampton.

31 3, 6 and 15 January 1947, Wavell-Pethick-Lawrence Correspondence, L/PO/8/43 and 12 and 26 February 1947, Wavell to Pethick-Lawrence, L/PO/10/24, IOR.

32 Files 37 (5)-E.II/47 and 37 (3)-E.II/47, NAI.

33 2 July 1947, Shone to CRO, T. No. 65, L/P&S/12/4639A, IOR.

34 9 July 1947, Symon to CRO, T. No. 72, L/P&S/12/4639A, IOR.

35 File No. 3 (16)-FSP/49 (MEA), NAI.

36 7 July 1947, Pearl S. Buck to Pandit, Correspondence File, Mathai Papers, NMML.

37 14 July 1947, Cabinet Memorandum, Item No. 106, Volume XII, *TOP*.

38 10 May 1947, EAD to Menon, T. No. 72, File No. 27 (12)-Eur/47, NAI.

39 13 May 1947, Menon to EAD, T. No. 130, File No. 27 (12)-Eur/47, NAI.

40 18 June 1947, EAD to Menon, T. No. 110, File No. 27 (12)-Eur/47, NAI.

41 19 June 1947, Menon to EAD, T. No. 183, File No. 27 (12)-Eur/47, NAI.

42 11 August 1947, Pandit to Nehru, File No. 20 (9)-Eur (Part I), (MEA & CR), NAI.

43 3 October 1947, Fortnightly Report from Moscow, File No. 20 (9)-Eur (Part I), (MEA & CR), NAI.

44 See Bhagavan, *The Peacemakers*; for a critical take, see Rakesh Ankit, 'In the Twilight of Empire: Two Impressions of Britain and India at the United Nations (UN), 1945–1947,' *South Asia: Journal of South Asian Studies*, 2015, 38(4): 574–588.

45 8 August 1947, Pandit to Bajpai, File No. 20 (9)-Eur (Part I), (MEA & CR), NAI.

46 16 September 1947, Kaul to EAD, File No. 27(11)-Eur/47, NAI.

47 27 February 1948, Quarterly Report for August–December 1947, File No. 20 (9)-Eur (Part I), NAI.

48 22 August 1947, Fortnightly Report from Moscow, File No. 20 (9)-Eur (Part I), NAI.

49 22 August 1947, Fortnightly Report from Moscow, File No. 20 (9)-Eur (Part I), MEA & CR, NAI.

50 13 August 1947, Pandit to Nehru, Correspondences File, Mathai Papers, NMML.
51 26 August 1947, Nehru to Pandit, Correspondences File, Mathai Papers, NMML, 23 August 1947, Bajpai to Pandit, Subject File Serial No. 56, Pandit Papers (I Installment), NMML.
52 18 August 1947, Pandit to Nehru, Subject File Serial No. 53, Pandit Papers (I Installment), NMML.
53 31 August 1947, Pandit to Nehru, Subject File Serial No. 53, Pandit Papers (I Installment), NMML.
54 6 September 1947, Notes of the Discussion of Zhdanov with Dange, Fond 17, Opis 128, No. 1127, http://digitalarchive.wilsoncenter.org/document/119260 (accessed on 8 December 2016).
55 12 September 1947, Roberts to Bevin, T. No. 690 (213/15/47), L/P&S/12/4639A, IOR.
56 30 September 1947, Pai to Bajpai, File No. 27 (12)-Eur/47 (EAD), NAI.
57 30 September 1947, Fortnightly Report from Moscow, File No. 20 (9)-Eur (Part I), NAI.
58 16 October, 8 and 16 November 1947, Pai to Bajpai, File No. 20 (9)-Eur (Part I), NAI.
59 16 October 1947, Pai to Bajpai, File No. 27 (12)-Eur/47 (EAD), NAI.
60 27 October 1947, Pai to Menon, File No. 27 (12)-Eur/47 (EAD), NAI.
61 27 October 1947, Pai to Bajpai and 8 December 1947, Pai to Delhi, File No. 27 (12)-Eur/47 (EAD), NAI.
62 1 and 8 December 1947, Fortnightly Reports from Moscow, File No. 20 (9)-Eur (Part I), NAI.
63 19 December 1947, File No. 20 (9)-Eur (Part I), NAI.
64 30 December 1947, Shone to CRO, L/P&S/12/4639A, IOR.
65 6 January 1948, Peterson to Attlee, 21/1/48, No. 13, L/P&S/12/4639A, IOR.
66 19 January 1948, Pandit to Nehru, Subject File Serial No. 53, Pandit Papers (I Installment), NMML.
67 23 January 1948, Nehru to Pandit, Subject File Serial No. 54, Pandit Papers (I Installment), NMML.
68 12 January 1948, Sahay to Menon and 22 January 1948, Menon to Pai, File No. 27 (12)-Eur/47 (EAD), NAI.
69 24 January and 6 February 1948, File No. 20 (9)-Eur (Part I), MEA & CR, NAI.
70 17 February 1948, Fortnightly Report from Moscow, File No. 20 (9)-Eur (Part I), MEA & CR, NAI.
71 11 February 1948, Pandit to Nehru, Subject File Serial No. 57, Pandit Papers (I Installment), NMML.
72 5 February 1948, Pandit to Bajpai, Subject File Serial No. 55, Pandit Papers (I Installment), NMML.
73 12 February 1948, Pandit to Nehru, Subject File Serial No. 57, Pandit Papers (I Installment), NMML.
74 26 February 1948, Pandit to Mathai, Correspondences File, Mathai Papers, NMML.
75 21 February 1948, Nehru to Pandit, Subject File Serial No. 54, Pandit Papers (I Installment), NMML.

76 4 March 1948, File No. 20 (9)-Eur (Part I), NAI.

77 2 March 1948, File No. 20 (9)-Eur (Part I), NAI.

78 14 March 1948, Pandit to Nehru, File No. 20 (9)-Eur (Part I), NAI.

79 27 February 1948, Quarterly Report, File No. 20 (9)-Eur (Part I), NAI.

80 16 and 19 March 1948, File No. 20 (9)-Eur (Part I), NAI.

81 4 March 1948, File No. 27 (12)-Eur/47 (EAD), NAI.

82 6 March, Abhyankar to Menon and 11 March, EAD to Moscow, T. No. 2225, File No. 27 (12)-Eur/47 (EAD), NAI.

83 15 March 1948, Moscow to EAD, T. No. 223, File No. 27 (12)-Eur/47 (EAD), NAI.

84 16 March 1948, Cairo to EAD, File No. 27 (12)-Eur/47 (EAD), NAI.

85 23 March 1948, Pandit to Nehru, T. No. 247, File No. 27 (12)-Eur/47 (EAD), NAI.

86 23 and 24 March 1948, Iengar to CC Desai, File No. 27 (12)-Eur/47 (EAD), NAI.

87 29 March 1948, Bajpai's note and 30 March 1948, Sahay's note, File No. 27 (12)-Eur/47 (EAD), NAI.

88 9 April 1948, Desai's Note (Chettur's Note, 6 April, DO 191-Secy/48), File No. 27 (12)-Eur/47 (EAD), NAI.

89 30 March 1948, Sahay's Note, File No. 27 (12)-Eur/47 (EAD), NAI.

90 30 March 1948, Pandit to Nehru, T. No. 262, File No. 27 (12)-Eur/47 (EAD), NAI.

91 30 March 1948, Pandit to Nehru, Subject File Serial No. 57, Pandit Papers (I Installment), NMML.

92 15 April 1948, Pandit to Nehru, Subject File Serial No. 57, Pandit Papers (I Installment), NMML.

93 2 April 1948, File No. 27 (12)-Eur/47 (EAD), NAI.

94 Quarterly report for 1 January–31 March 1948, File No. 20 (9)-Eur (Part II), NAI.

95 30 March and 15 April 1948, Pandit to Nehru, File No. 20 (9)-Eur (Part I), NAI.

96 20 April 1948, File No. 20 (9)-Eur (Part I), NAI.

97 19 April 1948, Mone (Food) to Menon (EAD) and 23 April 1948, Rahman (EAD) to Erzin, File No. 27 (12)-Eur/47 (EAD), NAI.

98 22 and 26 April 1948, Menon and Rahman to Kaul, File No. 27 (12)-Eur/47 (EAD), NAI.

99 1 May 1948, File No. 27 (12)-Eur/47 (EAD), NAI.

100 3 May 1948, Pandit to Nehru, Subject File Serial No. 57, Pandit Papers (I Installment), NMML.

101 20 May 1948, Pandit to Nehru, File No. 20 (9)-Eur (Part I), NAI.

102 5 May 1948, Nehru to Pandit, Subject File Serial No. 54, Pandit Papers (I Installment), NMML.

103 31 May 1948, Pandit to Nehru, File No. 20 (9)-Eur (Part I) and 4 June 1948, File No. 20 (9)-Eur (Part II), NAI.

104 6 May 1948, File No. 20 (9)-Eur (Part II), NAI.

105 9 February 1951, Record of the Discussions of J. V. Stalin with Comrades Rao, Dange, Ghosh and Punnaiah, www.revolutionarydemocracy. org/rdv12n2/cpi2.htm (accessed on 8 December 2016).

106 15 January 1950, Record of the Conversation between J. V. Stalin and S. Radhakrishnan, http://digitalarchive.wilsoncenter.org/document/119261 (accessed on 8 December 2016).

107 31 May 1948, Vishnu Sahay's Note, File No. 27 (12)-Eur/47 (EAD), NAI.

108 29 May 1948, Pandit to Nehru, No. 239, Subject File Serial No 28 (XV), Mathai Papers, NMML.

109 3 July 1948, Bajpai to Pandit, No 466-PASG/48, Subject File Serial No. 56, Pandit Papers (I Installment), NMML, 29 June 1948, Nye to Carter, L/P&S/12/4639B, IOR.

110 15 June 1948, File No. 27 (12)-Eur/47 (EAD), NAI.

111 21 June and 14 July 1948, Rahman to Kaul, File No. 27 (12)-Eur/47 (EAD), NAI.

112 10 July 1948, Pandit to Bajpai, Subject File Serial No. 55, Pandit Papers (I Installment), NMML.

113 22 July 1948, Bajpai to Pandit, 501-PASG/48, Subject File Serial No. 56, Pandit Papers (I Installment), NMML.

114 15 June 1948, Pandit to Menon, T. No. 341, Subject File Serial No. 10, Pandit Papers (II Installment), NMML.

115 17 June 1948, Menon to Pandit, T. No. 7023, File No. 27 (12)-Eur/47 (EAD), NAI.

116 File No. 27 (12)-Eur/47 (EAD), NAI.

117 21 June 1948, Nehru to Pandit, 885-PM, Subject File Serial No. 54, Pandit Papers (I Installment), NMML.

118 25 June 1948, Bajpai-Novikov Meeting (Sent to Pandit on 27 June 1948, No. 450-PASG/48, Subject File Serial No. 56, Pandit Papers (I Installment), NMML.

119 26 June 1948, Nehru to Menon, 903-PM, Subject File Serial No. 54, Pandit Papers (I Installment), NMML.

120 10 July 1948, Pandit to Bajpai, Subject File Serial No. 55, Pandit Papers (I Installment), NMML.

121 22 July 1948, Bajpai to Pandit, 501-PASG/48, Subject File Serial No. 56, Pandit Papers (I Installment), NMML.

122 R. H. Andrews, *A Lamp for India: The Story of Madame Pandit*, London: Arthur Barker, 1967, p. 253.

123 17 and 30 June, 23 July and 5 August 1948, File No. 20 (9)-Eur (Part II), NAI.

124 Quarterly Report for 1 April–30 June 1948, File No. 20 (9)-Eur (Part II), NAI.

125 6 July 1948, Moscow to FO, L/P&S/12/4639B, IOR.

126 3 August 1948, New Delhi to CRO, 48/C&D/19, L/P&S/12/4639B, IOR.

127 30 December 1948, New Delhi to CRO, 48/C&D/19, L/P&S/12/4639B, IOR.

128 5 August 1948, Pandit to Menon (Delhi), Subject File Serial No. 9, Pandit Papers (II Installment), NMML.

129 9 August 1948, Roberts-Pandit talk, L/P&S/12/4639B, IOR.

130 19 August 1948, Nehru to Pandit, Subject File Serial No. 54, Pandit Papers (I Installment).

131 19 August 1948, Nehru to Krishna Menon, Subject File Serial No. 54, Pandit Papers (I Installment), NMML.

132 20 August 1948, File No. 20 (9)-Eur (Part II), NAI.

133 Pandit, *The Scope of Happiness*, p. 248.
134 8 November 1948, Pandit (Paris) to Nehru, Correspondences File, Mathai Papers, NMML.
135 17 November 1948, Nehru (Cairo) to Pandit, Correspondences File, Mathai Papers, NMML.
136 6 September 1948, File No. 20 (9)-Eur (Part II), NAI.
137 24 September 1948, File No. 20 (9)-Eur (Part II), NAI.
138 7 October 1948, File No. 20 (9)-Eur (Part II), NAI.
139 21 October 1948, Dayal to K.P.S. Menon, Subject File Serial No. 3, Pandit Papers (II Installment), NMML.
140 23 October 1948, File No. 20 (9)-Eur (Part II), NAI.
141 27 October 1948, File No. 20 (9)-Eur (Part II), NAI.
142 9 November 1948, Pandit (Paris) to Dayal and 11 November 1948, Dayal to K.P.S. Menon, Subject File Serial No. 3, Pandit Papers (II Installment), NMML.
143 5 November 1948, File No. 20 (9)-Eur (Part II), NAI.
144 11 November 1948, Dayal to K.P.S. Menon, Subject File Serial No. 3, Pandit Papers (II Installment), NMML.
145 15 November 1948, File No. 20 (9)-Eur (Part II), NAI.
146 Fortnightly Report from Moscow for the Period Ending 31 December 1948, File No. 35-R&I (1949), NAI.
147 6 December 1948, Dayal to K.P.S. Menon, Subject File Serial No. 3, Pandit Papers (II Installment), NMML, 3 and 15 December 1948, File No. 20 (9)-Eur (Part II), NAI.
148 15 January 1950, Record of the Conversation between J. V. Stalin and S. Radhakrishnan, http://digitalarchive.wilsoncenter.org/document/119261 (accessed on 8 December 2016).
149 Fortnightly Reports from Moscow, 26 December 1948–31 January 1949, File No. 35-R&I (1949), NAI.
150 Fortnightly Report from Moscow, 26 January–10 February 1949, File No. 35-R&I (1949), NAI.
151 Fortnightly Report from Moscow, 15 January 1949, File No. 35-R&I (1949), NAI.
152 FO 371/101207, the National Archives (TNA), London.
153 13 January 1949, Dayal to Pandit, Subject File Serial No. 11, Pandit Papers (II Installment), NMML.
154 Fortnightly Report from Moscow, 15 February 1949, File No. 35-R&I (1949), NAI.
155 7 and 17 February and 1 March 1949, Pandit to Nehru, Subject File Serial No. 57, Pandit Papers (I Installment), NMML, 28 February 1949, Pandit to Bajpai, File No. 35-R&I (1949), NAI.
156 10 February 1949, Pandit's Record of Meeting with Molotov, D 1579-Emb/49, File No. 1 (33) Eur II/49, NAI.
157 Fortnightly Reports from Moscow, 11 February–25 March 1949, File No. 35-R&I (1949), NAI.
158 19 February 1949, Nehru to Pandit, No. 232-PM, Subject File Serial No. 54, Pandit Papers (I Installment), NMML.
159 15 March 1949, Nehru to Pandit, Subject File Serial No. 54, Pandit Papers (I Installment), NMML.

160 24 March 1949, Bajpai to Pandit, No. 29210, File No. 35-R&I (1949), NAI.

161 Fortnightly Report from Moscow, 11–25 April 1949, File No. 35-R&I (1949), NAI.

162 1 April 1949, From Moscow to FO, T. No. 263, L/P&S/12/4639B, IOR, Fortnightly Report from Moscow, 31 March 1949, File No. 35-R&I (1949), NAI.

163 14 July 1949, Dayal to Radhakrishnan and 21 July 1949, Dayal to K.P.S. Menon, File No. 3 (16)-FSP/49, NAI.

164 7 September 1949, Radhakrishnan-Vyshinsky Talks, Fond 82, Opis 2, No. 1196, Molotov Papers, RGASPI.

165 20 December 1949, Radhakrishnan-Vyshinsky Talks, Fond 82, Opis 2, No. 1196, Molotov Papers, RGASPI.

166 9 February 1951, Record of the Discussions of J. V. Stalin with Comrades Rao, Dange, Ghosh and Punnaiah, www.revolutionarydemocracy. org/rdv12n2/cpi2.htm (accessed on 8 December 2016).

167 30 April 1949, Fortnightly Report, File No. 35-R&I (1949), NAI.

168 23 May 1949, No. 268, Fond 82, Opis 2, No. 1199, Molotov Papers, RGASPI.

169 15 January 1950, Record of the Conversation between J. V. Stalin and S. Radhakrishnan, http://digitalarchive.wilsoncenter.org/document/119261 (accessed on 8 December 2016).

170 9 February 1951, Record of the Discussions of J. V. Stalin with Comrades Rao, Dange, Ghosh and Punnaiah, www.revolutionarydemocracy. org/rdv12n2/cpi2.htm (accessed on 8 December 2016).

171 Fortnightly Report from Moscow, 11–25 May 1949, File No. 35-R&I (1949), NAI.

172 Fortnightly Report from Moscow, 10 May 1949, File No. 35-R&I (1949), NAI.

INDEX

For Product Safety Concerns and Information please contact our EU representative GPSR@taylorandfrancis.com Taylor & Francis Verlag GmbH, Kaufingerstraße 24, 80331 München, Germany

Printed and bound by CPI Group (UK) Ltd, Croydon, CR0 4YY
01/05/2025
01858422-0001